Travels
in My Homeland

How splendid it is to set out on a new career and appear in the world of learning all of a sudden, carrying a book of discoveries, like an unexpected comet flashing in space.

XAVIER DE MAISTRE

ALMEIDA GARRETT

Travels
in My Homeland

*Translated from the Portuguese
and with an Introduction by
John M. Parker*

PETER OWEN/UNESCO

ISBN 0 7206 0663 2

Translated from the Portuguese *Viagens na minha terra*

UNESCO COLLECTION OF REPRESENTATIVE WORKS
European Series
This book has been recommended by the
Calouste Gulbenkian Foundation for the translations
collection of the United Nations Educational,
Scientific and Cultural Organization (UNESCO).

PETER OWEN PUBLISHERS
73 Kenway Road London SW5 0RE

First published in Great Britain 1987
English translation, Introduction and Notes © UNESCO 1987

Photoset and printed in Great Britain by
Redwood Burn Limited Trowbridge Wiltshire

Contents

Acknowledgement

In addition to books and articles on Almeida Garrett mentioned in notes, I wish to acknowledge a general debt to various items on the author by Professor Ofélia Paiva Monteiro, in particular her doctoral thesis *A formação de Almeida Garrett*, Coimbra, 2 vols, 1971.

J.M.P.

Introduction

Viagens na minha terra (Travels in My Homeland) was first published, following nineteenth-century practice, in the pages of a Lisbon weekly magazine, the *Revista Universal Lisbonense*. The first chapter appeared a mere six weeks after that 17 July 1843 on which the author set out to visit his old university friend, the opposition politician Passos Manuel in Santarém, and five more chapters were published before the end of the year. For unexplained reasons, further publication was suspended and on resumption, in mid-1845, with the magazine under new editorship, the initial chapters were reprinted in a revised version and the remaining chapters followed, at almost regular intervals, over the succeeding eighteen months. By the time publication was completed, on 12 November 1846, or very soon afterwards, the work was available in book form, in two volumes. An unsigned preface, generally attributed to the author, describes Garrett as 'orator and poet, historian and philosopher, critic and artist, jurist and administrator, scholar and statesman', dwells at some length on his classical education, the extent of his culture and his experience of life and people, of foreign countries and societies, and comments on the 'many works, in varied genres, with which, in his short life, this fertile writer has enriched our language'.

Garrett, as he is generally referred to, Almeida Garrett, as his name appears in editions of his works, João Baptista da Silva Leitão, as he was born,[1] was indeed still young in years and had undoubtedly enriched his country's literature in a variety of genres, as a glance at his output shows. In his student days at the University of Coimbra, where he read law (1816–21), he wrote poetry and plays, including a patriotic hymn inspired by the 1820 revolution, the poem *O retrato de Vénus* (Portrait of Venus, 1821), which led to a charge of obscenity, of which he was acquitted in court, and the plays *Lucrécia* (1819), on the conflict between natural man and social being, and *Catão* (Cato, 1821), whose central character embodies the problem of identity of thought and action, a timely topic in a revolutionary period. At the same time, Garrett was composing the shorter poems which were subsequently published (1829) under the title *Lírica de João Mínimo* (Poems of John Minimus), preceded by a narrative preface in which he relates how he came by the poems, whose authorship he attributes to the sexton of a church he had visited. The preface is dated from Birmingham in 1828, the year in which the poet was obliged to seek refuge in England for the second time. Several of the book's final group of poems are dated from England in 1823 and 1824, corresponding to Garrett's first period of exile, forced on him by the so-called 'Vilafrancada' of May 1823, the counter-revolutionary movement which proclaimed the restoration of absolute monarchy referred to in the first chapter of *Travels* and which sent many liberals in search of refuge abroad.

The greater part of Garrett's first period of exile was, however, spent in France, where he obtained employment as a commercial correspondent to support himself and his wife, after the British government refused financial aid to the refugees. While in France he wrote and published the two long narrative poems, *Camões* (Camoens, 1825) and *Dona Branca* (1826), which are generally considered to mark the beginning of the romantic movement in Portuguese literature, although Garrett, in his preface to the former, while claiming credit for its novelty, straightforwardly declined the epithet, asserting that he was neither classical nor romantic. However, his confession that he had ignored rules and principles, consulting neither Horace nor Aristotle, following in their stead the dictates of his heart and his natural emotions, places his intention firmly in the current of European reaction against seventeenth- and eighteenth-century neoclassicism. Both poems take their subject from Portuguese history, both replace classical mythology with other types of myth (e.g. Nordic sagas) or with national folklore and medieval atmospheres, both revolve around unhappy love affairs. In *Camões* Garrett clearly identifies his own situation with the exile of Portugal's national poet, who is portrayed as the typical passionate romantic bard; in *Dona Branca*, the love of a Christian princess for a Moorish chieftain permits a vision of religious universalism and serves as pretext for an attack on the custom of locking women away in convents.

The death of King John VI of Portugal in March 1826, followed by the decreeing of the 1826 constitution and an amnesty by Pedro IV,[2] allowed Garrett to return to Portugal and to his post in the Ministry of Home Affairs. In the two years during which he remained in his homeland, before the violent repression exercised by the despotic Dom Miguel forced thousands of liberals to flee the country, his pen seems to have been largely occupied with political journalism, in the periodicals *O Cronista* (i.e. The Chronicler, which Garrett founded and produced almost single-handed) and *O Português*, where he used his talents in the service of the 1826 constitution, the Charter, as it was known, until censorship forced both to close down. As one of the latter's editors, who were arraigned before the reactionary courts on a flimsy pretext, Garrett spent three months in prison, after which he left his homeland once more (June 1828) for England and later France. Further works of his were published in England: *Adozinda* and a new edition of his play *Catão* (both 1828), the already mentioned *Lírica de João Mínimo* and a *Tratado de Educação* (Treatise on Education), both in 1829, and an essay in political history, *Portugal na balança da Europa* (Portugal and Europe: An Assessment, 1830). *Adozinda* is of particular interest as the forerunner of a collection of balladry, along the lines of Walter Scott's *Ministrelsy* and

Thomas Percy's *Reliques*, which Garrett would eventually start to publish in 1843 and complete in 1851. From the letter to a friend with which the poet prefaced the London edition of *Adozinda*, we learn of his earlier interest in such collections of popular or folklore poetry, in line with the romantic tendency to seek inspiration in pre-Renaissance, non-classical literature – that is, to create links with certain medieval and popular traditions and the verse forms they used. We are told how his reading of Scott, Burns and the German poet Bürger gave him the idea of collecting similar material in Portugal and how *Adozinda*, which is preceded by an epigraph from one of Scott's ballads, was actually written during his months in prison, and that he took for its source a version of the popular ballad 'Silvana'.[3]

Once again, while Garrett's periods of exile bore literary fruits, his involvement in the liberal struggle led him to abandon the muse for more practical matters when, in March 1832, he left to join the constitutional forces, which had taken refuge in the Azores islands. There, while they prepared to attack mainland Portugal, Garrett was called upon to assist the economist and lawmaker, Mouzinho da Silveira, in drawing up the legal framework intended to reform national life in their homeland. Like Carlos in *Travels*, the poet was a member of the small constitutional army (7,500 men) which landed in northern Portugal and occupied the country's second city, Oporto, in July 1832. Despite overwhelming odds – the royalists had some 80,000 troops – a series of daring campaigns saw the opposing army defeated and the liberal cause triumph in May 1834.[4] The writer soon obtained a diplomatic posting as Portuguese chargé d'affaires in Belgium, an appointment which brought him many headaches, caused mainly, according to his official correspondence, by the government's failure to pay him his salary. He incurred many debts and was replaced in 1836, at which time he was also separated from his wife, Luísa Midosi, whom he had married in 1822 when she was barely fifteen years old – a biographical note which might partly explain his fascination with the adolescent figure of Joaninha in *Travels*.

On his return to Portugal, Garrett threw himself into parliamentary business, being responsible, among other things, for the introduction of a member's bill relating to literary and artistic copyright. In 1837 he was asked by the head of government, Passos Manuel – the politician who later invited him to visit Santarém (see *Travels*, ch. I) – to put forward proposals for the establishment of a national theatre and drama school. His subsequent involvement in the creation of dramatic texts was a direct result of the need for a national repertoire for the theatre. Starting in 1838, with the staging of *Um auto de Gil Vicente* (A Play by Gil Vicente), a play within a play, which brings together the great Iberian playwright and his contemporary, the poet Bernardim Ribeiro (see *Travels*, ch. X and n. 1), Garrett provided a series of dramas on subjects drawn from national history as well as a number of comedies and lesser, short pieces. *D(ona) Filipa de Vilhena* (1840) and Garrett's most famous play, *Frei Luís de Sousa* (first performed in 1843), are both based on different episodes from the sixty-year period of Spanish domination, while *O Alfagem de Santarém* (The Armourer from Santarém, 1842), referred to in *Travels* (ch. VII), goes back to the late fourteenth century and the threat of a Castilian succession to the Portuguese throne.

Such were, at the time of the preface to *Viagens na minha terra*, the works with which Garrett had enriched his country's literary and socio-political culture. He was subsequently to publish, among other works, more volumes of poetry, including *Folhas caídas* (Fallen Leaves, 1853), probably the most important collection of romantic poetry to appear in Portugal. Only one major genre is missing, the novel, and even here the author of *Travels* had not been idle, though, when *Viagens na minha terra* began to appear in the *Revista Universal Lisbonense*, he had not brought to completion any of the planned, and in some cases partly written, prose narratives written from as early as 1825. He was destined to publish only one other novel, *O Arco de Sant'Ana* (The Sant'Ana Arch, pt I, 1845; pt II, 1850), begun during the siege of Oporto in 1832, while the constitutionalists were resisting royalist attempts to recapture the city. In his preface to the first part of the novel, Garrett makes it clear that the medieval episode, in which King Pedro the Just administered a public whipping to the despotic Bishop of Oporto, was intended as a warning that the lackeys of the papacy were once more gaining control in Portugal and needed to be kept under surveillance. Although the author claims that most of the first part of the novel was written during the siege itself, the particular type of narrator contact with the reader, the constant digressions and the ironic humour used to achieve a certain distancing from the melodramatic excesses of romanticism, are factors pointing to a work of greater maturity written in the same period as *Travels*. It is interesting to note also that the novel's hero, Vasco, like Carlos in *Viagens na minha terra*, discovers that he is the illegitimate son of a Catholic ecclesiastic, a point whose symbolic importance will not be lost on us. The importance of ecclesiastical power in Portuguese history generally, but particularly once more in the 1840s, following certain anticlerical excesses during the heady days of the liberal triumph, can perhaps be gauged from the ecclesiastical presence in the four major romantic novels published in the course of the decade: in addition to those of Garrett, his confrère Alexandre Herculano published *O Monge de Cister* (The Cistercian Monk, 1841–3) and *Eurico, o Presbítero* (Eurico the Priest, 1844).

Despite the similarities which point to their proximity in time, to which we might add the tendency, explicitly recognized by the author, to mingle medieval history with his own nineteenth century in *O Arco de Sant'Ana*, as also happens in *Travels*, the latter is a different sort of book. Garrett himself refers to it as 'preposterous' and 'unclassifiable' (ch. XXXII), while in his preface he writes that it is possibly his 'most carelessly written work', leaving it to the reader to decide how he should interpret the ambiguity inherent in the adverb 'carelessly': without care or without cares? And we might well ask why Garrett did not expand the story of Joaninha, Carlos, Friar Dinis and the old grandmother into a novel, for what we have is an odd sort of mixture for a nineteenth-century romantic novel, the more so perhaps if we remember that Alexandre

Dumas père was publishing his most famous historical adventure novels in the same decade. In fact, Garrett makes clear from the outset that one of his points of reference predates the romantic novel, by quoting as his epigraph the first paragraph of Xavier de Maistre's *Voyage autour de ma chambre* and further invoking the same author and his book in his own opening lines. Subsequent references to Sterne's *Tristram Shandy* and *A Sentimental Journey* – from the latter the author of *Travels* quotes a paragraph (ch. XI) prior to embarking on the story of the 'maiden of the nightingales' – may be more significant for the form chosen.

Garrett was in a sense a divided spirit. His education had been eminently classical and conservative, ministered by an uncle who was a bishop, a savant and a neoclassical poet, an intellectual 'father' against whom the young man subsequently rebelled but whose world had a stability Portugal would not know again during the writer's adult life. Also, by the time he came to write *Travels*, Garrett was much disillusioned by the erosion and distortion of liberal ideals in the real conditions of contemporary politics. He was particularly bitter at the way certain groups had succeeded in manipulating the economic and legal reforms for which he himself had been partly responsible, to secure for themselves the main economic advantages under the new regime. This explains his violent, pessimistic attacks on the 'barons' which are at the heart of *Travels*.[5] It would also offer an explanation for his not wanting to camouflage his critical vision in the form of another historical novel: even if he could have found a suitable counterpart to the baron in earlier Portuguese history, the implications would not have been sufficiently clear to the reading public. At the same time, either he had no model for a contemporary novel – the preface to *Travels*, with its encomium of the author's knowledge of foreign literature 'ancient and contemporary', includes no mention of Balzac, Stendhal or even Dickens, despite the rapidity with which Sue's *Mystères de Paris* seems to have found its way to Portugal – or, if he was acquainted with any of their works, we may assume that the relative absence of the narrator from the diegetic world would not meet with his approval.

Whether or not these are the reasons, the fact is that the eighteenth-century models gave him much greater freedom of movement, allowing him to mingle different periods in Portuguese history, from the early medieval (St Iria goes back to the seventh century) to his own time, to mix history and fiction, literary genres and even styles. The English reader, accustomed to locating the rise of the modern novel in the eighteenth century, has to remember that not all countries had the social and economic conditions which made this possible. Identification of the novel as a dominant form with the rise and consolidation of a bourgeois culture makes it easier to understand why this begins to occur in Portugal only after the social upheavals of the earlier part of the nineteenth century, when the intelligentsia had returned from exile and were able to play an active role in the development of the country's cultural and political life in the urban centres. But their numbers were obviously small and Garrett makes clear, on various occasions, what he thinks of Lisbon as a centre of European civilization, as for instance (in ch. XXXVIII) when he compares it, humorously, to the situation in the provinces, which lacked any pretension to a cultural life, making it possible to view the capital's cultural manifestations, in retrospect, with a slightly less jaundiced eye.

This view of Lisbon has, however, another, perhaps more significant, aspect. Lisbon is at once the home of the 'blessed regime which governs us', as Garrett sarcastically terms the government of Costa Cabral, and the domain of the hated 'barons': it has ceased to be a worthy symbol of the nation. This the author goes to look for in Santarém, the ancient town, nowadays less than an hour's ride from Lisbon on the metal railways whose viability Garrett doubted in 1843. Santarém, redolent with national history which is everywhere inscribed in stone; with ancient monuments closely linked to Portugal's existence as an independent nation. But also the centre of a region in which some of the civil war's last decisive battles were fought, itself the last stronghold of the royalists: where, in a sense, everything began to go wrong for the liberals, or

14

constitutionalists as they were known. European travellers in the eighteenth and nineteenth centuries, especially the newly rich British bourgeoisie, toured the Continent to acquire and accumulate culture, and travel literature became one of the genres of a period that also saw the appearance of a multitude of treatises and speculative disquisitions on the arts. Garrett, modestly one might say, while restricting his tour to a small area of his home country, moulded these two genres into one, for he not only reports and describes what he sees, but speculates on matters literary and artistic; and, to give his readers still better value for their money, he also included a romantic tale of love with an unhappy ending, which intertwines with and exemplifies his central theme.

That the story of the 'green-eyed maid' is in no way separate from the mainstream of the book and was not intended to be, the narrator makes clear (in ch. XXXII). After describing his book as 'preposterous' and 'unclassifiable', he notes how the thread of his stories and observations intertwines in such a way that the reader needs a good deal of patience to untangle it and keep track of it. The noun that corresponds to the verb translated here as 'intertwine' (*enredar-se*) is also the Portuguese word for the plot of a narrative (*enredo*). There is, then, a central thread, or plot, to the book as a whole, of which the story of Joaninha and Carlos is a part, a very important part, clearly, as is shown not only by the amount of space given to it by the narrator, but by his eventual participation in it when, at the end of the book, he makes direct contact with Friar Dinis. This central thread is the formal organization of Garrett's central theme in *Travels*, which might be stated succinctly as: What went wrong with Portugal? In this sense, Santarém, by its historical importance, serves as a microcosm of the country as a whole: it is the symbol both of nationality, or national pride, and of the degradation and erosion of that same sense of national identity and pride. There is clearly a point in Portugal's history when, for Garrett, this process began. Although he does not spell it out, he seems to locate it in the period of Castile's political control of Portugal (1580–1640) and the corresponding cultural domination by the Jesuits: the

Philippine style of architecture corresponds directly to Jesuit philosophy and marks a point when churches ceased to be built *because* people believed and wanted to pray, and were erected *in order to* make them believe and pray (ch. XXVII). While the author-narrator is critical of the treatment given to the religious orders by the liberals, he clearly feels strongly about the power they wielded in civil society, particularly when they no longer had the moral authority and when their main concern was to prevent the modernization of Portugal and Portuguese society. His dilemma and his own divided nature are well reflected in the novella, not only through the portrait he, as narrator, paints of Friar Dinis, but in the monk's relationship with Carlos and with the grandmother, Francisca. A useful summary of this intricate problem is to be found in the paradoxical nature of Joaninha's observation of the friar in chapter XIV: 'a complex mixture of eagerness and dejection, of faith and unbelief, of liking and aversion', which the narrator sees as embodying 'the vacillations of the century' – particularly his own, perhaps.

Certainly his own. He describes his journey to Santarém as an odyssey, *his* odyssey, and the novella, or what we are told of it at that point, while the travellers rest in the vale of Santarém, is its first episode. While the connection with Homer's *Odyssey* must not be hammered, it is interesting to recall that Odysseus was unable to save his comrades who had devoured the oxen of Hyperion, the Sun, which may not be all that unsuitable a comparison for the behaviour of the 'barons' who had been Garrett's comrades, among whom he includes Carlos (see ch. XLIX). The old lady endlessly winding her yarn does not fail to recall Penelope to the narrator, a comparison he passes on to the reader, who can understand it both in terms of a country in stagnation, because its rightful king (Pedro IV) is not on his throne, and, as happened in Ithaca, as one being bled dry by those who wished to usurp that throne (Dom Miguel and his supporters). The old lady's name (Francisca) and her self-imposed religious vows seem to point, once again, to the religious orders, her blindness requiring no further explanation. Carlos will eventually lay the blame for his behaviour entirely at

God's door, disclaiming all personal responsibility (ch. XLVIII); in the opening book of *The Odyssey*, Zeus says: 'What a lamentable thing it is that men should blame the gods and regard *us* as the source of their troubles, when it is their own wickedness that brings them sufferings worse than any which Destiny allots them.'

The symbolic line can be pursued further. Helder Macedo[6] has pointed to a national literary source for the green-eyed Joana and her accompanying nightingales in the *Menina e moça* of the sixteenth-century poet-novelist Bernardim Ribeiro (cf. ch. X n. 1), which gives the romantic nature of the novella a decidedly Portuguese and pre-romantic origin. R. A. Lawton[7] views Joaninha in a Neoplatonic light as a younger sister of Dante's Beatrice, but also sees in her a female form of Johannes, the source of light in the masonic cult to which Garrett has been linked. It is clear, certainly, that she represents everything that is pure and innocent, yet at the same time strong, passionate and self-confident, an ideal Portugal, perhaps, whose Garden of Eden is destroyed by the warring factions and to which Carlos has just sufficient conscience to realize he can no longer aspire. Georgina's name marks her out as a symbol of Georgian England, with its material progress and its liberal Toryism, which presumably seemed to Garrett to have the best of both worlds, retaining the excellencies of the past, which were carried forward into the present. Does Garrett mean us to understand that Carlos would have had to abandon his native land for good in order to accept the love of Georgina? In other words, is he suggesting that the English system could not be transferred to Portugal?

Possibly this presents an over-simple view of the novella, which is complicated by the psychological experience of men and women in love; or more precisely of a man, or type of man, undergoing a sort of sentimental education from which he learns very little, because he is essentially in love with himself and the women he claims to love are mere reflections of his own narcissistic self-regard. Carlos is emotionally a child, or at most an adolescent: his behaviour on discovering that Laura is engaged makes this clear, but it also explains his reaction to Joaninha. Of course the vision of woman as an angel figure is a romantic *topos*, and Carlos repeatedly uses the word 'angel' or 'angelic' of the three sisters as well as of Joaninha. Carlos's letter to Joaninha, which occupies the book's final chapters, is one of Garrett's master strokes in *Travels*. He makes use of an earlier literary form, the epistolary, in order to allow his central character to take over the narration and fill in certain important gaps in the story. At the same time he reveals much about himself, for while the author offers him the opportunity to plead his case, he also gives him enough rope to hang himself.

It has been customary in Portugal to identify Garrett biographically with Carlos, attributing to the former the latter's love affairs in England and specifying real siblings for the three young Englishwomen. Perhaps Carlos's own comments with regard to his supposed affair with the nun Soledade (ch. XLVIII) could be taken as a warning to avoid such identifications, which in any case add nothing either to one's enjoyment or one's interpretation of *Travels*. Where Garrett might be said to equate himself with Carlos serves, if anything, to distance the two and to point up the fictional nature of the novella with its historical background and its framework of real events relating to the author's visit to Santarém. As Helder Macedo has shrewdly noted, Garrett takes Carlos's place by occupying his semantic space in the final confrontation with a changed Friar Dinis, where each recognizes that there have been mistakes on both sides. Ten years after the liberal victory, the old lady continues to wind her yarn, but now she is not merely blind, she is totally oblivious to the world about her, a dead woman waiting to be buried, as the narrator tells us in chapter XLIII. This comes shortly after his indignant outburst, at the end of the previous chapter, when, infuriated by the desecration of King Fernando's tomb, he prophesied that another ten years with the 'barons' ruling the roost would see the last breath depart from Portugal's dying body. He himself lived little more than ten years after his visit to Santarém, but he saw the final defeat of Costa Cabral and played a part, as Foreign Minister, in the so-called 'regenerator' government which at last succeeded in unifying the national bourgeoisie and completing the phase of adaptation to the loss of Portugal's main colony, Brazil, and to the collapse of the old regime. Garrett became a peer of the realm and was criticized for joining the legion of the hated 'barons', but I believe one should view his peerage as no more than a just, though tardy recognition of the unstinting manner in which he put his many talents so exclusively in the service of his country and, in particular, of the ideals he tried so hard to keep alive. *Travels in My Homeland* provides some indication of how difficult this was.

THE TRANSLATION

The translator of any work belonging to an earlier century faces an initial dilemma which seems to offer three solutions. He may opt to attempt a reproduction in his own language of the period style corresponding to the original work – clearly a daunting task in itself, made more difficult by having to decide just which periods correspond in the two cultures concerned: what are considered innovatory aspects of Garrett's style in the Portuguese literary code are already found in eighteenth-century English prose. Or the translator may go to the other end of the scale and update the original completely, casting it in modern dress, producing a version entirely in the style and obeying all the norms of our contemporary language. Not all works are susceptible to such treatment, it seems to me, particularly where the author's material and points of reference are very much of his own time and clime, which I consider to be the case with the present work, which offers the additional problem of different stylistic registers, features of the spoken language mingling with passages of high-flown rhetoric. I have chosen a middle course in trying to produce an English version that should not seem very strange to the contemporary reader, while retaining something of the flavour of Garrett's mode of writing in the context of his areas of reference.

Garrett did not publish a revised edition of *Travels*, and his own partly corrected copy of the first edition cannot be considered a final version. However, while I have made use of several existing editions, I have in most cases resolved doubts by reference to Augusto da Costa Dias's edition (Lisbon: Portugália, 1972), which incorporates the author's corrections and additions. In the Portuguese editions, Garrett used a number of English as well as French words and expressions. These are all italicized in the present edition, followed by an asterisk.

JOHN M. PARKER

I

·:·

How the author of this learned book decided to travel in his homeland, after having travelled in his bedroom; and how he decided to seek immortality by writing down his travels. – Departure for Santarém. – Arrival at Terreiro do Paço[1] to board the steamboat for Vila Nova; what happens to him on board. – The *Dedução Cronológica*[2] and downtown Lisbon. – Lord Byron and a good cigar. – A difference of opinion between the men from Ílhavo and the men from Bordas-d'Água:[3] baggy trousers win the day.

THAT a person who lives near the Alps, in Turin, which is nearly as cold as St Petersburg, should travel around his bedroom, is understandable.[4] But in this climate, with this God-given air, in which orange trees grow in the back garden and the undergrowth is a mass of myrtle, even Xavier de Maistre, if he were writing here, would at least go as far as the backyard.

I myself, on these stifling summer nights, often travel as far as my window to get a sight of the snippet of Tagus at the end of the street and to delude myself with the greenery of some trees that drag out a laborious infancy among the rubble heaps down on the Cais do Sodré. And I have never written down these travels of mine or my impressions of them; well, there was so much to see! My pen was always ambitious: poor yet presumptuous, it needs a broader theme. That is just what I shall give it. I shall go to Santarém, no less, and I swear that everything I see and hear, everything I think and feel, shall be chronicled.

For a long time I had had this vague idea, more of a notion than a plan, of touring the rich plains of our Ribatejo and paying my respects to the most historical and monumental of our towns on its lofty height. I am prevailed upon by the insistence of a friend;[5] my mind has been made up by the fatuous statements of a newspaper which, for sensationalism, decided to headline my visit as having a specific political design.[6]

For that very reason, then, I shall go: *this is a formal statement of intent*.

It is the 17th of the month of July, in this year of grace 1843, a Monday, an ordinary day and a good beginning. St Paul's is striking 6 a.m. and here am I walking to Terreiro do Paço. I arrive very early, putting to shame the earliest risers among my travelling companions, who all pride themselves on being earlier risers than myself. I have all but crossed the square when I hear the heavy, urgent rumble of an *ancien régime* carriage: it is our leader and commander, the captain of our enterprise, the Count of T., arriving in state.

Our other companions have now arrived. The bell rings for the last time. We are off.

In a steamship regatta[7] our boat would certainly win no prizes. And if, with the coming of progress, there should be established Isthmiads or Olympiads for this sort of course, and should there be some Pindar eager to run behind the winner in strophes and antistrophes and crown him with immortal hymns, there will not be even a sad, shrivelled epode for this weary Vila Nova runner. It is a serious, sensible boat and does not go in for such escapades.

Here we go, then, at our leisure, observing the majestic, picturesque amphitheatre formed by Lisbon's east end, which, seen from the river, is the most beautiful and impressive part of the city, the most characteristic too, for here and there one can make out, or more exactly conjure up, some rare traces of our good old Lisbon of the chronicles. Down-river from the foundry[8] everything is prosaic and bourgeois, nasty, vulgar and tasteless, rather like a passage in the *Dedução Cronológica*, with the occasional sprinkling of an attempt at the height of bad taste, like one of the less mediocre stanzas of the *Oriente*.[9]

So the ordinary people, whose taste is always better and purer than that of the pale scum that floats on the surface of every population and entitles itself in superior fashion *society*, their favourite outings are to the Madre de Deus, the Beato, to Xabregas and Marvila and the gardens of Chelas. To one side the majestic sweep of the Tagus at its greatest expanse and power, more like a small Mediterranean sea; to the other, cool gardens and shady trees, palaces, monasteries, all places sacred to glorious or fond memories. What other way out of Lisbon can compare in beauty to this one? Except for Belém, not one. And Belém, even so, is more barren.

We have already greeted Alhandra, breeder of bulls, and Vila Franca, which was de Xira, then da Restauração, and then de Xira again, when the so-called Restoration,[10] as always happens to all restorations and always will, fell into such loathing and execration that not even a wretched town wanted to be named after it. 'It was not so much a case of restoring or not restoring, but of our getting rid of a government of jokers, which is the most odious and disgusting of all possible governments.' Such was the reflection one of our travelling companions contributed to the considerations on Vila Franca that I had unthinkingly begun to voice.

But I have no hatred at all for Vila Franca, nor even for that notorious pilgrimage the old monarchy went and made there. It was something that was in the run of events and simply had to happen. This necessary and inevitable upheaval the world is going through will take a long time and will be resisted by a good deal of reaction before it is complete. . . .

In the meantime let us light our cigars and leave the aristocratic precincts of the stern; to the prow, the domain of smokers' freedom!

I don't recall that Lord Byron ever celebrated the pleasure of smoking on board ship. It is remarkably forgetful of the most seafaring, sailorly poet there ever was, who even poetized seasickness, that most prosaic and nauseating of life's miseries! But on a day like this, to feel on one's cheek and in one's hair the refreshing breeze skimming off the waves, while lazily inhaling the narcotic fumes of a good Havana cigar, is one of the few truly good things there are in this world.

Let us smoke!

Here is a *campino*[11] thoughtfully smoking his cigarette, he will give me a light.

'Here you are, sir . . .' – offers another courteously, a very different type, whose features, dress and manner form a singular contrast with those of the Mozarab from the Ribatejo.

Our cigars were lit and we took stock more leisurely of the company we were in.

The group we had joined was certainly remarkable and interesting, and stood out picturesquely from the remainder of the passengers, who were a hybrid mixture of ordinary, characterless dress and features such as abounds in the vicinity of a large maritime and commercial city. Not so this somewhat isolated group we had chanced upon. It was made up of a dozen men. Five of them were the type of those famous athletes from Alhandra, who every Sunday go to gather the *pulverem olympicum*[12] in the bullring at Sant'Ana and who, at the imperious, irresistible shouts of *à unha, à unha, à cernelha*,[13] rush to grapple with animals more noble if not more powerful than themselves, to the sound of tremendous applause and in exchange for the few coppers which express the always noisy and equally empty enthusiasm of crowds. My five warriors were returning home, still in their bullring clothes, still bruised and covered in glory from the previous day's contest. But alongside these five and arguing with them – I shall say why directly – were six or seven men who looked in every respect their antipodes.

In place of the yellow knee-breeches and floral waistcoat typical of the *forcado* performer, these others wore the wide Greek skirt used in Ovar and the braided Sicilian tunic of worsted. The *campino*, like the *saloio*,[14] has the stamp of African races; these others are of Pelasgian stock: regular, mobile features, an agile frame.

Now the northerners were arguing with the southerners. The dispute had been interrupted by our arrival at the ship's prow. But one of the men from Ílhavo – a fine, poetic figure of a man – turned to face us and said, in an emphatic voice: 'Now here's someone who'll decide for us. It's like this, gentlemen. These fellows, just because they wrestle with bulls, think they're better than anyone, that no one can match them. And you gentlemen, if you are from Lisbon, will probably agree. But we...'

'None of us is from Lisbon, except the gentleman who is just coming.'

It was the Count of T. who was approaching.

'I know him, he's one of us!' exclaimed one of the *forcados*, the moment he saw him. 'He's a proper gent. I've never seen him at a branding, it's true, but from Valada here to Almeirim there's no better horseman than he, come rain come shine, and he must know a real bull and what it means to work with cattle.'

'Let us hear the dispute, then.'

'It's not a dispute,' answered the man from Ílhavo, 'but if his lordship here rides near Almeirim, it's to Almeirim that we're going, that just the other day was waste land and is now a garden, God bless it! But it wasn't the bull-herders who made it, it was our people who hoed and cultivated it and made it what it is, turned the sand of the heath into soil.'

'That's true enough.'

'So it is! For it's a mighty feat to grow wheat here in this loamy soil on the banks of the Tagus, just like sowing seeds in butter. It's work done by God Himself, with His own hand, watering, fertilizing and all. And what God doesn't do, they don't, for they cannot even make these mounds firm by planting trees. They have put in a few farther up, but it's precious little for a river like this and the fine soil that is carried away by the floodwaters. But us now, one foot on board, the other on land, at one moment we can be weeding the corn on the moorland, at another we are on our way down-river with the pole against our chest and the boat sticking in the sand because there's not enough depth . . . but always toiling for dear life.'

'It's strength we're talking about,' retorted the bull-herder, to shift the argument into the area that suited him. 'It's strength we're talking about. When a countryman throws himself on a bull's horns where a whole company of fisherman couldn't grab him, begging your gentlemen's pardon, by the arse! . . .'

And he added strength to his argument with a triumphant guffaw, which was echoed by the interested bystanders who had squeezed together to hear the arguments.

The men from Ílhavo were somewhat discountenanced; while not losing their sense of superiority, they were intimidated by the hullabaloo.

They were like the opposition benches in parliament when they see their orators' best phrases and strongest arguments drowned by the offensive hubbub of the ministerial rabble.

But the orator from Ílhavo was not one to accept defeat so easily. He looked at his fellows, as if consulting and encouraging them, with a meaningful nod, and facing us, his right hand extended towards his adversaries: 'Well then, if it's strength you're talking about, what I'd like to know, and these gentlemen shall tell us, is which is the stronger, a bull or the sea?'

'Well, I'm blowed! ...'

'We should like to know.'

'The sea, of course.'

'So between us, who battle with the sea a week to ten days on end in a storm, from Aveiro to Lisbon, and these fellows who scrap with a bull one afternoon, which of us is the stronger?'

The *campinos* were crestfallen; this time an impartial public applauded the opposition and the Vouga defeated the Tagus.

II

————— ·:· —————

The travels are declared to be typical, symbolical and mythical. – The author modestly sings his own praises. – On the march of civilization: it is shown that the march is led by the Knight of La Mancha, Don Quixote, and his squire, Sancho Panza. – Arrival at Vilo Nova da Rainha. – The torment of Tantalus. – Virtue as its own reward and a Jeremy Bentham sophistry. – Azambuja.

THESE interesting travels of mine shall be a masterpiece, erudite, sparkling with new ideas, something worthy of our century. I need to inform the reader of this, so that he may be forewarned and not think that they are just another batch of these fashionable scribblings entitled *Travel Notes* or something similar, which weary the printing presses of Europe without the slightest benefit for science or for the advancement of the species.

First of all my book is a symbol . . . a myth, a Greek word, and a Germanic fashion, that is put into everything nowadays and used to explain everything that . . . can't be explained.

It is a myth because . . . because. . . . Without further ado I shall lift the veil and state openly to my benevolent reader the profound idea that is concealed beneath this frivolous appearance of a brief trip seemingly taken in play, while all the time it is a serious, sober, thoughtful business like a new tome from the Leipzig fair, not one of your penny dreadfuls from the boulevards of Paris.

Some years ago there was a deep, abstruse philosopher from over the Rhine[1] who wrote a work on the march of civilization, of the intellect – what we might call, to be better understood, *Progress*. He discovered that there are two principles in the world: *spiritualism*, which marches on heedless of the material, earthy side of this life, eyes fixed on its great, abstract theories, a stiff, spare, hard, inflexible belief which can be suitably embodied, symbolized by the famous myth of the Knight of La Mancha, Don Quixote; and *materialism*, which, taking not the slightest heed of these theories, in which it does not believe and whose impossible applications it declares to be Utopias each and every one, can be properly represented by the rotund and well-fed person of our old friend Sancho Panza.

But, as in witty Cervantes's story, these two completely opposed and contradictory principles nevertheless are always together, the one some way behind, the other going on ahead, often getting in each other's way, rarely helping one another, but always *progressing*.

And this is what is possible for human progress.

And here is the chronicle of the past, the history of the present, the programme for the future.

Our present-day world is a vast Barataria governed by King Sancho.

Don Quixote's turn will be next.

Common sense shall come with the millennium: the kingdom of the children of God! It is guaranteed in the divine promises ... like the constitution promised by the King of Prussia; and he has not failed yet, because – because the contract has no fixed date: he promised, but he did not say for when.

Now this journey of mine up the Tagus symbolizes the march of our social progress: I hope the reader has understood this by now. I shall be careful to remind him from time to time, for I very much fear he will forget.

We are arrived at the dismal wharf at Vila Nova da Rainha, which is the ugliest piece of alluvial soil on which I have ever set foot. The sun is burning hot as it has not yet been this year.

An enormous agglomeration of calashes, mules, donkeys and muleteers awaits us in this African desert. We must needs choose between the two torments: the calash or the mule. The lesser of the evils ... it shall be the latter.

And over there – oh, torment of Tantalus! – I can see two powerful, sleek Spanish she-mules harnessed to a vehicle which, in these parts and in comparison with the others, looks to me more splendid than a Hyde Park landau, more elegant than a Longchamps *calèche*, more comfortable and springy than the Princess Helena's sprightliest britzka. And yet – oh, magic power of situations! – it is nothing more than a substantial, handsome, curtained four-wheeler.

Berobed manes of old-time judges, venerable locks with curls and ringlets, what will you say, o revered shades, if from that limbo where you await the resurrection of Pegas[2] . . . and of book five – you can see this spurious, degenerate successor of yours, in wide trousers, green tailcoat, white hat, colourful cravat, carrying a rubber switch, about to mount a poor little *Palito Métrico* mule[3] like a callow second-year student, while casting envious looks at that natural, appropriate and requisite mode of magisterial transport? Oh, what shall you say? With what just disdain shall you not look upon such degradation and malfeasance!

I was communing silently with myself in these weighty meditations and irresolutely turning over in my mind the massive doubt: whether the correct administration of justice was sufficient reason for a magistrate to go on foot! . . . The Sancho Panza of the flesh wrestled within me with the Don Quixote of the spirit, when Providence, which never abandons us in the direst straits and temptations, brought me a generous offer from a friend and travelling companion on the steamship, Senhor L.S.: the envied carriage was his and he gave me a seat in it as far as Azambuja.

Virtue is its own reward, according to an ancient philosopher, and I do not believe in Bentham's famous quip that ancient wisdom is all sophistry. The latest thing is also the oldest, no doubt, but the thing of old that still persists has been confirmed by experience not available to novelties. Jeremy Bentham perpetrated his sophistry like the next man.

We move slowly across that poorly built embankment which rises but a few spans above the low, salty ground. In winter it cannot be traversed without danger; even now one moves with some discomfort and apprehension. We are in Vila Nova and at the door of the disgusting caravanserai which is the only shelter for the traveller on what is now the busiest highway in the kingdom.

This repulsive hamlet looks to be dirtier and more desolate, more ruined and abandoned, now that it has next to it the landing-place for the steamboats which are the comfort, the life, the soul of the Ribatejo. I imagine that a bedouin village, in the foothills of the Atlas Mountains, must be cleaner and more comfortable.

Oh, Sancho, Sancho, you too shall not reign among us! The worm-ridden throne of your predecessor, adversary and sometimes master collapsed; they whipped your buttocks so as to remove the spell from the beautiful *del Toboso*; they then proclaimed you King of Barataria, yet in this Lusitanian province of yours the paternal rule of your stupid materialism cannot even install itself for the comfort and salvation of the body, since the soul. . . . Oh, the soul! . . .

Let us talk about something else.

Let us be gone, and quickly, from this dunghill. The road is monotonous, arid, unfreshened by trees: but for the occasional, stunted olive tree, which at long, irregular intervals exhibits its gnarled trunk and twisted boughs, adorned with sickly little branches, on which the natural pale green of the leaves is more ashen and lack-lustre than usual. And yet the soil, with the odd exception, is excellent, and with a little work and some insignificant expense would yield as good a road as the best in Europe.

A friend of mine, a secretary of state, used to say that for the streets of Lisbon to be improved on an equal footing, ministers ought to be obliged to change street and district every three months. When the law of ministerial responsibility is drawn up, at the Greek Calends, I shall propose that every minister be made to travel this Portugal of his once a year at least, to discharge his obligation.

Here is Azambuja, a small but cheerful town, with obvious signs of life, its houses clean and comfortable-looking. It is the first place to indicate that we are on the fertile banks of the Portuguese Nile.

We hasten to dismount at the elegant establishment which simultaneously accumulates the three distinct functions of the town's only hotel, restaurant and café.

Heavens! What witch is this at the door? What den of vice within?! . . . My pen falls from my hand.

III

—— ·:· ——

The reader is disappointed by the prosaic sincerity of the author of these travels. – What should an inn be like in these days of romantic literature? – The discussion of this momentous problem is interrupted in order to attend, in prose and verse, to a very nice point of political economy and social morality. – How many souls must be given to the Devil and how many bodies delivered to the cemetery in order to make one rich man in this world. – How it came to be discovered that the science of our century is an awful idiot. – King in reality and king by right. – Beauty and falsehood are not good bedfellows. – The author sets out for the pine forest of Azambuja.

I am assuredly about to disappoint the benevolent reader; my inescapable sincerity is about to lose me whatever good opinion I had earned in the first two chapters of this interesting journey.

What, after all, did he expect of me now, after I had dared to declare myself a writer in these times of romanticism, this century of powerful feelings, of descriptions made in broad, *incisive* strokes, engraved upon the soul and throbbing with blood in the heart?

At the end of the preceding chapter we stopped at the door of an inn. What inn should it be, now, in the year 1843, under the very nose of Victor Hugo, with Doctor Faust running round in our heads and the *Mystères de Paris*[1] in everyone's hands?

Can today's taste stand Cervantes's classical *posada*, with its fat, ponderous *mesonero*, its muleteers with their jokes and the blanket-tossing of some poor simpleton of a Sancho – Sancho, the invisible king of our century, *on whose behalf kings reign and lawgivers decree and decide what is just*?! Sancho tossed in a blanket by low muleteers?! Not in our day.

With clover shall I crown my sword,
With carrots, beetroot and lucerne,
Harmodios to sing and Aristogitons
Who have ye from the tyrant yoke
Delivered of that useless, old
Worm-eaten science that raised from earth,
Uplifted, set aloft that which
In man there is of Being divine,
And for great feats and virtues great
Did from the flesh his spir't separate. . . .[2]

No – go to the Devil, you generation of steam and pottery; macadamize roads; make railways; build flying machines, like Icarus, to cover faster and faster the numbered hours of this material, coarse and humdrum life that you have made of the one God gave us, which was so different from the way we live today. Go on, money-grubbers, go on! Reduce everything to figures, reduce all the considerations of this world to equations of material interest: buy, sell, speculate. At the end of it all, what profit will there have been for the human species? A few dozen more rich men. I ask the political economists and the moralists if they have calculated the number of individuals who must be condemned to misery, to excessive labour, to depravity, to villainy, to wanton ignorance, to insurmountable wretchedness, to absolute poverty, in order to produce one rich man. The British parliament should be able to tell them, after so many commissions of inquiry there, they must have computed the number of souls[3] that must be sold to the Devil and the number of bodies that must be delivered before their time to the cemetery to make a wealthy, noble textile manufacturer like Sir Robert Peel, or a mine-owner, a banker, a gentleman farmer or whatever: every rich, well-to-do man costs hundreds of unhappy wretches.

Therefore the happiest nation is not the wealthiest. Therefore the utilitarian principle is the castor oil of injustice and condemnation. Therefore . . .

There are more things in heaven and earth, Horatio,
Than are dreamt of in your phylosophy [sic][4]

This century's science is an awful ass.

And, therefore, conceited and puffed up with foolish pride.

★   ★   ★

On with the description of the inn. It cannot be classical, otherwise it will be hissed at by all those bearded, moustachioed, cigar-smoking young men who compose deep, abstruse literature all the way from the door of the Café Marrare to the Café de Moscow. . . . [5]

But at this point I am struck by an inexplicable incoherence. Our society is materialist, yet our literature, which is the expression of society, is all excessively, absurdly and preposterously spiritualist! Sancho, king in reality, Quixote, king by right.

That is the way it is and it is easy to explain. It is literature which is the hypocrite: there is religion in poems, charity in novels, faith in newspaper articles – just like those people who give alms to be mentioned in the *Daily*, succour orphan girls in the *Gazette* and provide for widows on theatre bills.

And they talk about the Gospels! It must be mockery. If they read them, they will find that the left hand must not know what the right hand is doing. . . .

On with the description of the inn and an end to all these digressions.

It cannot be classical, that is clear, this description of ours. Then it shall be romantic. Not that, either. Why not? I have only to put in a *Chourineur*[6] sharpening a huge knife a foot and a half long, fit to carve up any man or beast that gets in his way; a *Fleur de Marie*,[6] to do and say all sorts of mawkish things to an itsy-bitsy little rosebush, sweetie thing, that died, poor wee thing; and a German prince in disguise, great at fist fighting, bulging with pounds sterling, skilled in thieves' and blind men's slang . . . and there you have Azambuja with an inn that has no need to envy the most perfect, fashionable hostelry in this elegant, sensitive, authentic, natural century!

That is how I should go about the description, I know full well. But there is a fatal, insuperable impediment, as with the famous salvo that did not happen. . . .[7] It is that it wasn't anything like that.

And I do not wish to malign the good people of Azambuja.

Better those others do not read my book, because I aim to live and die faithful to Boileau: *Rien n'est beau que le vrai.*

It has long been said that honour and profit are not good bedfellows and, I say, nor are beauty and falsehood; and that is the best possible Portuguese version of Boileau's famous, gospel hemistich. For the most part the attractions of present-day literature remind me of those beauties that tempted the saintly anchorites in the Thebaid. Poor St Anthony or St Pachomius (Pachomius fits better here)[8] were open-mouthed at first, but a feeling in their bones made them look at the temptresses' feet. . . . Heavens, the cursed one! His feet were what he couldn't disguise. And at the saint's first *abrenuntio* the beauty disappeared in clouds of sulphur and there was the Devil, black, ugly and caprine as only the father of falsehood can be and always was.

None of that, then: the truth and only the truth. All there was at the inn in Azambuja was a poor old woman I called a witch, because, well, what was I to call the dirty, ragged old woman who was at the door of that repulsive place?

There was this old woman, with her younger companion, younger but no less loathsome to look upon than she herself, and a half-paralysed, half-crazy old man, sprawled in a corner there for all the world as if he had come to the tavern just for a rest because he had already drunk the place dry.

We were dying of thirst, but the water there is like drinking fever. The wine was ghastly. Lemonade? No lemons and no sugar. A local was dispatched to the shop at the other end of the town. He brought back three lemons, which put me in mind of some that used to hang, when I went there on holiday, at the door of the famous eating joint in Leiria.

The sugar would be better in the last scene of *Monsieur de Pourceaugnac*.[9] But it was all mixed together with the fever water, we drank it, resumed our journey and up to now it has done us no harm, despite being the most abominable, unpleasant and filthy beverage imaginable.

We travelled on in the same manner until we reached the famous Azambuja pine forest.

IV

————— ⋅∴⋅ —————

How the author rode on thinking and musing, and what he
was thinking and musing about on the road from the town
of Azambuja to the famous pine forest of the same name. –
The Greek poet and philosopher, Demades, and the
English poet and philosopher Addison: the tail-coat and the
Athenian pallium, together with other important matters
in which the author wished to show the profundity of his
learning. – Discussion of the very serious problem of
whether it is necessary for a minister of state to be ignorant
and unlettered. – Admirable zigzag reflections on the
subject of *re politica* and *re amatoria*. – It is eventually
discovered that the author had been dreaming throughout
the chapter and the benevolent reader is requested to turn
the page and move on to the next chapter.

I shall always place modesty first among all the good qualities.
Even above innocence? Yes, certainly. Innocence can be lost
through a single mistake; only serious lapses, only real crimes
can deprive one of modesty. An accident, a chance happening,
can destroy the former; the latter, only an opportune, deliberate
and intentional action.

I still recall quite well those two verses of the poet Demades,
which offer an authoritative argument against my theory; I
thought I had a less-favoured memory. I shall set them down
here, so that this great book of my travels shall not be without
the merit of learning and shall not be called a mere fashionable
pot-boiler. I am determined to make my reputation with this
book:

> Αιδὼς τε κάλλεος καί ἀρετῆς πόλις
> Πρῶτοη ἀγαθῆ ἀναμαρτηαία, δεντερον δέ ἀισχυνη.

> (Of beauty and virtue the fortress is
> Innocence first – and the same again.)

35

But authority is answered by authority, and text by text. And I have my Addison here in my pocket – one of the few books I am never without – and I set the English philosopher upon the Greek and emerge victorious, because Addison places nothing higher than modesty, and Addison, despite his tailcoat, is a much greater philosopher than was Demades for all his tunic and his Athenian pallium.

This time the learned and amiable reader will be spared further quotations: let him buy a *Spectator*, which is a work one just cannot be without, and read *passim*.

I like, as can be seen, to counter the objections that can be made; I even suggest them myself, so that I am not told afterwards: 'Ha, ha! Trying it on?!' – 'Not a bit of it, that's not my style.'

In honesty, then . . . here is what people might say: 'Addison was a secretary of state and so. . . .' – 'And so what? Can you not conceive of a secretary of state being a philosopher, a minister being a poet, an elegant, witty, talented writer? No, I see you cannot; you have the fixed idea that a minister of state must needs be some vulgar, petulant bore. But this happens in civilized countries like ours, where it is no longer of any importance to the public weal, where neither people nor ruler care any longer into whose hands they deliver themselves and in what heads they place their trust. In England, which has yet to reach our stage of perfection, things are not like this, nor were they in Addison's day. Let them try asking Queen Anne to make places in her cabinet[1] for a trio of ignorant, ill-bred brutes for no other reason than that one of them was good at speculating with public moneys, another had some good tricks for *canvassing*★ in certain elections, while the third was an important figure at Freemasons' Hall!'

Of course there is not the slightest allusion in any of this to the blessed regime that governs us: I am talking about modesty and we live in Portugal.

Yet modesty can be almost entirely a failing in a man if it be excessive and come close to timidity, to what society calls *lack of savoir-faire*. In a woman it is always a virtue, enhancing the charms of those who are beautiful, veiling the shortcomings of those who are not.

For my part, I know no object in all nature that is lovelier, more bewitching, more able to transport the spirit and inflame the heart, than a young maid when modesty brings a blush to her cheek and innocence gently lowers her eyelids. . . . Though she has little sparkle in her eyes and her features be not regular, her figure lacking in elegance, at that moment you will see her as an angel. And such an angel is the modest maid on whose countenance is ever etched a paradise of virtues. . . . I know of one beauty with eyes *black as the night* or *sapphirine (dial. poet. vet.)*,[2] with cheeks of *milk and roses*, teeth like *pearls*, bosom of *ivory*, *ebony* tresses (the allusion is varied, there is plenty of choice), who provided ample material for dozens of sonnets – when the sonnet reigned supreme – and in our day would inspire myriads of nonsensical, vaporous songs, intoned tearfully to the accompaniment of the harp or sobbed to the lute. Except for the lyre, which is classical, all instruments, including the bandore, are equal before romantic law.

But now then, that beauty, because of something modish about her, a brazen look in her eyes, a boldness about her face and a lack of composure in her manners, loses all the charm and almost loses the very beauty with which nature had endowed her. . . .

Just look at those ruby lips. Does flowering May ever produce a rose button so lovely at break of day? . . . And now look how a coarse laugh strips it so hideously with its ill-timed hilarity. . . .

Her prestige has vanished.

There was not a man, young or old, worldly or erudite, who would not have given half of his pleasures, his books, his life, for just one kiss from that mouth. Now perhaps not even constant *avances*★ can gain her the favours of a professional lover. . . . And she will have to pay him in advance, and at a price!

★　　★　　★

But what can all this have to do with the journey from Azambuja to Cartaxo? The closest and most genuine relation possible. Because while I was thinking or dreaming these things, I rode all the way until I was in the Azambuja pine forest.

There we stopped and I awoke.

I am subject to these distractions, to this day-dreaming. What can I do about it? Walking, talking, writing, I dream and walk, I dream and talk, I dream and write. I have to confess quite frankly to being a somnambulist, a somniloquist, a. . . . No, it is better with its Greek look (my Hellenic bump is in an astonishing state of tumescence today!) – let us say, somnilogic, somnigraphic. . . .

My honest and *conscientious* opinion is that the reader should skip these pages and go on to the next chapter, which is of another nature altogether.

V

———— ⋰ ————

The author comes to the pine forest of Azambuja and cannot find it. – He labours to explain this amazing phenomenon. – A fine burst of romantic style. – A recipe for composing original literature with little effort. – A classical transition: Orpheus and the wood on Maenalus. – The author descends from these lofty, sublime considerations to life's material realities: he is deserted by the hospitable carriage and has to ride the drover's pitiful mule. – The animal's admirable jogtrot. – Recollections of the Marquis of F., who was very fond of jogtrotting.

SO this is the pine forest of Azambuja?[1]

Not possible.

This the ancient forest feared almost religiously as a Druids' wood? And I who, as a child, could never hear stories about Pedro de Malas-Artes[2] but I straight away imagined the scene somewhere near here! . . . I who was expecting to come at any moment across the grave of Captain Roland and the lady Leonarda! . . . Oh, one more illusion I had to lose. . . .

In the name of all the curses and hells that adorn the style of a genuine romantic writer, tell me, tell me: where are the serried groves, where the awful sites of this bosky mass? Can it be possible? Can this be the pine forest of Azambuja? . . . I had them all ready, *cut out*, to place them here, all Schiller's friendly *Highwaymen* and the elegant criminals from the *Auberge des Adrets*,[3] and am I to lose my master-works? Because it is the same as losing them, having nowhere to put them! . . .

Yes, benevolent reader, and I shall take this opportunity to explain to you how we compose our literature nowadays. I no longer care about keeping the secret; after this disaster I no longer care one bit. You shall know then, reader, how we produce what we make you read.

Take the case of a novel or a drama. Do you imagine we are

going to study the history, the nature, the monuments, the paintings, the tombs, the buildings, the memoirs of the period? Don't be a simpleton, reader, and do not suppose that we are either. Drawing characters and situations from life and giving them the true colours of history . . . that is difficult, lengthy and delicate work, it needs study, talent and, most of all, special skill! . . . Not a bit of it: the business is done much more easily. Let me explain.

Every drama and every novel need:
One or two ladies (more or less naïve),
A father (noble or ignoble),
Two or three children, between nineteen and thirty years of age,
An old retainer,
A monster, whose job it is to perform the wicked deeds,
Several rogues and a few persons to act as go-betweens.

Now then, we go to the French models, Dumas, Eugène Sue, Victor Hugo, and we *cut out*, from each of them, the figures we need, stick them on a sheet of paper in a fashionable colour, green, grey, blue – the way English girls do in their albums and *scrapbooks*★ – and arrange them in the groups and situations that suit us; it doesn't matter if they are not very plausible. Then one ransacks the old chronicles for a handful of old names and rare words: the names are used to characterize the notables, the rare words *illuminate* them (hack-painter style). And that is how we compose our original literature.

And that is the precious work that I have just lost!

It just cannot be! A handful of skimpy, stunted pine-trees, through which the surrounding vineyards and olive groves are almost visible! . . . It is the most complete and utter disappointment I have ever had in my life – a right swindle, to use a good old-fashioned Portuguese expression.

And yet this is where it should be, and where it is, geographically and topographically speaking, the well-known and demarcated site of the pine forest of Azambuja. . . .

Can some Orpheus have passed through and used the magic powers of his lyre to carry with him the trees of this ancient, classical Maenalus of Lusitania's highwaymen?

I am not very slow to admit miracles when I cannot find some other way of explaining phenomena. The pine forest of

Azambuja has moved. Which of the many Orpheuses that one hears and sees around was the one who worked the miracle is more difficult to say. There are so many of them and they all sing so well! Who knows? Maybe they got together, formed a joint-stock company and negotiated a harmonic loan, and that way the miracle would be worked more easily. That is how everything is done nowadays. It is the way the treasury went over to the bank and the bank to the mutual insurance companies . . . why shouldn't they do the same with the Azambuja forest?

But where is it then? Will somebody tell me? . . .

Yes, sir, I shall: *it has been consolidated.* And if you do not know what that means, read the budgets, look at the lists of taxes, run your eyes over the votes of confidence, and if you still do not know how and where the Azambuja pine forest was *consolidated*, give up geography, which is clearly not your speciality, and go for finance, for which you have a flair. We shall have you elected for Arcozelo or for the eternal city – it's the same thing, you shall be on the finance committee, then *lord*★ of the treasury, minister: it is the *ladder*, it would not offend the mangy Constitution of '38, let alone the Charter.[4]

★   ★   ★

The worst thing is that, in the midst of these fields where once was Troy, in the midst of these sand dunes where once the pale fears of the Azambuja pine forest took refuge, my dear, kind carriage abandoned me. I was left like good old Xavier de Maistre, when, half-way round his room, his chair overbalanced and he fell, or almost fell – I cannot quite recall – flat on the floor.

I very nearly threw myself on the ground, like a spoilt child, when I saw our comfortable vehicle return to Azambuja and saw before me the sorry-looking donkeyish mule that, alas and alack, was to be my mode of transport from there to Santarém.

Ah well, what has to be, has to be, and there's nought to be done about it. Consoling myself with this true and *elegant* proverb, I lifted my spirit to the demands of the situation and decided to show myself a man of strength and endurance. I resignedly bestrode the rack of that ragged saddle, took in my left hand the unfeeling reins of raw leather and launched the creature into its fastest pace, which was a comfortable, extremely pleasant jogtrot such as would give endless delight to my respectable and eccentric friend, the Marquis of F.

He had a penchant, a passion, a craze, a mania for jogtrotting, did that remarkable gentleman, the last aristocratic man of letters this country produced. He just adored jogtrotting, the noble marquis did. I met him in Paris towards the end of his life, when he was eighty or thereabouts. He would quit his comfortable, well-sprung English carriage, and go riding in a certain hired cabriolet that he had picked for the hard, sharp vertical motion with which it shook one up and down. He made me try it one day: it was splendid. The jogging of that execrable Babieca[5] was transmitted from the old Norman stallion to the shafts and from the shafts to the shell of the cab complete and undiluted! I never saw anything like it. The marquis said it had tonic and purgative qualities; I described it as a most violent laxative.

He was one of the most extraordinary men, certainly the most remarkable Portuguese, I have ever known, that nobleman. He was as ugly as sin and as elegant as a monkey, and women adored him. He was a second son and lived from his earnings in the diplomatic missions to which he was always attached. He lived in great style and bequeathed considerable wealth at his death. When he printed one of his works, he would have a single copy made, which he kept for himself, and break up the types. . . . If I start telling stories about the Marquis of F., I shall never stop.

Let us spur on for Cartaxo, it is getting late.

VI

—— ·:· ——

It is shown that old Camoens had no choice but mingle the legends of classical mythology with those of Christianity. – Father José Agostinho is first considered right then wrong. – In the midst of these academico-literary disceptations the author comes to discover that one needs faith for everything in this world. – *This world*, because, as far as the other is concerned, he knew it already. – *The Lusiads, Faust* and the *Divine Comedy*. – Camoens's misfortune in being born before the romantic period. – The Styx and Cocytus are shown to be better places, after all, than Hell and Purgatory. – The author goes in search of the Marquis of Pombal and comes upon him in the Blessed Isles of the poet Alcaeus. – A game of whist between the illustrious deceased. – The marquis shows pity for Richard Smith and J. B. Say, poor fellows. – The marquis and his eyeglass answer the author's pretentious questions. – Return to the real world and arrival in Cartaxo.

THE most remarkable, I am not sure if I should, or at least if I shall continue to, say the most inexcusable defect that critics and disparagers have so far dug into in that *Iliad* of modern nations, the immortal *Lusiads*, is undoubtedly the heterogeneous and heterodox mixture of theology and mythology, of the allegorical myths of paganism and the austere symbols of Christianity. To tell the truth, and despite the rude gestures one might feel like making at Father José Agostinho,[1] even so, to see father Bacchus clothed *in pontificalibus*,[2] before the altar-piece of some saint or other, probably saying his *Dominus vobiscum* to some Bacchic or corybantic acolyte who answers *Et cum spiritu tuo!* – it cannot be, it's just too much. . . . And then there is that famous closing conceit, worthy of the *Fénix Renascida*:[3] The false adores the one true god!

For as long as I can remember, I have read and admired *The*

43

Lusiads; I am moved, I weep, I take pride in the greatest work of creative genius that has appeared in the world between the *Divine Comedy* and *Faust*. . . .

The Italian put his faith in God, the German in scepticism, the Portuguese in his native land. One has to believe in something to be great, not only a great poet, great in anything. An old nurse I had when I was little, Brízida, was a great teller of fairy stories, because she sincerely believed in witches. Napoleon believed in his star, Lafayette believed in Louis-Philippe's monarchist republic, and so that we too may dare to *celebrare domestica facta*, even in our day, our great men all believe in something, some in the Credit Agency, some in the idle rich, some in Master Adon-Hiram,[4] and some in the beauty and reality of the constitutionalist system by which we are fortunate to be governed.

But these beliefs are for those who used them to become important. What does a poor fellow like me have left to believe in? Me, despite the critics, I still believe in our Camoens. I always have.

And yet, since the age of innocence, when I so enjoyed those battles, those adventures, those love-stories, all those scenes that are so natural, so well portrayed, until my present inevitable age of experience, this prosaic age when the most beautiful creations of the human mind seem like foolish antics in the face of the real world, and the noble impulses of the heart just enthusiastic fancies; until this age of nostalgia for the past and hope in the future, but not of pleasure in the present, this age when my patriotism (might this too be illusion?) and my personal sense of the *beautiful* make reading *The Lusiads* a quite different pleasure, different from but not inferior to previous times – I have always been aware of that important defect in our great poem, and try as I would I could never find an excuse for it, let alone a justification.

But we keep on learning until we die, according to the adage, and so it is. There is another moral aphorism too, equally applicable to literary matters: that in order to find an excuse for other people's faults, one must consider, put oneself in the same circumstances, find oneself involved in the same difficulties.

Here am I, now, finding any excuse for poor Camoens, in order to justify him, and ready (for such are the charities of this world) to take to the field, lance at the ready, and to do battle with each and every adversary who attacks this weakness of his. Why should this be? Because my hour has come, and *si parva licet componere magnis*[5] (today the Latin bump is the swollen one) I now find myself in the same difficulty with this chapter as our bard with his poem.

I have forestalled any remarks with the above text: I am fully aware who Camoens was and who I am, but it is a case of a cleft stick, which is the same despite the difference of those who are in it. The author of *The Lusiads* found himself caught between his country's creed and the wonderful traditions of classical poetry, which was his teacher and his model.

There were no romantics, no romanticism yet, in those days, the world was very backward. The odes of Victor Hugo had not yet unseated those of Horace; the curses of Canidia[6] were thought more lyrical, more poetic than the nightmares of a condemned man in a chapel; people wept reading Ovid's *Tristia* because they could not snivel over Lamartine's *Méditations*. Andromache bidding farewell to Hector at the gates of Troy; Priam prostrate at the feet of his son's killer; Helen torn between remorse for her crime and love for Paris – they had not yet been eclipsed by mother Eve's ravings at the gates of the earthly paradise. The combat of Hector and Achilles, and of the Argive and Trojan hosts, had yet to be cut down to size by the pitched battles between good and bad angels, bombarding their way through the clouds. Dido weeping for Aeneas had not yet been reduced to a snivelling Alfama wench lamenting her Manel[7] who is off to India.

The world really was backward. Milton had not yet taken Homer's place, nor Shakespeare that of Euripides, and Lord Byron over and above them all: in a word, the world was not yet anglicized, so that, putting the *march of the intellect* on the same level, it is all a bad business.

So now, then: our Camoens, the creator of the epic and – after Dante – of modern poetry, found himself in a quandary: he mixed his religious beliefs with his poetic creed and committed, *tranchons le mot*⋆, a lapse of taste.

And here I shall echo the words of the bard Elmano:[8]

> Camoens, oh great Camoens, how much alike
> I find thy fate and mine when I compare!

Now I too am going to commit a lapse of taste, in this fine chapter of my masterpiece. What choice have I? I need to talk to one of the illustrious deceased; I need to summon the shade of a great genius who now dwells among the dead. So where shall I go? To Hell? I hope that divine justice took pity on him in his final hour of repentance. To Purgatory, to the Empyrean? Despite the example of the *Divine Comedy* I do not dare make a comedy with such settings – and, well, I don't know, but I do not like to play with such things.

I can see no other way than to resort to the blessed Elysian fields, the Styx, Cocytus and its environs: they are neutral ground where one can parley with the dead without serious involvement and . . .

And here I am, making the same mistake as Camoens and falling into the hands of the critics, with their darts raining down on me, because I did this, that and the other . . .

But, gentlemen, consider, come now: what is one to do? I do not know what cunning Dante had that he was able to baptize Publius Virgilius Maro to act as his guide in the regions of the Christian Hell, Purgatory and Paradise, and with such good fortune that he was neither burned by the Inquisition nor admonished by the Crusca,[9] not even mutilated by the censors, persecuted by the police for abuse of freedom of the press, nor yet sent to be judged by his peers. . . . They hadn't yet discovered the liberal skullduggery practised nowadays, and the charters that the people had were their freedom won and upheld at sword-point, with much courage and few words, much patriotism, few laws . . . and even less reports. In Florence there was neither gazette to praise the ministers' follies, nor were there ministers to pay for the gazette's follies.

Dante was outlawed and exiled, but he did not stop writing: he belaboured to his heart's content the enemies of freedom in his native country.

We could do with a battalion of poets like him!

Let a wretched bard nowadays, in the age of enlightenment, write what Dante wrote in the dark ages! Even the philosophers would cry Scandalous! Professed atheists would shout out against the irreverence; people without religion, not even that of Mahomet, would clamour on behalf of religion; they would start putting hoods on each other's heads, then fall upon the poet and, if they could not hang him, they would at least declare him a republican, which according to them is a very serious insult.

Enough! Long live Camoens and his wonderful hodgepodge, it is the most convenient invention in the world. I shall go along with it and the critics can carp all they like.

I wish to search the world of shades for no less a person than the Marquis of Pombal; I have a serious question to ask him before I reach Cartaxo. And we are already riding among the rich vineyards that surround it with a zone of freshness and greenery. Quick, the golden branch to open the dreaded gates to my wish! Quick, the honeyed sop to throw to the three jaws of the great dog![10] Let us go. . . .

But in what part of these regions shall I find King José's prime minister? Where are Ixion and Tantalus, where dwell Sisyphus and other rogues of that sort? No, this is a very gloomy district and is likely to have as mayor some madman who will redden my ears.

In the Elysium with father Anchises and other classical greybeards of that ilk? How should I know? Surely not. He must be in those Isles of the Blest referred to by the poet Alcaeus, who set the tyrannical souls of Harmodios and Aristogiton to walk there among the eternal greenery. . . .

Well, I never! What's this? Sebastião José de Carvalho e Melo, Count of Oeiras and Marquis of Pombal, in the company of his political enemies. . . . That is where you are wrong. There are no longer political friends and enemies once you leave office and renounce all pretension to it. So once past the portals of eternity it is certain that one no longer thinks of these things. C.J.X.,[11] who died in the act of signing an edict, had already dropped his pen by the time he got there via Prazeres,[12] no less! . . .

The fellow must be in the Isles of the Righteous. Let us try there . . .

There he is. There's the good marquis playing whist with Baron Bidefeld, with the Emperor Leopold and the poet Dinis.[13] The game must be interesting, perhaps all these people have bets – all these shades in a circle about them. What a scowl the marquis gave some poor soul who went and put his nose into his cards! Imagine who it was! That nosy Monsieur Talleyrand. He almost fell on top of him. But he didn't see anything: the noble marquis was always good at concealing his hand.

He has already seen me.

'What did you say? Ah! Yes, sir, I am Portuguese and I have come to ask your lordship a question, to ask you to clear up an important point for me.'

He flourished his fearful eyeglass at me.

'Why did you order the Ribatejo vineyards to be torn up?'

He screwed his eyeglass into his brow and smiled.

'They have increased a hundredfold, now they have even invaded the pine forest of Azambuja. You committed an unnecessary despotic act and now . . .'

'Now who drinks all that wine thereabouts?'

I didn't know what answer to give him. He shook his head of curls, turned his back on me, took Colbert by the arm, passed close by Richard Smith[14] and J. Baptiste Say, who were arguing, gave a pitying shrug of his shoulders and entered a lush avenue that led into those delightful gardens, disappearing from our sight.

I came back up into this world and found myself mounted on the ass and right outside Cartaxo's grand café.

VII

— ·:· —

Important reflections on the Bois de Boulogne, sprung
carriages, Tortoni's and the café at Cartaxo. – On cafés in
general and how they are characteristic of a country's
civilization. – The *Alfageme*. – Unintentional hecatomb
carried out by the author. – Cartaxo's history. – It is shown
how Great Britain always owed all her power and glory to
Portugal. – Shakespeare and Lafite, Milton and Château-
Margaux, Nelson and the Prince de Joinville. – Monsieur
Guizot is proved to be obviously the ruin of Albion and of
Cartaxo.

To return at midnight from the Bois de Boulogne, the wood
par excellence, descend, amid clouds of dust, the long stadium of
the Champs-Élysées, snatching a passing glimpse of the Luxor
obelisk, the trees in the Tuileries, the column in the Place
Vendôme, the heteroclite magnificence of the Madeleine, then at
last feel the two powerful English greys that carried us in one
gallop to the Boulevard de Gand brought to a masterly halt; and
then to half open a lazy eye, raise oneself a little from the
delightful comfort of the silk cushions and say, 'Ah, we are at
Tortoni's.... How delightful, an ice-cream in this heat!' – is
assuredly one of the finest pleasures in the world, one feels that
this is life: a half-hour of such an existence is worth ten years as
king in any other part of the world.

Well, believe me, dear reader, I know something of the
pleasures and disappointments of this world; take my word, it is
that of a man of experience: the pleasure of arriving in that
manner at Tortoni's, getting down from that elegant barouche
that bowls along on the softest springs that English skill has
fashioned from pure Swedish steel, cannot equal, cannot
compare with the pleasure and consolation of body and soul that
I felt on dismounting from my jogtrotting mule at the door of
Cartaxo's grand café.

Do you have any idea of what the Cartaxo café is like? Of course you don't. They just do not travel, do not go out, see nothing of the world, these Lisbon people! If they spend their life between the Chiado, the Rua do Ouro and the São Carlos theatre, how can they extend the sphere of their knowledge, develop their minds, put themselves on a par with the century?

Crown yourselves with lettuce and go and play billiards or write sonnets to your latest lady-love; go on, you are no good for anything else, my dear Lisbonese. Or debate the insipid horrors of some melodrama that was hissed off the stage at Porte Saint-Martin and escaped to hide in the Rua dos Condes.[1] You can go to the bullfight as well – their horns are padded, there is no danger . . .

Travel? . . . What travel! As far as the Cova da Piedade, at most, on days when they have bareback riders. Then you shall be 'little lettuces'[2] for ever and imagine all the squares in the world are like the Terreiro do Paço, all the streets like the Rua Augusta, all the cafés like the Café Marrare.

Well, they are not, and the Cartaxo one less than any.

The café is one of the most characteristic features of a country. The experienced, sharp-witted traveller can arrive anywhere, go into the café, look at it, examine it, study it, and he knows all about the country he is in, its government, its laws, its customs, its religion.

Take me blindfold wherever you like and remove the blindfold only in the café: I promise you that, in less than ten minutes, I shall tell you which country I am in, if it be a sublunary land.

We entered the Cartaxo café, Cartaxo's grand café, and never did a Turk lower himself cross-legged on to the silk divan of the most splendid harem in Constantinople with as much spiritual pleasure and bodily satisfaction as when we sat down on the hard, rough boards of the narrow, blotchily painted benches which adorn that magnificent Borda-d'Água establishment.

Its classical simplicity can be described in a few lines. It would be a parallelogram little bigger than my bedroom; on the left, two pine tables; on the right, the glass counter whereon are exhibited the obligatory bottles of almond, cinnamon and clove liqueur. From the ceiling, laboriously fashioned by no ordinary pair of scissors, hang paper droppers, inviting to lascivious repose the restless race of flies. An admirable coolness reigns in that enclosure.

We sat down, took a deep breath and entered into conversation with the master of the house, a man of between thirty and forty, with a lively, pleasant face, nothing like the nasty, repulsive villains one so frequently comes across in similar places in my country.

'So what's the news here around Cartaxo, landlord?'

'News?! Nothing in these parts except what comes from Lisbon. Here is yesterday's *Revolução* . . .'[3]

'Newspapers, my dear fellow! We've had enough of them. Tell us some local news. What is happening to. . . ?'

'Master J.P.,[4] the Armourer?'

'How do you mean, the Armourer?'

'That's what they call Master J.P., of course! Some gentlemen from Lisbon, who stayed at Senhor D.'s, gave him that name, and we know what it means. It stuck and now nobody calls him anything else but the Armourer. But for my money either he isn't the Armourer or he won't be for much longer. He's not the one, no. I know what I'm saying.'

The conversation was taking an interesting turn, especially for me. We tried to go into it more deeply.

'That's quite a story, landlord! So you think this Armourer business is to do with . . .'

'I think it's what it is, what everyone thinks. And we know a bit, here in Cartaxo, about what's going on around us. The real Armourer, they say he was a sword-maker or weapon-maker, a knife-grinder or something of the sort, in Ribeira de Santarém, and that he was an honourable man and sided with the people,[5] and didn't want to have anything to do with parties, for he said: "We shall never lack a king to hang us and a pope to excommunicate us. So let the others fight and let us work and earn our living." But that he didn't want foreigners: he said this land is ours and shall be governed by our own people. And more of the same, until they finally called him a traitor and took away everything he had. But that the Constable, who was an upright character and a true nobleman, helped him and would not let them dispossess him. Isn't that the way it was?'

'Yes, indeed, my friend. And then what?'

'Well, then you conclude that when there were noblemen like

the saintly Constable, there were also armourers like the one from Santarém. That's all.'

'Exactly, but why did they give Master P. the name of Armourer of Cartaxo?'

'I'll tell you. The man was nothing special. He spoke well and had the gift of the gab with the people. So he made himself a judge and set things to rights hereabouts – God knows the things he set wrong as well –, made a name for himself with the ordinary people and now he does what he likes with them. As long as it always suits him to do good, all well and good. . . . Can't I get you anything?'

The good fellow clearly did not want to say any more and we should not bother him. We sacrificed several lemons, which we squeezed into deep goblets – *vulgo* three-pint mugs – and with water and sugar we offered the due libations to the genius of the place.

Unfortunately the sacrifice was not altogether bloodless. Many hecatombs of myrmidons[6] fell in the holocaust and gave it a smell and a taste which may or may not have pleased the divinity, but made the priests feel terribly sick.

We left and went to visit our good old friend D., who is the life and soul of the Ribatejo. He already knew of our arrival and was on his way to greet us.

Together we went for a stroll around the place.

Cartaxo is one of the prettiest villages in Portugal, clean and bright; it looks like the residential suburb of a city. There are no monuments here, no ancient history: the town is new and its growth and prosperity date back thirty or forty years, from when its wine started to be known. It has now declined from what it was, owing to the stagnation of that business, but it is still, nevertheless, the best thing in the Borda-d'Água area.

It has no ancient history, as I said, but it does have a very important recent history.

What memories there are here of the Peninsular War! What fantastic drinking bouts were indulged in here by the most famous generals, the most distinguished military men of our *old and faithful ally*, which then at least still drank our wine!

Nowadays, not even that! . . . Now they drink that Jacobin concoction from Bordeaux and those bitter lemonades from Burgundy. Who would expect that of conservative Albion!

How can a loyal British throat, roughened by the anarchist acids of those French *vins* very *ordinaires*, give proper voice to *God Save the King*★ in a national *toast*★?! How, without Oporto or Madeira, Lisbon or Cartaxo, can a British subject raise his voice in that harmonious, insular cacophony that is peculiar to him and part of his respectable national character? Yes, it is; do not laugh: an Englishman sings only when he drinks ... or rather when he has 'had a drop'. *Nisi potus ad arma ruisse.* Alter to: *Nisi potus in cantum prorumpisse....* And how, when he has 'had a drop' of *that*, can he raise his voice in that sublime and tremendous popular hymn, *Rule, Britannia!*★

Go on, drink French mouthwash, my English friends; go on, pay the earth to drink those lemonades from the burgraves and margraves of Germany – you may call them, to deceive yourselves, you may call them *hoc*, call them *hic*, call them the whole *hic haec hoc*, if it pleases you, and in a few years we shall see your national character reduced to an *acetate*.

Oh, blind nation that God wishes to destroy! Can you not see that you are nothing without us, that without our alcohol, whence came your wit, your science, your courage, you will infallibly go back to your ancient, lazy, Saxon uncouthness!

From those treacherous French shores, whence you now receive the poison that is corroding your nature and your power, shall ere long arrive another Bastard William, to conquer and chastise you, to make you repent, later, the criminal error you make today, o faithless islanders, by abandoning our alliance. Our alliance, yes, our strong alliance, without which you are nothing.

What is an Englishman without Oporto or Madeira, without Carcavelos or Cartaxo?

Had Shakespeare sought his inspiration in Lafite or Milton in Château-Margaux, or chancellor Bacon diluted himself in the best Burgundy ... we should see what poor vinegary jingles and what wretched distempered quibbles they would have produced.

For all his diets Newton never thought of drinking Johannisberger; Byron would rather have drunk gin, or Thames or Pamisos water, than those dregs from the sands of Bordeaux.

Deprive your admirals of their port wine and no one will be afraid that you might have another Nelson. Making you drink his mouthwash is part of the Prince de Joinville's plan: it amounts to so many points a hand that you give him for his game.

It is Monsieur Guizot who is ruining England with his alliance; he it is too that is ruining Cartaxo. For that reason, I want nothing more to do with the doctrinaires.[7]

★   ★   ★

Twelve years ago Cartaxo once more figured conspicuously in Portuguese history. During the terrible, long-drawn-out struggles of the last war of succession, the Marquis of Saldanha had his headquarters here for quite a time.

Some dithyrambs were composed, some echoes of the old Bacchic songs from the days of the Peninsular War still came to life at the sound of the constitutional hymns.

But the liberal regime, except at election time, is not a good thing for the wine-growing industry, or so they say. I don't believe it, though, and I have good reason, which can wait until another opportunity.

VIII

———— ∴ ————

Departure from Cartaxo. – The heath. – The author finds himself in imminent danger of turning poet and writing verses. – The Emperor Dom Pedro's last review of the liberal army. – The Battle of Almoster. – Waterloo. – The author makes a solemn declaration that he is not a philosopher and reaches the bridge over the Asseca.

IT had struck five in the afternoon; the heat was abating. We mounted and rode among the lush vines that are the glory and beauty of Cartaxo. The mules were refreshed and livelier and soon we found ourselves out on the heath.

What a fine, vast plain! No longer oppressed by the sun's rays, how soothingly it is outlined against the horizon! What a delightful, woody aroma is given off by these pungent, tenacious plants with which it is covered and which stay green and glossy in the heat of Portugal's July sun.

The gentle feelings aroused in the spirit by the refreshing view of a young wheatfield in the Ribatejo in early April, undulating sensuously in the mild spring breeze; the bucolic delight of a Minho cornfield at watering time, in mid-August, when the stalks leap in the splashing water, surrounded by oak trees classically wedded to vines hung with bunches of black grapes – both scenes possess a poetry so charming and tender such as I never found translated even in the best verses of Theocritus or Virgil, or in the most perfect prose of Gessner or Rodrigues Lobo.[1]

The sombre, solemn majesty of an ancient, bosky wood, the silence and dark of its densest thickets, the solitary shelter of its clearings, all this is grandiose, sublime and inspires lofty thoughts. One cannot help meditating there: the soul is cut off from the senses because of the gentle torpor into which they fall ... and God, eternity – man's primitive, innate ideas – are left alone in one's thoughts. . . .

55

That is how it is. Yet I have but to sit, at sunset, on a rock in the wild, deserted moorland, coated only with low, wild grazing, eaten short by the cattle, and it tells me things about heaven and earth like no other spectacle in nature. There is something vague, hazy, filmy in such a scene that does not exist in any other.

It is not the sublimity of the mountain, or the majesty of the wood, or yet the delight of the valley. There is nothing very specific there, nothing that can be positively defined. There is the solitude, which is a negative idea....

I love the heath.

And I am not fanciful, and as for romantic God, save me from that, at least from what the word means in today's slang.

Well, the heath between Cartaxo and Santarém, at the hour of day when we crossed it, was beginning to take on that hue and I was just discovering in it that indefinable charm.

I felt in the mood for writing poetry.... To what? I do not know.

Fortunately I was not alone and got out of yet another vexation.

But it was just as if I were writing poetry, as if I were actually composing a poem, because I allowed myself to fall into a real poetic state of distraction and silence, my vital energies ceased to function and I was aware only of my inner existence.

Suddenly my lethargy was broken by a voice exclaiming: 'It was here! ... This is where it was, without a doubt.'

'Where what was?'

'The Emperor's last review.'

'The last review?! What do you mean, the last review?! When? Well?...'

Then I came completely to myself and remembered, with bitterness and disillusionment, the tremendous sacrifices to which my generation was condemned, God knows why – God knows whether it was to expiate the guilt of our forefathers, or to purchase the happiness of our descendants....

The truth of the matter is that the Emperor Dom Pedro had indeed reviewed the liberal army there for the last time. It was after the Battle of Almoster, one of the bitterest and bloodiest of that dreadful war.

Civil war is always dreadful.

And it is difficult to say for whom it is more dreadful, for the victors or for the vanquished.

Set aside personal questions and examine the matter in good faith: you will see that, for the whole of each faction into which the nation was divided, the gains, if there were any, for the victors do not make up for the sufferings and sacrifices from the past, less still their responsibility for the future. . . .

I am no philosopher. In a philosopher's eyes, civil war and war between nations are both wars to be condemned – the one no more than the other . . . unless the philosopher happens to be Hobbes, which is a different matter.

But I am no philosopher. I was on the field of Waterloo, I sat by the bronze lion on that mound of earth soaked with the blood of all those thousands, I saw – twenty years after – I still saw the glint of the white bones of the victims who sacrificed themselves for goodness knows what. . . . The nations said for freedom, the kings said for royalty. . . . Neither gained very much from that victory, nor for very long. . . .

But that is enough. I was there and I felt my heart quicken with the recollections, the memories of the great feats and gallantry that occurred there.

Why is it that all I feel here is sadness?

Because fratricidal struggles can inspire no other sentiment and because. . . .

I mulled over these bitter thoughts by myself and all the beauty of the heath vanished before my eyes.

In this unpleasant frame of mind we reached the bridge over the Asseca.

IX

SOME fifty or sixty years ago there lived here, in this good land of Portugal, a very odd character who undoubtedly had a gift for discovering national subjects for the stage; at times he even showed skill in sketching out the scenario and some ability in assembling the characters. But when it came to putting them in motion, to giving them life, to making them speak . . . it was the end! He was a hopeless bore.

He left an enormous collection of plays that no one, or scarcely anyone, knows, and not one of which would probably bear staging. Yet few of them could not be patched up and made stageworthy. What a rich, fertile wellspring for a middling dramatic talent! What fine, Portuguese things might be extracted from the thirteen volumes – there are thirteen large volumes – of the theatrical works of our Ennius, Manuel de Figueiredo![1] Some of his plays, with very little work, more life in the dialogue, a more spirited style, would make excellent comedies.

I am thinking of the following:

O casamento da cadeia (The Prison Wedding), perhaps the title is different but that is the subject – a comedy with skilfully drawn characters based on an old law of ours that forced men to get married in prison when it was felt that they could thereby remedy certain damage to a lady's reputation.

O fidalgo de sua casa (Lord in His House), a very witty satire on a particularly common national foible.

As duas educações (Two Upbringings), a fine comedy of manners. It concerns two youths, both given foreign upbringings, one French, the other English, neither Portuguese. It is exceedingly comic, convincing, or, as the fashionable expression has it, 'excitingly modern'.

O cioso (The Jealous Husband), an updated version of Ferreira's old comedy, with all the seeds of a truly rich and original composition.

O avaro dissipador (The Spendthrift Miser), whose very title reveals the wit and inventiveness of the man who devised such a topic, one never before used by any dramatic author of any country, yet which is a common foible seen every day in the real world.

There are many more, not just these, of this prolific author's compositions, which, if sifted through the filter of good taste and livened up particularly in their style, would make a reasonable repertoire to make up for the dearth of material in our theatres.

One of the dullest, however, perhaps the one that will generally be considered the dullest, but that amuses me because of the pleasant, familiar naïveté of its maudlin, gloomy banality, is the one with the title *Poeta em anos de prosa* (A Poet in Times of Prose). And it was because of this one, all because of this one that I let myself be led into the dramatic and literary digression at the beginning of this chapter: it stuck to my pen because it had got stuck in my head, and unless it first got out the chapter would not get started.

A Poet in Times of Prose! Oh, Figueiredo, Figueiredo, what a great man you were to invent a title that is a book in itself! There are books, and I know a good many, that should have no title, and whose title is nothing to do with them.

Kindly tell me what is the use, the meaning of *Wandering Jew*, placed on the title-page of that interminable, mercenary novel that is all over the place, more wandering, more aimless, more undying than its prototype?

And there are titles too which should have no book, because no book can be written that represents them as they deserve.

A Poet in Times of Prose is one of them.

I do not read a single one of those really beautiful works that are seldom written today, works, that is, that are simple, true and therefore sublime, without exclaiming to myself with sincere dejection: *Poet in Times of Prose!*

Well, is this a poets' century? Or do we have poets for the century? . . .

Yes, we do. I know three: Bonaparte, Silvio Pellico and Baron Rothschild.

The first made his Iliad with the sword, the second with patience, the third with money.

They are the three agents, the three entities, the three deities of our time.

Either we slash with Bonaparte, or buy with Rothschild, or suffer patiently with Silvio Pellico.

Anyone who writes any other sort of poetry – or prose, for that matter – is a fool. . . .

These most judicious reflections occurred to me concerning the previous chapter of this masterpiece of mine, and I set them down here for the instruction and edification of my benevolent reader.

I finished them when we reached the bridge over the Asseca.

I forgot to mention that of those three great poets only one is translated into Portuguese: Rothschild. The translation is not literal, it is bastardized and much polluted by misprints, but as there is no other. . . .

Now where did this name Asseca come from? Somewhere near here there must be a site, place or what have you with the name Meca, and perhaps this is the origin of the admirable Portuguese saying that has still not been properly studied as it ought to be and surely contains some important, primitive moral axiom: '. . . he travelled through Seca [Asseca?] and Meca and olive groves of Santarém'.[2] Those olive groves are just ahead. It is as good an etymology as the next man's.

The Asseca bridge cuts through a vast tract of meadow land that must be an enormous marsh in winter; even now it is oozing water everywhere.

This place is noteworthy in modern history. Here, during a skirmish with our troops, Junot was seriously wounded, wounded in the face. *Il ne sera plus beau garçon*, said the French negotiator who came after the battle, to arrange an exchange of prisoners or something like that, I believe. But the negotiator was wrong, Junot continued to be very good-looking and elegant afterwards.

I regret never having seen either Junot or One-arm,[3] the two foremost notables I heard acclaimed as such and whose names I knew . . . I am mistaken: I knew Bonaparte's name first. And I remember perfectly well I never convinced myself that he was the ugly, awesome monster priests and old women made him out to be at that time. I always supposed that for him to arouse such hatred and ill will he would need to be a really great man.

I have been a Jacobin since I was little, of course, and when I was little I suffered for it. I got my ears boxed by my father, because at the St Lazarus fair in Oporto, instead of penny whistles or bookmarks with saints' pictures or similar trifles such as the other lads were buying, I bought – guess what! – a picture of Bonaparte.

It was a jinx, as a lady of my acquaintance, who believes in them, would say; it was a jinx that has still not gone away and has pursued me all my life.

Who could have said at that time, when, because of that first political sin of my childhood, because of that first harsh and – begging the forgiveness of my dear father's respected memory! – extremely unjust treatment brought about by my mere instinct for liberal ideas, who could have said that I would suffer persecution for them all my life; that, when I was barely out of puberty, I would have to go to that same France, the home of those men and ideas with whom my nature sympathized for reasons unknown to me, in search of shelter and protection?

I saw hardly any of those I so desired to meet: the ruins of the great empire were scattered, her generals dead or exiled, or wearing, from cowardly self-interest, the colours of the victor. . . .

Of all the great figures of that time, the one I knew best and had most contact with was a lady, the epitome of charm, of affability and talent. Our contact was brief, but it was enough to enchant me and to fashion in my mind a model of feminine courage and excellence that turned out to be very bad for me later.

It is difficult afterwards to reach the same level. . . .

This is how I made her acquaintance.

61

I can still see him – poor fellow! – poor Count of S., noble, witty, gentlemanly, whom one forgave all his caste prejudices, and he had them all, because of the superior politeness and elegant affability that distinguish the genuine aristocrat (old style). I can see him now, already sexagenarian, much more than *ci-devant jeune homme*★, his neck held stiff by his inflexible cravat, his feet sticking to the doorstep, like Ovid's – not held fast by nostalgia, but paralysed by incipient cachexia, his youthful spirit reacting and insisting.

'Come on!' he said. 'I'm fine today, I feel a different man. I want to introduce you to Mme de Abrantes. She is so aged! Women are not like us, they age so quickly. . . .'

And the poor old fellow's legs trembled and he choked with coughing.

We took a *citadine*★ and went to an elegant, new street, not inappropriately called the Rue de Londres, where we found that beauteous star of the empire surrounded by all the splendour of her decline.

I do not wish to give the idea that she was a beauty, far from it. The Duchess of Abrantes was neither beautiful, nor young, nor noticeably handsome. But half an hour of conversation, of contact, was enough to reveal so much charm, such naturalness, such affability, so true and perfect an embodiment of the Frenchwoman, who is the most alluring woman in the world, that one said to oneself unthinkingly: 'How comfortable one feels here!'

We talked about Portugal, about Lisbon, about the empire, the Restoration, the July revolution (it was 1831), Monsieur de Lafayette, Louis-Philippe, Chateaubriand – her great friend –, the Sacré Coeur and its elegant votaries[4] – we talked about the arts, poetry, politics . . . and I had not the courage to end the conversation.

Benevolent and patient reader, what I do still have is a conscience, a bit of a conscience: let us be done with these constant digressions and divagations of mine. I am fully aware that I left you waiting for me half-way across the Asseca bridge. Forgive me, I beg of you. Let us spur on our mules and be on our way, it is getting late.

Here we are in one of the loveliest and most delightful places on earth: the vale of Santarém, home of nightingales and honeysuckle, encircled by fair yews and lush bay trees. Paris has nothing like this, nor all of France, nor any other Western country but ours, and it makes up for the many things we do not have.

X

———— .:. ————

The vale of Santarém. – The author takes a fancy to a
window seen through some trees. – Conjectures about said
window. – Similarity between a poet and a woman in love
and undoubted inferiority of the man who is not a poet. –
Nightingales. Remembrance of Bernardim Ribeiro and his
Saudades.[1] – How the author had his romance wellnigh
complete, but for a white dress and a pair of black eyes. –
The eyes turn out to be green, to his great surprise and
amazement. – His conjectures about the mysterious
window are shown to be true. – The maiden of the
nightingales. – The ladies' rebuke, to be much feared; the
dandies' criticism, to be much derided. – Here begins the
first episode of this odyssey.

THE vale of Santarém is one of those places privileged by
nature, pleasant, delightful spots where plants, air and situation
are in the most gentle and perfect harmony: nothing there is
grandiose or sublime, but there is a certain symmetry of colours,
sounds and disposition in everything one sees and hears, that it
can seem that only peace, health, spiritual tranquillity and
heart's ease must dwell there, that love and kindness must reign
supreme. Evil passions, petty thoughts, the burdens and base
things in life can flee only far away. From this spot one can
imagine the Eden that the first man lived in with his innocence
and the virgin purity of his heart.

To the left of the vale, sheltered from the north by the
mountain that rises almost sheer, there is a clump of greenery of
great lushness and variety. The yew, the ash and the poplar join
their friendly branches; honeysuckle and musk-rose drape their
garlands and festoons one to another; periwinkle, fern and
hollyhock cover and carpet the ground.

The beauty of the scene is further enhanced by what one can
see through a gap in the trees, the half-open window of an old,

but not dilapidated cottage, having an appearance of rough comfort, its walls darkened by time and by the southern gales to which it is exposed. The window is wide and low; it looks more ornate, perhaps older, than the remainder of the building, though this is hardly visible . . .

The window awoke my interest.

Who might have the good taste and good fortune to live there?

I stopped and stood ogling the window.

It charmed me, it had me there as if spellbound.

I thought I caught a glimpse of a white curtain . . . and a figure behind it. . . . Imagination surely! If the figure were female! . . . My romance would be complete.

How beautiful it must be to see the sunset from that window! . . .

And to listen to the song of the nightingales! . . .

And watch dawn break on a May morning! . . .

Can there be anyone there to make the most of it, of that delightful window? . . . Someone who appreciates and can enjoy all the tranquil pleasure, all the innocent joys of the spirit that seem to flutter around it?

If it be a man, he is a poet; if a woman, she is in love.

They are the two most similar beings in nature, a poet and a woman in love: they see, feel, think and speak as other people neither see, nor feel, nor think, nor speak.

The greatest passion, the purest affection of a man who is not a poet contains a certain amount of common human prose: it is an alloy essential to the production of his finest gold. A woman, no. A woman in love really becomes sublime, immediately becomes divine, she is all poetry, and neither physical pain, material interest nor sensual enjoyment bring her down to the reality of prosaic existence.

While I was lost in these meditations, a nightingale started the loveliest, most exquisite song I can remember hearing for a long time.

It was over by that window!

Another answered immediately from the other side, and the two of them joined in a contest that was so balanced, in alternate verses that were so measured, so modulated, so perfect, that I lost myself in my romance oblivious to everything else.

I remembered Bernardim Ribeiro's nightingale, the one that fell into the water, of sheer exhaustion.

The trees, the window, the nightingale . . . the hour of day, late afternoon . . . what more was needed to complete the romance?

A female figure to come and sit at that balcony, in a white dress – oh, it must be white! . . . – her forehead resting on her left hand, her right hand hanging down, her eyes raised to the sky. What colour eyes? I don't know, what does it matter? That would be putting too much detail in the painting and it should be in large, broad lines, so as to be romantic and vaporous, drawn with the vagueness of ideal poetic sentiment . . .

'The eyes, the eyes . . .', I said, by now thinking aloud, but still enraptured, 'the eyes . . . black.'

'Well, they were green!'

'Her eyes green . . . hers, the figure at the window?'

'Green as two priceless, gleaming, transparent oriental emeralds.'

'No, really! . . . Is that a joke or is there really a pretty woman there?'

'There is no one there – no one whose name is mentioned now, but there was . . . oh, there was an angel who must be in heaven.'

'I was right then, when I called that window . . .'

'It is the window of the nightingales.'

'The ones that are singing.'

'Yes, they are there still as they were ten years ago – the same or another pair, but the *maiden of the nightingales* has gone and never came back.'

'The maiden of the nightingales?! What story is this? So that window really does have a story?'

'It is a complete romance, *all done* as the French say,[2] and it can be told in a few words.'

'Let us hear it. The maiden of the nightingales, the green-eyed maiden! It must be very interesting. Let us hear the story, straight away.'

'All right. Let us dismount and rest a while.'

This dialogue obviously took place between myself and one of my travelling companions. We did indeed dismount; we sat down and this is the story of the *maiden of the nightingales*, as it was told to me.

It is the first episode of my odyssey. I am afraid to start it, because the ladies and the men of fashion in my country say that Portuguese is not suitable for it, that French has a certain *je ne sais quoi*. . . .

I think the ladies are ill-informed and I know that the men of fashion are a bunch of fools, yet I am always a bit apprehensive, because, when all's said and done, I may laugh at the latter, but be it poetry or a novel, music or drama, if the ladies do not like it, it is because it is no good.

Nevertheless, fair, gentle readers, let us understand one another: what I am going to relate is not a novel, it has no complicated adventures, no unexpected events, no rare situations or incidents; it is a simple, naïve little story, unpretentiously and honestly told.

This chapter's end shall serve as a prologue and the subject matter of my tale shall go into the next.

XI

———— ·:· ————

Concerning the only privilege of poets, one which the philosophers wanted to gain for themselves, but which they were not awarded, while the novelists were. – Aristotle and Anacreon as examples. – The author, having declared, in the ninth chapter of this work, that he was not a philosopher, now confesses, with near solemnity, that he is a poet and as such means to conserve his right. – How His Majesty the King of Denmark had less sense than Yorick, his jester. – Yorick's teaching. – The author takes it as the basis for his admirable system of transcendental physiology and pathology relating to the heart. – By means of a strict, rigorous deduction in the most thoroughgoing logic, we arrive at the reason why poets were granted the indefinite right to be always in love. – All these theories are applied to the present situation of the author at the moment when he embarks on the episode promised in the previous chapter. – Modesty and polite diffidence cause him to doubt his qualification for the enterprise; he requests his female readers to take a vote. – It is agreed that the vote shall not be nominal and explained why. – Dido and her sister Annie. – A start is made at last to the promised story. – How the old woman was sitting winding yarn on the doorstep and called her granddaughter, Joaninha, when the yarn became twisted.

THE sole privilege of poets is this: that they can be in love until they die. And it is the only one, to my knowledge. Everyone else has his time of life and after that is not allowed to fall in love. The philosophers tried to obtain the same benefit, but this was not allowed them by Queen Opinion, who is absolute monarch and judge supreme, against whom no one appeals or complains.

Anacreon sang his passion when his hair was white and no one thought it strange. Aristotle's beard was scarcely grey at the time of that last love affair, yet his good reputation still suffers even now because of it.

Now I am certainly no philosopher, as I have said before. I am a bit of a poet, as a matter of fact I have suffered some quite severe attacks of that disease and might well use them to excuse certain weaknesses of the heart. . . . But not a bit of it: I have no wish to excuse myself as if I were at fault, preferring to defend myself as one who has reason and justice on his side.

I agree with my friend Yorick, the King of Denmark's very sensible jester who some years later was resuscitated in Sterne with such an elegant pen, indeed I do. 'I have been', says he, 'in love with one princess or other almost all my life, and I hope I shall go on so till I die, being firmly persuaded, that if I ever do a mean [petty] action, it must be in some interval betwixt one passion and another: while this interregnum lasts I always perceive my heart locked up [my feelings cold] – I can scarce find in it to give misery a sixpence: and therefore I always get out of it as [fast as] I can and the moment I am rekindled, I am all generosity and good will again.'[1]

Yorick is right, he was much more right and sensible than his august master the King of Denmark. Generalize the principle only a little more and it will become indisputable and absolute for ever and in everything. Man's heart is like his stomach, it cannot be empty, it always needs nourishment as only the affections can give it, healthy and in abundance; hatred, envy and other evil passions are stimulants that merely irritate without giving sustenance. If reason and morality tell us to abstain from these latter passions, and if philosophical or other fancies forbid us the former, what nourishment will you give to the heart, what shall it do? Gnaw away at itself, consume itself. . . . Life is thus soured, the dissolution of our moral existence is hastened and the health of the spirit becomes impossible.

Anyone who can live that way, lives to do evil or to do nothing at all.

A man who does not love, does not passionately love his child, if he has one, or his mother, if she is still alive, or the woman he prefers to all others, such a one is he and God protect me from him.

Above all, let him not be a writer, for he would be a terrible bore. Perhaps this is the reason for the limited permission given to poets to be for ever in love.

Novelists enjoy the same charter and have the same obligations. It is like the privilege of being an appeal court judge, which noblemen used formerly to obtain, when being an appeal court judge was worth something . . . and how!

How, then, can I, who have to insert in this serious odyssey of my travels the most interesting and mysterious love story ever told, or sung – how am I to do it, who have nothing left to love in this world but a memory and a hope: a child in a cradle and a wife in the grave? . . .[2]

Will this be enough? Tell me, fair readers: can the life of the heart take nourishment from this alone?

'Yes, it can.'

'No, it cannot.'

'The opinions are divided, I request a vote.'

'Nominal?'

'No, certainly not.'

'Why?'

'Because there are many things that one thinks and believes and even says in conversation, that one does not dare confess publicly, declare openly, stating one's name . . .'

Ah, yes . . . so that's how it is! How well I understand you, ladies: always keep a way out for difficult cases, for extraordinary circumstances. Isn't that it?

Well, I shall do the same.

And although today it is a month since, on a day like today, a day for ever memorable in my life, a vision appeared to me, a heavenly vision that took my heart by surprise, in a strange new manner, and of which I could certainly not say, as Dido did to her sister Annie, I recognize the ardour of my former flame – *Agnosco veteris vestigia flammae* – since the vision passed by and disappeared . . . but it left engraved upon my heart the certainty that. . . . Although this is all true, I shall confide no more, ladies, but it shall be enough for you to know that I am suitably qualified to be the teller of my tale, and my tale is this.

It was the year 1832, a summer's day like today, hot and dry, but with a clear, peaceful sky. On the doorstep of that house among the trees sat an old woman well over seventy, though she did not show it. She wore a sort of purple tunic, held in at the waist by a broad black leather belt, which set off the pallor of her face and of her long hands, which were thin but not bony as old women's hands usually are. Her head was covered with a scrupulously white kerchief, arranged in a special fashion, like a nun's wimple; a linen pinafore, every bit as white, which covered her bosom and which likewise simulated the form of a nun's scapulary, completed the old woman's strange dress. She was sitting on a low chair of the most classical shape: it looked like a textual reproduction of the one Raphael used as a model in his beautiful picture of the Madonna della Sedia.

By way of an historical note and an artistic illustration, may I be permitted to add here, in parenthesis, that not long ago I saw in the house of an ordinary cobbler, in Lisbon's Bairro Alto, just such a chair, with pyramid-shaped mouldings, simple, undistinguished, but elegant.

Let us return to the old woman.

There she was, sitting in the aforementioned chair, and in front of her she had a reel which moved in a regular motion at the pull of the thread that passed into her hands and was wound on to the already large ball.

That was the only sign of life in the entire scene. But for this, the old woman, the chair and the reel would all look like a charming sculpture by António Ferreira or one of those true-to-life paintings by the Morgado de Setubal.[3]

The perfectly visible motion of the reel was regular and corresponded to the almost imperceptible movement of the old woman's hands. The movement was regular, but it lasted a minute, then stopped, then went on for another two or three minutes and stopped again; it carried on with this intermittent regularity like the pulse of someone trembling with the ague.

But the old woman did not tremble, in fact she held herself very straight and erect. The interruptions to her work occurred because the labour within her spirit doubled in intensity from time to time and suspended all outside movement. But the interruption was short and limited; her will reacted and the reel started moving again.

There was a strange look in the old woman's eyes, though: she faced west and neither took her eyes away from that direction nor in any way lowered them to the reel, which was a little to her left. They did not blink and the blue of the pupils, which must have been as bright as sapphires, looked dull and lifeless.

The motion of the reel came to a sudden halt, the old woman calmly lowered her hands and the ball of yarn to her lap and called into the house: 'Joaninha?'

A sweet, clear yet strong voice, one of those voices we seldom hear and that echo inside us, never more to be forgotten, answered from within: 'Yes? I'm coming, Grandmother, I'm coming.'

'Sweet child!... She heard me immediately! Never mind, come when you can. It is only the yarn that has got twisted.'

The old woman was blind, blinded by gutta serena, and was patient with the resignation that God's compassionate providence almost always grants to those in this world whom He has destined to the harsh trials of such unrelieved suffering.

XII

—— ∴ ——

How Joaninha unravelled her grandmother's yarn, and
what further happened. – What sort of girl Joaninha was. –
The author gives signal proof of naïveté and good faith by
admitting to a serious flaw in his ideal; he insists, however,
that it is an adorable defect. – Why a woman whose hair
loses its curl is like Samson shorn of his locks. –
Astonishing monstrosities of nature that disprove the
dandies' age-old credo. – Joaninha's green eyes. – The
author strenuously professes the religion of black eyes. –
The danger in which he finds himself in the presence of a
pair of green eyes. – Of how, while grandmother and
granddaughter are engaged in intimate conversation, Friar
Dinis arrives and they interrupt their conversation. – Who
Friar Dinis was.

'HERE I am, Grandmother, is it your thread?... I shall put it
right for you,' said Joaninha, coming from inside the house with
her arms stretched out towards the old woman. She embraced
her with ineffable tenderness, kissed her several times and,
taking the ball of yarn from her hands, rapidly unravelled the
thread and gave the ball back to her.

The old woman smiled that satisfied smile which expresses
the soul's tranquil joys and which appeared to be saying: 'How
happy I am, despite being old and blind! Praise be to God!'

This last phrase, the blessing of a thankful heart that wafts
gently heavenwards like the fumes of holy incense rising from
the altar, this last phrase overflowed from her heart and emerged
articulated by her lips: 'God be praised, my child, my Joaninha,
my dear granddaughter! And may God bless you too, child!'

'Do you know what else, Grandmother? That is enough work
for today, it is time for tea.'

'Let us have tea, then.'

Joaninha went into the house and fetched a small round table.

She covered it with a gleaming white cloth, placed fruit, bread, cheese and wine on it, and moved it close to the old woman. Then she took the ball of yarn from her hand and moved aside the reel. The old woman ate a few golden grapes from a bunch which her granddaughter chose and placed in her hands, drank a little wine and fell silent and still, but without that expression of happiness and contentment which shone in her face only a moment before.

Joaninha's lively features reflected the same alteration, in sympathy.

Joaninha was not beautiful, perhaps not even comely, even in the suggestive, popular sense that the word has in Portuguese; but she was the embodiment of sweetness, the ideal of spirituality. Natural grace and an admirable symmetry of proportion had endowed that countenance and sixteen-year-old body with all the noble elegance, all the unassuming ease of manner, all the graceful suppleness that the art, the manners and the experience of the court and of the most select company eventually confer on a few rare and privileged creatures in this world.

But in this case, nature had done it all, or nearly all, and education nothing, or close to nothing.

Few women are much shorter, yet she looked tall, because her body was elegantly proportioned, so slender and *élancée*★.

And it was not the stiff, upright elegance of the perpendicular English *miss*★, who looks as if she had been moulded in one piece. No, she was lithe and supple like the trunk of a sapling, which is straight, yet pliable, strong with the sap that gave it life, and yet so tender that a strong wind snaps it.

She was white-skinned, but not the incongruous whiteness of blondes, nor yet the smooth, hard, marmoreal whiteness of redheads – rather, that modest white of wax lit by a pale shade of Bengal rose.

And of other roses, rosy roses that show up all the naturalness of blood flowing freely through the heart and running at will through arteries not dominated by nerves: but there were none of those in her face, which was as serene as the sea on a still day when the wind is sleeping. In her case, passion lay sleeping.

But let the faintest breeze spring up and its gentle breath is enough to ruffle the glassy surface of the sea.

74

Let the most candid, gentle flutter of the heart whisper, in the first stir of passion, and you shall see how the muscles of that peaceful cheek, now quite motionless, begin to twitch.

Her nose, slightly aquiline: her mouth, small and delicate, neither favoured nor despised the smile, but its natural, usual expression was one of simple gravity, without the slightest harshness or pedantry.

There are some little rosebud mouths, all prim and pursed with pedantry, that are the most abominable and blighted wee thing that God allows to happen to his female creatures.

In perfect harmony of colour, shape and tone with the delicacy and sweetness of her features, her hair, of so dark a brown that it bordered on black, fell, on either side of her face, in three long, unequal and loosely curled corkscrews, whose wavy spiral became gradually looser and lessened towards the end, until it was almost straight where they touched her neck.

In terms of style – in the style of the foremost and most beautiful of the arts, the *toilette* – this is a fault, I know.

Oh, the promises that are made, the prayers that are said to St Barometer, on the eve of a ball, to ask him for a dry, mild atmosphere that will keep intact, at least until the seventh quadrille, the precious creation of curl papers and hot iron. Macassar and lacquer that cost so much time and work, so many worries and fears.

I know, of course, that it is a fault, then. All right, I suppose it is ... but what an adorable fault! What delightful visions it evokes of abandon – excuse the Gallicism! –, of trust, of total, generous surrender to one's every whim, of complete and utter abdication of self-will!

As a rule, women appear to place the same faith in their hair as did Samson: what went from him when his was cut, they believe goes out of them together with the hair that loses its curl, is that it? Perhaps I am close to believing it: inflexible curl, inflexible woman.

Our beaux deny that such a thing as the corkscrew curl exists *in rerum natura*; they say it is like the phoenix, which came about because our ancestors did not know Greek.[1] I shan't go so far, because I have seen nature's negligence produce amazing monstrosities.

Anyway, let us leave in suspense the examination of this

profound and interesting problem. It is postponed to an *ad hoc* chapter and we shall return to my Joaninha.

Those charming curls fell on either side of her sweet face, and the rest of her hair, which was plentiful, curled and twined itself with simple elegance down from the crown of a small, narrow, perfectly shaped head.

Her eyebrows, which were also nearly black, were drawn in a well-defined curve and her long, silky lashes shaded the pallor of her cheek.

Her eyes, however ... strange whim of nature, which chose to cast a note of admirable discord in the midst of all this harmony! Like a bold and forceful maestro who, in the midst of the most classical and logical phrases of his composition, suddenly throws in a sharp, strident note, which no one expects and which seems to throw the musical rhythm into anarchy ... the dilettanti shudder, the professors cross themselves, but those whose ears take music to the heart and not to the head quiver with admiration and enthusiasm ... Joaninha's eyes were green ... not the treacherous, pale green of the feline race, that evil, discoloured green that is no more than an imperfect blue; no, they were green as green could be, bright and shining like emeralds of the highest carat.

They are the rarest and most fascinating eyes that exist.

I, for whom black eyes are a religion, which I was born in and hope to die in ... who on rare occasions have allowed myself to incline to the perverse heresy of a blue eye and suffered the well-deserved fate of any renegade.... Firm and unshaken, now more than ever, in my principles, sincerely convinced that there is no salvation without them, I confess, nevertheless, that once, one single occasion when I beheld such a pair of green eyes, I was beside myself, I felt my Catholicism shaken to its foundations; I fled from myself in horror and sought to revive my wavering faith in the contemplation of the eternal verities, which can be found solely and uniquely where all faith and belief exist ... in a pair of truly and sincerely black eyes.

Joaninha, however, had green eyes, and the effect of this rare feature in her countenance, though at first sight so dissonant, was in reality astonishing. First it fascinated, it perturbed one; then it caused an inexplicable, uncertain feeling that was painful and pleasurable at the same time; eventually, by degrees, it set up a magnetic current that was so powerful, so charged, so unbreakable, that one lost all memory of anything else and the will and the intelligence were totally absorbed.

All that needs be added, and the portrait is complete, is a simple, dark-blue dress, black belt and apron, and flat shoes with the laces wound around the ankle. Her foot small and narrow; a shapely leg, from what one could see.

Such was the ideal, highly spiritual figure who stood leaning on the table from which the good old woman had just eaten, contemplating the inexpressible look of sadness that was spreading gradually over her wasted, faded face and was mirrored, as I said, in the watcher's countenance.

The old woman gave a deep sigh and, in an effort to take her mind off the thoughts that were distressing her, groped with her hands in search of her ball of yarn: 'My ball of yarn, child, I can't sit doing nothing, it isn't good for me.'

'Let us talk, then, Grandmother.'

'All right, but give me my ball of yarn. I can't explain why, but when I am not working, something is working inside me that tires me much more. They are right when they say that idleness is the worst sort of labour.'

Joaninha gave her the ball of yarn and arranged the reel for her.

The old woman felt something on her hand, raised it to her mouth and seemed to kiss it, then said: 'I saw it, Joaninha!'

'What, Grandmother? What did you see?'

'I saw it, child, I saw it . . . not with these eyes which God closed for ever – praise be to him for everything! – I saw it by feeling it, the tear, yours, it fell on my hand and now it is here in my breast, because I drank it, Joana. Already, my child! It is too soon for you to start, leave it to me, I am used to it, but you, only sixteen and without sorrows!'

'None at all, Grandmother! And the two of us alone in the world, you in this state, me at my age, and . . .'

'And God in heaven to take care of us. . . . But what is that? Look, Joana, I can hear footsteps on the road, see what it is.'

'I can't see anyone.'

'But I can hear. . . . Wait, it is Friar Dinis, I recognize his footsteps.'

The old woman had barely spoken the name, when, from behind some olive trees in a bend in the road, on the Santarém

77

side, appeared the tall, thin, bent figure of a Franciscan friar, leaning on a rough staff, dragging his yellow sandals, his pale grey hat swaying on his head, who was coming towards them.

It was in fact Friar Dinis, the austere superior of the convent of St Francis in Santarém.

XIII

—— ·:· ——

On monks in general. – The monk considered in social and artistic terms. – The monk is proved to be a more poetic figure than the baron. – Don Quixote and Sancho Panza again. – About the baron: classification and description according to Linnaeus. – The story of the house that Jack built. – Eugène Sue's glaring mistake: it is shown that the Jesuits are not cholera morbus and the *Wandering Jew* must be rewritten. – How the monk did not understand our century, nor our century the monk. – How the baron took the monk's place and all that we lost thereby. – The only voice to be heard in the desert of present-day society: the barons shouting in guineas. – How that money is counted and paid for. – The author's artistic preference for the monk: he confesses and explains his preference.

MONKS ... monks ... I do not like monks. As we saw them still in this century, as we understand them today, I do not like them, I have no use for them, in moral and social terms.

From an artistic point of view, however, the monk is very necessary.

In the cities, those solemn, serious figures with their habits reaching to their feet, most of them picturesque, some elegant, passing among the crowds of monkeys and dolls in tight jackets and bucket hats, which are typical of Europe's foppish species – they broke the monotony of that ridiculous picture and gave the population some character.

In the country the effect was greater still: they were a typical feature of the landscape, they gave a touch of poetry to the most prosaic situation on hill or in vale, and they were such necessary, obligatory figures that in many scenes of this sort the picture is no longer the same without them.

Apart from this, the convent in a village and the monastery out in the wilds gave colour and comfort and put soul and majesty into things: they protected the trees, blessed the springs, filled the land with poetry and solemnity.

Something that the rapacious barons who have taken their place cannot and do not know how to do.

The monk is much more poetic than the baron.

The monk was, to a certain extent, the Don Quixote of the old society.

The baron is, in almost every respect, the Sancho Panza of the new society.

Except in elegance. . . .

Because the baron is the most inelegant and stupidest animal in creation.

Not excepting the asinine family, which is illustrated by such distinguished personalities as our friend Sancho's *Rucio*, the Maid of Orleans' donkey and others.

The baron (*Onagrus baronius*, Linn.; *L'âne baron*, Buff.) is a monstrous variety sired on the ass of Balaam, as far as concerns the essentially Judaic and usurious part of his nature, in infernal coitus with Martin, the bear in the Jardin des Plantes, in respect of the foppishly Frenchified and sordidly revolutionary side of his character.

The baron is, thus, usuriously revolutionary and revolutionarily usurious.

For this reason he is covered all over in monarchico-democratic stripes.

This is the true, thoroughbred baron; those lacking these features belong to a diferent species and we are not concerned with them here.

Now – while not losing sight of the barons –, coming back to the monks, I say that they did not understand our century, nor have we understood them. . . .

For this reason, we fought for a long time. Eventually we won and we sent the barons to expel them from the face of the earth. Which was as stupid a thing as ever was done. The baron bit the monk, he devoured him . . . and kicked out at us afterwards.

And how are we now to kill the baron?

Because the story of this world is the story of the house that Jack built. Here is the dog that bit the cat that killed the rat that gnawed the rope, etc. etc: it keeps going on like this. . . .

But the monk did not understand us, and so he died, and we

did not understand the monk, so we made the barons, and we shall die from them.

They are the disease of the century: it is they, the barons, who are the cholera morbus of present-day society, not the Jesuits. Our friend Eugène Sue was totally mistaken in the *Wandering Jew*,[1] which needs to be rewritten.

Now the monk was the first to err, by not understanding us, our century, our inspirations and aspirations; that way he put himself in a false position, cut himself off from social life and made his demise a necessity, something infallible and irreparable. He was afraid of freedom, which was friendly to him, but meant to reform him, and he joined forces with despotism, which only liked him depraved and loose-living, because otherwise he was no use to it.

We too erred, by not understanding the monk's excusable mistake, by not giving him a different social function and thus avoiding the baron, who is a much more noxious animal and more of a rodent.

Because, do not be deceived, the world was always thus and always will be. However beautiful the theories that are worked out, however perfect the constitutions one sets out with, the *status in statu* takes shape straight away: either with monks or with barons, or with freemasons, a tendency begins to organize itself that is different from, if not opposed to, the manifest, visible tendencies of the great social body. This is the natural opposition to Progress, which has its opposition like all sub- and superlunary things, and it sometimes proves a healthy corrective, moderating its speed, at others impedes it excessively and improperly; but, after all, it is a necessity.

Now I, as an advocate of Progress, would rather have monks than barons as opposition. The point was how to contain it and make use of it.

Progress and Freedom lost, they did not gain.

When I remember all these things, when I see the convents in ruins, the expelled monks begging and the barons riding in carriages, I miss the monks – not as they were, but as they could have been.

And I know that I am not being misled by poetry, because I react strongly and with inflexible logic against poetic illusions when serious matters are involved.

I know, too, that I am not one to be enamoured of paradox, nor one of those restless, contradictory spirits who are always sighing for the past and are never content with the present.

No, indeed. The monk, who is a patriot and liberal in Ireland, in Poland and in Brazil, could and should be so here, and we would be much better off than we are with half a dozen unlettered curates to say mass for us and a couple of dozen barons, not to act as that healthy opposition, but to exert all the moral and intellectual influence on society, because here there is no other.

Otherwise, tell me: where are our universities, and what else does the one we do have do, other than award its third-rate degree of bachelor in law and medicine? What does it write, what does it debate, what are its principles, what doctrines does it profess, who knows anything about it or hears anything from it except the occasional timid, fearful echo of what is said and done elsewhere?

Where are our academies?

What forceful words resound in our pulpits?

Where is our parliamentary eloquence?

What poet sings loud enough to be heard by the brute stones and hard oaks of this materialist forest to which the utilitarians have reduced us?

If we exclude the feeble cries of the liberal press, and that partly throttled by the police, the only voice to be heard in the immense silence of this desert is that of the barons shouting their guineas and sovereigns.

Ten guineas for a voter!

Another two hundred guineas for tobacco!

Three thousand guineas for the preservation of an amphigory.

Five thousand guineas for highways for acronauts!

Six thousand guineas for this, ten thousand guineas for that!

Before long they will be counting in hundreds of thousands.

Counting costs *them* nothing.

Those who count the cost are the ones who pay for all these paper balloons: the country and industry.

*   *   *

This chapter must be considered as an introduction to the next chapter, in which Friar Dinis, Father Superior of the convent of St Francis in Santarém, makes his entrance.

I have already been told that I have a monkish nature, because I cannot write a story, a play or a novel without slipping in my bit of monk.

Camões has one, Fr José Índio;

Dona Branca three: Fr Soeiro, Fr Lopo and the Blessed Fr Gil – that makes four;

Adosinda has a hermit, a sort of monk – five;

Gil Vicente has another, that is to say it really has only half a monk, André de Resende, and what is more it is not a speaking part – five and a half;

The *Alfageme* three-quarters of a monk, Froilão Dias, a novice in the order of the Knights of Malta – six and a quarter monks;

Frei Luís de Souse is full of monks, counting them there must be three, four, half a dozen monks – that is already twelve and a quarter.

Some people, excluding myself, would include *O Arco de Sant'Ana* in this sum, and there are no less than two monks and a lay-brother.

So here am I with no less than fifteen and a quarter monks on my back. With our Friar Dinis we have a whole friary.

Well, gentlemen, I don't know what to do with them: the fault is not mine. From 1100-odd, when Portugal became a nation, until the 1830s, when some say she was restored and others that she went to the devil, I don't know of any public or private event that took place, or could take place, in this land without a monk being a part of it.

The only way to get round it is to follow the recipe given in the fifth chapter of this work.

Follow it who will; not I, I neither want to nor do I know how.

XIV

———— .:. ————

Having at last got over his distractions and divagations, the author goes straight on with the promised story. – How Friar Dinis gave his sleeve to be kissed by grandmother and granddaughter, and what else took place between them. – The friar chides the old woman and we begin to see where the story is leading.

THIS chapter has no divagations, nor reflections, no considerations of any sort: it will go straight on with the story, without any distractions.

Friar Dinis came up to the two women and said: 'Our Lord Jesus Christ be praised!'

Joaninha stepped towards him to kiss his sleeve. He added: 'God's blessing and the blessing of our holy father St Francis be upon you, child.'

'Benedicite, Father Superior,' said the old woman, bending forward and half rising from her seat.

'In the Lord's name, amen!' replied the friar, coming closer and putting his arm where she could kiss it. 'Well here I am, Sister, what do you want of me? How are things here? Are we taking comfort, being patient and suffering with eyes on the Lord?'

'I have no eyes except for Him, Father.'

'Now, now, Sister Francisca, always the same thought, the same complaint! I have reprimanded you so many times and you do not improve.'

'I did not complain, Father. God knows that I do not complain . . . not for myself, at least.'

'For whom, then?'

'Oh, Father!'

'Sister Francisca, I am afraid to understand you. I do not know the affections of the flesh nor do I concern myself with the fragile thoughts of this world. I am a friar, Sister. I no longer belong to

84

the number of the living. I put on this shroud so as not to be one of them, I put it on in an age when mockery and scorn are a friar's only patrimony, when ridicule, derision and insults – the worst and cruellest of persecutions – are all we can hope for. I wanted to become a friar and I became a friar knowing and seeing all this. I became a friar in the midst of it all, when I was already old and experienced in the ways of the world, knowing it all too well and certain as to what awaits me and the profession I have embraced. What do you want of a man who has taken the decision to cut the ties that bind humanity to this wretched life on earth in order to live only on his hopes for the next one? That is why I put on this habit. And yours, Sister, why did you put yours on? Is it for amusement, is it a whim, a comedy with God? Tear it off quickly, deck yourself in worldly finery, do not try God's patience by wearing the sackcloth of patience outwardly and keeping your heart within quite unrestrained by penance and mortification.'

With her hands clasped together, her face and sightless eyes raised towards heaven, the old woman offered up to God all the bitterness of that severity, which she did not think she deserved and seemed not to understand. Joaninha, who had gradually moved closer to her grandmother and was more or less supporting her from behind with one arm, gripped the back of the chair with her other hand and fixed her piercing, brilliant gaze on the friar. Her face bore an indefinable expression: it was tinged, distinctly yet simultaneously, with a complex mixture of eagerness and dejection, of faith and unbelief, of liking and aversion.

It might have been said that the vacillations of the century were embodied and symbolized by those green eyes and that pale face.

'Father!' the old woman replied, with sincere humility in voice and gesture. 'If I deserve it, punish me. God, who sees and hears me, knows only too well that I speak truly and from the heart and will forgive me because I am weak and because I am a woman.'

'And did He not say to the weak: *Take up thy cross and follow me*? Who obliged you to make the vows you made?'

'It is true, Father, it is true. I know just what I promised, that I dedicated myself to God, body and soul, that I do not belong to myself, that my affections are not mine to bestow, but . . .'

'But what? Sister Francisca, God is not deceived. Your vows were not made in a monastery, nor professed before an altar with all the church ritual. But I have already told you that in your inner conscience, in God's presence, they are as binding, or even more so, than if they had been. Renounce them if you wish: no law, no human power constrains you. Tell me once and for all, tell me you want to be released and I shall not come here again.'

'For pity's sake, Father! In God's name! But just one question, one only, and I promise not to think, not to speak any more about. . . . Where is he?'

'Leave us, Joana.'

Joaninha clasped her grandmother to her with both arms and, without a word, without a single gesture, went slowly and silently into the house.

'And what about her, Father?' said the old woman without waiting for a reply to the first question she had asked so anxiously. 'What about her? Must I separate from her, must I give her up too?'

'She is innocent and as long as she stays that way . . .'

'As long as she stays? My Joana is an angel.'

'Blasphemy, blasphemy! May the Lord not punish you for it. Joana is good and God-fearing, let us hope that He keeps her in His grace. The other one . . .'

'What has become of him, Father? Oh, tell me and I promise . . .'

'Do not make promises which you cannot fulfil. Your grandson is with those miscreants who have come from the islands, he is amongst those who disembarked in Oporto . . .'

'Oh, my darling child, and may I not embrace you? . . .'

'Indeed not. Win or lose, all association, any possibility of harmony between ourselves and those men has come to an end. Our obligation is to destroy them, their one desire is to exterminate us.'

'My God! My God! Have we come to this? Then there is no mercy on earth or in heaven?'

'God's mercy is exhausting. If there was ever mercy on earth, I do not know where it is. The weak use the word irreverently for their own cowardice.'

'And is it cowardice to wish for peace, to want unity, to plead for indulgence? Does not God command us to forgive those who trespass against us and love our enemies?'

'Ours, yes. His, no.'

'Have mercy on me, Lord!'

'If your sorrows are of flesh and blood, if they are earthly thoughts, as, unfortunately, I see they are, weak, faint-hearted woman, take comfort, because it is clear and certain to me that those men are going to win.'

'Which men?'

'Those enemies of the altar and of truth, those men who have been led astray by the specious doctrines of our century. They have high hopes and make great promises, they are in the full vigour of their illusions. While we carry the burden of many centuries of disillusion, the sins of thirty generations that have gone before us and the unbelievable corruption of the present. . . . We are destined to succumb. Our temples will be destroyed, their ministers outlawed, the name of God blasphemed at will in this accursed land!'

'And are they all so lost, so abandoned by the hand of God . . . all of them?'

'All. What do you think, Sister? That ours are any better, the ones who say they are for us? That there is more faith in their credo, much more truth in their religion? O almighty God!'

'You make me tremble, Father!'

'And so you should. Ungodliness and greed have taken root in every heart. *Doubt* is the only principle, *wealth* the only aim, of all these people. Liberals and royalists, none of them has faith. The liberals still have hope, but it will not last for long. Let them win and they will see.'

'And will they win?'

'Of course.'

'No one else says so.'

'I say so.'

'And all those thousands of soldiers on the government side!'

'And as many millions of sins against it. It is not possible, not possible. God's mercy is exhausted and the day longed for by the impious is at hand. Their mission is easy and rapid – the only thing they can do, the only thing they know how to do, is destroy. Building is not for them, they have nothing to build

87

with, they do not believe in anything. The Christian symbol is not only a religious truth, it is an eternal and universal principle. *Faith, hope and charity*. Without belief, without hope . . .'

'And without love!'

'Woman, woman! Love is the last of the virtues . . .'

'But it is through it and only through it that we attain the others.'

'No, weak, woman, no. Once and for all, Sister Francisca, let us stop fooling ourselves. Between me, between the God I serve and His enemies there is no compromise. On this point I do not know the meaning of indulgence. I see the fate which awaits me in this world, and I do not tremble in the face of it. Those who are afraid must take a different path. Not I.'

'Father, I am not afraid or anxious for myself. I am weak and a woman and in every tribulation and misfortune I shall glorify my God and bear witness to my faith. But . . . but my grandson is my blood, my life, he is the only child of my beloved only daughter. He knew no other mother than I, and I love him for his sake and for hers. I cannot abandon him, I cannot stop thinking about him. God's will . . .'

'God's will is that the just shall depart from the impious, that the blessed lambs shall go to one side and the cursed kids to the other – oh, Sister, I am not made of stone, no I am not, and my heart breaks too to have to say it –, but that boy is damned and between him and us is the abyss of hell.'

'God have mercy!'

Pale and drawn, his face sallower and more deathly pale than ever, Friar Dinis pronounced these last terrible words with a tremor, but forcefully. His eyes, which were normally sunken and hollow, receded still farther within their fleshless sockets; his staff quivered in his left hand, while his right hand, raised in the air, seemed to convey to the sinner the awful curse that came from his lips.

'Curses! Curses on you,' the friar went on, 'ungrateful child, deprived, perverse heart!'

'My God, do not listen to him!' the old woman cried out, falling on her knees and prostrating herself on the hard earth. 'My God, do not confirm those dreadful words. Do not listen to him, Lord, and allow the precious blood of Thy son and the blessed suffering of His mother, o my God, to protect the head of my poor child from the cruel words of this pitiless, loveless man.'

The old woman would have said more: the heartbreaks that had been piling up in her soul, which could contain them no longer and was overflowing, were now all ready to come out, to pour out in tears and sobs in the presence of her God, whom she always saw on His throne of mercy, whom she could not find it in her to see as the inflexible and terrible God of vengeance announced by the friar. But the flesh was less willing than the spirit, the strength went out of her body: she was overcome by a deathlike swoon, fell silent and . . . her life came to a standstill.

Friar Dinis watched her in this state for a few moments and appeared moved, but his nerves were cords of tempered steel and did not vibrate when struck so softly. He took two paces towards the house door, knocked with his staff and said, with a strong, firm voice: 'Joana, come to your grandmother, she is not feeling well.'

Then he left the way he had come and, without once turning his head, strode quickly on and was soon hidden behind the olive trees on the road.

XV

———— ∴ ————

Portrait of a Franciscan friar which was not sent to the Holy
Land warehouse and is not said to be in the Academy of
Fine Arts. – We see that Friar Dinis's logic was not at all
similar to Condillac's. – His opinions on liberals and
liberalism. – That power comes from God, but how and for
what? – That the liberals do not know what liberty and
equality are; and what monks would be for, if they were
what they should be. – Textual proof that man does not live
by bread alone; the question is then asked by what did Friar
Dinis live.

W HO was Friar Dinis?

He said it himself: a man who had become a monk when he
was old and weary of this world; who had taken the habit at a
time when mockery, scorn and contempt pursued that
profession; who was aware of it, knew what it meant and for
that very reason had defied it.

Rare, strong characters like this always appear at the demise of
great institutions, so that they do not perish without a protest,
so that it cannot be said of any durable, time-honoured ideology
that there was no one to honour it in its final hour with a noble,
glorious devotion worthy of the human spirit at its best.
For man is a great, sublime creature, whatever the philosophers
say.

Such was Friar Dinis, a man of austere principles, of rigid
beliefs and of a stubborn, inflexible logic, a logic which,
however, rejected any form of analysis and which, with the
strength of the great intellectual and moral truths in which he
had steeped his spirit, descended from them with all the
tremendous weight of a most severe and oppressive synthesis
that crushed every argument and destroyed every rational proof
which opposed it.

Condillac called synthesis the method of the benighted. Friar

Dinis laughed at Condillac . . . and I think I feel inclined to do the same.

Despotism he detested as no liberal contrives to hate it, but he ridiculed the philosophical theories of the liberals, which he considered absurd: he rejected them for, in his view, falsifying every sane idea, every just sentiment and every viable kindness. For man, in whatever state, and for society, in whatever form, there were no laws other than those of the Ten Commandments, nor, said he, were any constitutions necessary other than the Gospels. Strengthening them is superfluous, inproving them impossible and deviating from them monstrous. From the height of evangelical perfection, which is the monastic state, down, there are rules for everyone there: all that is needed is to observe them.

According to his principles, for one man to have power over another was always a usurpation, regardless of the way such power was constituted. All power was in God, who delegated it to father over son, thus to the head of a family over the family, and thus from one of these over the State, but to govern according to the Gospel and with all the republican austereness of the early Christian principles.

Thus had Saul been anointed and after him all the kings of the earth – otherwise they were not kings.

Anything else was anarchy, usurpation, tyranny, sin – absurd, untenable and impossible.

And about this he did not argue either, because he could not conceive how: it was dogma.

With regard to the application of these principles he did raise doubts, or rather he disputed, with his iron logic. The old laws, old customs, men of former times, he did not spare these any more than those of the present. The tyranny of kings, the greed and pride of the great, the corruption and ignorance of priests: no popular orator ever lashed them more pitilessly and more harshly.

Nevertheless he obviously defended the principle of the old monarchy as the true one, even if those who invoked it were lying hypocrites.

With regard to the doctrines of the constitutionalists, he did not understand them and claimed that their most zealous apostles did not understand them any better; they lacked common sense, they were intellectual abstractions.

Now I would like to laugh at the friar . . . but I don't see how I can.

So-called liberalism he *could* understand: 'It comes down', he said, 'to two things: to *doubt* and *destroy* as matters of principle, to *acquire* and *grow rich* as the end in view. It is a completely material sect, in which the flesh commands and the spirit obeys. It has a great power for evil and can do no real, true, lasting good. To cure a country that is ruined, like all those in Europe, by means of a liberal revolution, is the same as bleeding a consumptive – the loss of blood relieves the lungs for a while, but his strength ebbs away and death is the more certain.'

Of the great, eternal principles of Equality and Liberty he said: 'When the liberals actually practise them, I shall become a liberal too. But there is no danger of that, because they do not even understand them! To understand liberty one has to believe in God. To believe in equality, one must have the Gospel in one's heart.'

The monastic institutions were, in his understanding and in his system of thought, an essential condition of existence for civil society – for a normal society. He did not gloss over the abuses that occurred in converts, nor did he conceal the monk's faults, criticizing their laxness more severely than anyone, but he maintained that, without that embodiment of evangelical perfection, the Christian way of life would lose its norms, harmony would be completely destroyed and society would hurl itself, more quickly and irreparably, into the abyss of stupid, brute materialism where all social links would rot away and disappear and selfish individualism – the last phase of over-civilization, which borders on the far side of savagery – become more and more isolated and exclusive.

Such were the principles of this extraordinary man, who added to a vast erudition his deep knowledge of man and of the world in which he had lived until he was fifty years old.

How and why had he abandoned secular life? How and why did a man with such an active, superior mind concern himself only with the obscure duty of superior of his friary, a position he had accepted out of obedience, and limit his relations outside the cloister almost entirely to that house in the valley where he saw no one but the old woman and the child?

Despite his ascetic rigour, was there something which

attached that mind to this world of ours? Might that heart, withered by the mortification of those austere and terrible meditations on the life eternal, consumed by his abstention from all pleasure and all desire in the present, still perhaps have some fibre sufficiently alive to quiver with recollections, with sad memories, with regrets for the past?

In his convent he had nothing more than a bare cell, with a crucifix as its only ornament and a breviary as his only book. In that one family with which he had contact, there were, as I have said, the old woman, who was blind and infirm, Joaninha, to whom he barely spoke, and an absent member, a youth of whom nothing had been heard for nigh on two years. In political intrigues, in ecclesiastical business and all else in our world, he played no part. What did he live by, then, this man who assuredly was not one of those who live by bread alone?

And this was one of the few Latin texts that he repeated, the favourite topic of the rare sermons he preached: *non in solo pane vivit homo* – Man does not live by bread alone.

He did live by something, then, this man. Prayer and meditation were not enough for him, because he left his monastery and it was not to preach or to pray. . . . Every Friday he was a certain visitor at the house in the valley, at the same hour, in the same manner. . . .

There, then, was a part of the friar's life, this monk who had not wholly cut himself off from the earth, a part which, say what he will, he had yet to *castrate* for the sake of heaven.

The point is, half a century of worldly life leaves many roots which do not die just like that. Maybe, though, the root is but one, yet deep and strong with fibre and sap, and though the leaves die, the branches go dry and the trunk rots, it continues to live.

Let us hear something about that life.

XVI

—— ·:· ——

Inquiry into the friar's life. – Just why was he a Franciscan?
– Concerning martyrs of old and martyrs of today. – Some
details about Friar Dinis, before and since he became a
monk. – Emigration. – An incomplete explanation. – How
the old woman had lost her sight and Joaninha her smile. –
Friday, a day of ill omen.

LET us hear something about the friar's life, his secular life,
since his life in the cloister was bare and non-existent,
monotonous and simple, as we have seen.

In civil life his name was Dinis de Ataíde and he had followed
a career first in the army, then as a scholar. He had fought in the
Peninsular campaigns with distinction and almost with
enthusiasm, and been there almost to the end. However, either
because he was discontented with the service or because he cared
little for military glory, he entered the magistrature, for which
he was qualified, and in 1825 was due to move from the post of
district judge in the Ribatejo, which he had held twice, to the
appeal court in Oporto.

He went to Lisbon to receive his letter of appointment, kissed
the King's hand and from there one day took the road to
Santarém, and arriving in that town left servants and horses at
the inn, while he went and rang the bell at the door of the
convent of St Francis.

The servants waited several days in vain: he did not return.

Dinis de Ataíde disappeared from secular life and two years
later appeared Friar Dinis da Cruz, the austerest monk and most
eloquent preacher of that time. He preached but rarely, and only
on doctrine, but he was a torrent of vehemence and plenty, a
power!...

Among the monastic institutions, which had all by then
declined considerably in splendour and reputation, the order of
St Francis was perhaps the one that had fallen lowest in public

repute. The more severe the rule, the more obvious any laxness on the part of those who profess it; the licentiousness of the Franciscans had become a byword with the people. There were so many of them everywhere and they mixed with all classes, therefore the people became so accustomed to the appearance of those black shrouds – no longer so austere, and once it ceased to be that ... ridiculous – and they turned up in such places, at such times of day and in such a way that the people had lost all respect, esteem and consideration for them. They had no authors any more, few preachers and those of no repute: in all senses it was the brotherhood that had fallen lowest in the general decadence of the orders.

Friar Dinis went to it for that very reason. He wanted to be a monk, the nineteenth century's despised, taunted monk.

For some spirits, much more courage and enthusiasm is needed to face this martyrdom than had been necessary in former times to seek the noble persecution of blood and fire.

Then they fought with honour, they fell with glory, often they triumphed by dying...

Now, it is all suffering.

The world applauded those great sacrifices and witnessed those gigantic combats with interest, admiration and wonder. And the tyrant trembled before his victim, or even fell at his feet, defeated, converted and repentant...

Nowadays, the people pass by and laugh, their kings occupy themselves otherwise and the Church itself is not aware that it has martyrs.

'Well it has,' Friar Dinis would say, 'and it has more need of them to redeem itself than it once did to found itself.'

That is why Dinis de Ataíde did not wish to be a Benedictine, a Hieronymite or a Carthusian, and became a Franciscan.

From all his possessions, which were considerable, he took only the modest amount of money needed to pay the dower and endowment for his admission to the monastery. He settled the remainder entirely on Dona Francisca Joana, the old woman, now blind and infirm, whom we encountered at the beginning of this story, winding yarn on her doorstep, at the house in the valley.

The old woman's only family was a grandson and a granddaughter.

95

The granddaughter was Joaninha, only child of her only son and now orphan of both parents.

The grandson, also an orphan, had been born after his father's death and had cost the life of his mother, the old woman's dearly beloved daughter.

Until the splendid settlement made by Friar Dinis, the family, which was of good, honourable stock, could be said to be poor; thereafter, they lived reasonably well. But the old woman had never wanted to change the modest condition in which she had lived until then. They had a plentiful supply of bread, oil and wine from their own land, which was managed by a trusty old servant; they dressed and lived as people of medium station but independent means.

In former times, when Dona Francisca's two children were alive, Friar Dinis, then Dinis de Ataíde and district judge, had been a frequent visitor at that house. Since the death of the son and the son-in-law, who had both perished tragically the same day while crossing the Tagus in a fishing-smack, at a time when the river was in flood, he had never returned.

Until he became a monk, the years went by and he was made superior of his monastery.

By now the old woman's daughter and daughter-in-law had also died.

And it was remarkable that, at the very hour when Friar Dinis was taking his vows in the convent of St Francis of Santarém, Dona Francisca put on the purple tunic which she never gave up wearing.

But one day Friar Dinis came to the door of the house in the valley and said: 'God be in this house!'

The old woman shuddered, but soon recovered. She sent out the children, who were playing near her, shut herself in with the friar and they talked all day long. They prayed and wept, this much was heard, but what they said and discussed was never known.

The priest went away at nightfall; the old woman continued to pray and to weep, and she wept and prayed all night.

This was on a Friday. From that day on, on the Friday of every week, Friar Dinis came and spent a few hours with the old woman.

He was not her confessor, but he directed her as if he were, in each and every way, except where Joaninha was concerned.

There was an obvious affectation in the friar's manner, a premeditated, unalterable and systematic intention to abstain completely from anything that might interfere, however remotely, with that likeable child.

Joaninha was not afraid of him, but the respect he inspired in her was tempered by an instinctive aversion which, by virtue of an extraordinary, inexplicable contradiction, allowed her to sympathize with everything he said and stood for: teachings, opinions, sentiments, everything about the priest appealed to her, except his person.

Not so Carlos, her cousin, our Joaninha's companion and only friend, the old woman's other grandchild, from her daughter. He was already in his final year at Coimbra University, about to graduate in Law, when Friar Dinis da Cruz began once more to visit the house which Dinis de Ataíde had quitted.

Concerning Carlos the monk's attention was detailed, vigilant and anxious. The books he read, the friends he went about with, the ideas he embraced, the tendencies he favoured: Friar Dinis concerned himself with everything, and everything gave him cause for concern. He said little to him directly, but had long discussions about him with his grandmother.

Of late he appeared to be satisfied with the way the young man seemed to be shaping.

'He is God-fearing, he is neither covetous nor servile by disposition, he is not a hypocrite, he has not yet been bitten by the liberal craze. He will be a worthy man,' said the monk to Dona Francisca, with genuine satisfaction and interest.

However, the memorable year of 1830 was more than half through and Carlos, who had graduated in early summer, had spent his time between Coimbra and Lisbon, returning home to his family only towards the end of August. He returned sad, melancholy and thoughtful, quite different from the way he had always been, since he was a young man of cheerful disposition and pleasure-loving by nature.

He arrived on a Friday, Friar Dinis's day for visting the valley. After the first greetings and embraces, when the two of them were alone, 'I don't like the look of you,' said the priest.

'What do you mean? What is the matter?'

'The matter is that you have come back different from when you went away, Carlos.'

'I am different, it is true, but you need not be upset at seeing me, as the upset will not last long.'

'What do you mean by that?'

'That I have decided to emigrate.'

'To emigrate? You?... Why? What for? What madness is this?'

'I have never been more sane.'

'Carlos, Carlos! Not another word on the subject. What bad company have you been keeping? What evil books have you been reading? You were such a ... Carlos, I forbid you to think such madness.'

'You forbid ... me ... to think! ... Well, I ...'

'Yes, I forbid you to think. Read your Horace, if you are tired of the pandects. Take your Virgil into the garden ... or go for walks, go hunting or riding, do what you will, but do not think. I am here to do your thinking for you.'

'Why? Must I always be a child? Is my life to be like this? Horace! I am in a fine mood now to read Horace ... what an excellent occupation for a man twenty-one, to scan iambs and trochees.'

'Well read your Bible, then. That is poetry scanned in the spirit, it delights the mind and heart.'

'I don't want to be a monk, did you know?'

'Nor do I want you to be a monk.'

'Thank God! I thought. ... Still, in the times we live in ...'

'The times we live in are times of presumption and immorality, and I want to spare you both of them, Carlos. Your grandmother knows my intentions concerning you, and she approves of them ...'

'My grandmother ... approves of many things I disapprove of.'

'How can you say that, Carlos?! What do you mean?'

'Just that, sir, and that I leave for Lisbon tomorrow to board ship for England.'

'Carlos!'

'It is a considered and unshakeable decision. I want nothing to do with this country, nor with this ...'

'With this what, Carlos?'

'Do you want me to say it? I shall tell you: with this house.'

The monk was choking and stammered, with a mixture of anger and amazement: 'May I know why?'

'Because I am sickened and humiliated at having an outsider in charge here. . . . Because I have always suspected, because I now know . . .'

'You know what?'

'I know, Father Dinis, but do not ask me what I know.'

The monk trembled and his face turned yellow, purple, ashen, black, his eyes receded still more and flashed like two live coals within their sockets. He made a great effort to speak and said, with a hollow, cavernous voice, as if from the tomb: 'Well I am asking, and may God permit . . .'

'Father, do not swear and curse!' Carlos interrupted, firmly and calmly. 'Your intentions may be good, perhaps. . . . I believe they are good, offspring of a proper remorse . . .'

'What are you saying, Carlos . . . what did you say? Oh, my God!'

The tables had been turned: Friar Dinis looked like the pupil, his voice had a suppliant tone and he no longer trembled with anger but with distress. Carlos, on the other hand, spoke with the severe, earnest tone of a man who is sure that he is right and is noble in his resentment. The young man's words were sharp, it was obvious that he felt what he said and that he was trying to soften them by the inflexion of his voice.

'What I am saying, Father Dinis, what I am forced to say to you is this: My grandmother consented, out of feminine weakness, to something to which I cannot and must not consent. What we have in this house is not . . . is not mine, the bread we eat . . . is bought at a cost . . . Father! It is clear that we cannot speak further about this matter. I leave for Lisbon tomorrow. Grandmother!' added Carlos, changing his tone and calling into the house, 'Grandmother.'

The old woman came out and he told her of his intention, which he attributed to his political opinion, inveighing against Dom Miguel, showing himself an enthusiastic supporter of the liberal cause and claiming that during the year he had declared his sympathies in Coimbra, and subsequently in Lisbon, so outspokenly that only a prompt flight could save him. . . . The old woman wept, pleaded, begged . . . all in vain. Friar Dinis witnessed it all without a word. That afternoon he went back to the convent earlier.

Very early next morning, clinging to his grandmother and his young cousin, who were weeping bitterly, Carlos said a last farewell to that dear house and to that beloved valley where he had been brought up. . . . That night he was in Lisbon, a few days later in England and some months afterwards on the island of Terceira.

On the Friday after Carlos's departure, Friar Dinis came to the valley and had a lengthy conference with Dona Francisca.

The old woman spent the next three days locked in her room weeping. . . . At the end of the third day she was blind.

Joaninha was a child at the time and seemed not to understand what was happening. But, observing her closely, one could see that she increased her love and affection for her grandmother and that she never again smiled at the monk. . . .

He aged ten years that day. The sunken eyes, that were the dominant feature of that ascetic countenance, receded still farther; his tall, upright figure became bent; the nervous twitch, which affected him on occasions, became a habit; his limbs stiffened, the flesh fell from the muscles of his face and his skin, which was already deeply lined with cares, became furrowed and creased in a network of grooves, as if it had been toasted on a grill.

There were no more days of happiness in the valley. Friday, however, was the fateful, ill-omened day. Friar Dinis now came only in the late afternoon and did not stay long, but it was enough. They waited for that hour with longing and with fear. The comforting news and the terrifying rumours were brought by the monk. The rest of the week was spent weeping and waiting.

And two years had gone by in this way, until the Friday on which we saw those three creatures together at the door of the house. Another week went by in the same way, until our story finds them again.

XVII

—————— ∴ ——————

How, come another Friday, grandmother and granddaughter waited for the friar, who appeared, contrary to habit, from the direction of Lisbon. – Why the liveliest conversation is often most likely to stop and break off suddenly. – A new proof of two of our ancients' major axioms, namely, that the habit does not make the monk, and that when neighbours quarrel truth will out. – The old woman reproaches the priest, thereby lifting a corner of the veil that conceals the mysteries of our story.

THAT week in the valley, unlike so many that had passed amid vague feelings of sadness, sorrow and melancholy, was spent in positive anxiety and acute distress caused by the monk bringing reliable news that Carlos was in Oporto as a member of King Pedro's small army.

Unconfirmed rumours, of the sort that circulate in a country in such times and which magnify, exaggerate and confuse events, had travelled as far as the secluded peace of the valley with news of bloody encounters, of violent upheavals, of acts of sacrilege and irreverence, and of terrible deeds of revenge and retaliation committed by attackers and defenders alike.

Friday arrived. The hours of that day, awaited as always with a mixture of longing and fear, were counted out minute by minute, the minutes growing longer, heavier and slower as the last one approached.

The sun was already down . . . and no sign of Friar Dinis!

In their usual places near the door of the house, Joaninha straining her eyes, the old woman pricking up her ears, the two women eagerly examined the space towards the east, hoping and fearing all the time, the one to see the well-known figure appear, the other to hear the familiar sound of the friar's footsteps.

And they were still so engrossed, so intent on this concern, that they did not notice a monk who was walking towards them, with laborious but impatient strides, from the other direction, that is from the Lisbon road.

He came right up to them without their hearing him and a familiar voice, hoarser and deeper yet than they had ever heard it, pronounced the customary greeting: 'God be in this house!'

'Amen!' they both answered automatically, with an involuntary shudder, immediately turning in the direction from which the voice had come.

'Heavens!' said the old woman, coming to her senses. 'Father Dinis, where have you come from to be so late?'

'I have just arrived from Lisbon.'

'From Lisbon? God reward you!... You went for news?...'

'Yes. I went for news of this dreadful war, God's awful visitation on this execrated land of Portugal...'

'Well tell me...'

'Good news, I bring good news.'

'Sit you down, Father, sit you down. Joaninha, fetch a chair. Rest yourself.'

'This is no time to rest, it is a time to watch and pray.'

'What happened then, Father? Don't keep me in this awful suspense. Tell me, where is he? Has anything terrible happened to him, O God in heaven!...'

'And what does it matter to me what has happened or might have happened to one more among so many lost souls? He will get his deserts, he will go the way of the others. .... He walks in the darkness with them and like them he can only end up in the depths.'

The monk's last words, spoken roughly, in an indifferent, disdainful tone, were followed by the strained silence that accompanies a pause in any serious, intimate conversation, when the thoughts are so many that they fall over one another and cannot find a way out in speech.

Friar Dinis was lying.... In the harshness of those words he was lying to his heart, though not to his mind. Just as an epispastic is applied to the skin in order to move an inflammation underneath it, he chafed his breast with the harsh austerities of his doctrine and rigid principles in order to assuage the acute pain and grief that consumed him.

The monk was on the outside, the man on the inside.

An ordinary observer saw only the monk's habit and cord that shrouded the corpse. One who looked deep into his eyes and listened carefully to the inflexions of his voice, would say: 'Priest, you are lying without knowing it. You are sincere in your faith, in your austerity, in your self-denial, but your sacrifice is like Abraham's on the mountain, and God knows that you have not the strength to carry it out.'

Not so the old woman, who trembled at Friar Dinis's harsh words and believed the coenobite's heart to be dead to all affection and all human feeling.

She, who in the silence of her sleepless nights and in the perpetual darkness of her sad days had struggled for so long, struggled in vain to detach from worldly affections that poor heart of hers that she wanted to sacrifice to the Lord – she saw, with pious envy and admiration, the superhuman strength she supposed the monk to have, and, despairing of being able to accompany him to those heights of evangelical perfection, she sank back, more depressed and more wretched then ever, into the weakness that was hers as a woman and a mother.

Oh, no one who has not suffered this agony can know what is torment, what is hell on earth!

But does God allow those to suffer in this way who do not have great guilt and great, irreparable errors to expiate in this world?

I firmly believe he does not.

Eventually, wearied and exhausted by such a relentless struggle, the old woman lost control of her reason at the monk's last words and, in an outburst of tears, cried out: 'Dinis ... Friar Dinis, in the name of that sacred token I have in my possession, for the sake of that precious cross on which my unhappy daughter wept her last tears, Dinis!'

'Silence!' shouted the monk, wrenching from his breast a cry that made all the echoes in the valley moan. 'Silence, woman! Do not invoke the devil I carry incarnate in my breast, which all my penances can barely hold in check ... which perhaps death alone will be able to expel. Woman, woman! This corpse, which is already dead, which has rotted away in all other respects, for it is being eaten, without even feeling it, by all the worms of destruction ... this corpse has one live spot in its heart ... and your egoism has put its finger on that very spot, woman! ...

Oh sin, that are ever against me! Eternal justice of God, when will you be satisfied?'

The monk's voice had burst out with great violence, but fell to a low, awesome whisper when he spoke this last mysterious imprecation. The final syllables virtually died on his agitated lips and, as he brought them out, he collapsed, exhausted, his strength quite spent, on to the chair that Joaninha had brought.

The old woman was aghast and bewildered, and trembled at what she had done, like the sorceress who trembles before the foul spirit that her spells have summoned, terrified by her own powers.

Words cannot describe the next few seconds.

The priest lifted his face, looked first at her, then at Joaninha and, like someone emerging, with great effort, from the enormous weight of water that engulfed him, shook his head, sucked in a deep breath of air and said, in his ordinary voice, only fainter: 'Carlos, Madam ... Sister, Carlos is alive. And here, by way of the French consul, is a letter from him.'

He took a letter from his sleeve and handed it to Joaninha.

XVIII

―――― ·∴· ――――

We discover that there are great, astonishing secrets
between the monk and the old woman. – Joaninha's pious
deception. – Struggle between the habit and the monk.

THE friar handed the letter to Joaninha, who glanced at the
envelope and became hesitant and nervous, like someone afraid
and eager by turns to be told a piece of news. He, with a quiver
of alarm in his voice, added: 'Goodbye, it is getting late! ...
Read the letter and next Friday ... you can tell me what it says.'

'Well, I never!' said the old woman timidly. 'Don't you want
to hear what he has to say?'

'Next Friday,' the priest went on, not hearing or not taking
notice of the question, 'next Friday I shall take care of the reply
and get it to him by the same route. ... Just one thing. Not a
word about me. As far as Carlos is concerned, I am ... dead.'

'Dinis!' cried the old woman beside herself. 'Dinis!'

The monk all at once recovered his severe tone and answered
solemnly: 'What, Sister?'

'Just that,' said she, once more timid and submissive, 'it was, I
wondered. ... Are you not going to listen to his letter?'

Friar Dinis did not answer, but remained seated. His head
sank on to his chest and, clutching his staff to him, he gave no
further sign of life.

The old woman listened in silence for a few moments and,
with her very acute hearing, the piercing sight of the blind,
obviously realized what was happening, so that, with a calmer
and more relaxed voice, she said: 'Open it, Joana. Read it, my
dear.'

Joaninha opened the letter and eagerly scanned the few lines
that were in it.

'Aren't you going to read it?' said her grandmother
impatiently. 'Read it, read it aloud, Joana.'

'The letter is just for me,' she answered coldly.

'What do you mean, just for you?' asked the grandmother.

'This letter is for me alone. There is nothing in it that . . .'

'Nothing in it?!' the grandmother retorted. 'Well! Read it aloud. Whatever it says, read it and let us hear it.'

Joaninha still seemed to hesitate. She glanced at the monk and saw that he maintained the same impassive posture; she turned to her grandmother and saw how eager and apprehensive she looked. . . . She read the letter.

The letter was indeed only for her and it was a very simple letter: all it contained was the innocent expression of a never-forgotten brotherly affection, endless memories of the past, little hope for the future, almost none of their meeting again at all soon. All of this, however, concerned his cousin; for his despairing grandmother, or for anyone else . . . not a word.

Joaninha carried on reading, her voice growling fainter and fainter. At the end she added some kisses and loving thoughts, and some mumbled, unfinished sentence in which he asked his grandmother's blessing.

The old woman shook her head sadly and said: 'Well, well . . . God be praised!'

Joaninha blushed to the roots of her hair. Just as well her grandmother could not see her! But Friar Dinis did and, with a trembling hand and tears in his eyes, he made a silent, meaningful sign of approval and gratitude. Joaninha blushed again, then went pale as death: it was the first time she had told a lie . . . and Friar Dinis, the austere Friar Dinis, approved!

The friar rose and, without a word, took the road to Santarém.

A choking sound of strangled sobs could be heard some way off. . . . Could it be him?

Grandmother and granddaughter embraced and wept.

Neither of them said a word about the letter; the old woman had noticed Joaninha's pious deception . . .

Oh, what an existence, the four of them! The monk, the old woman and those two children! And most people, who are *real* people, live that way. . . . And they like it, they like life just as it is, they are attached to it! Oh, what an enigma is man!

Another week went by, the monk came again on the usual day, took the reply to the letter – a reply that Joaninha alone wrote and saw – and forwarded it in Lisbon via the safe route he had mentioned.

They heard that it had been delivered, but weeks and weeks went by and became more than a year ... but no other letter came.

In the meantime the civil war continued and, after all its tremendous episodes, the great drama of the Restoration was drawing rapidly to a close. It was the middle of '33. The Algarve operation has gone miraculously well for the constitutionalists. Dom Miguel's squadron had been captured and Lisbon was in their hands. The royalists' vain, belated efforts to take the capital had occupied the remainder of the summer. October was already stripping off its last fruits and the leaves were beginning to go pale and fall, when, one Friday at sunset, Friar Dinis appeared in the valley, more bent and tremulous than ever. He had been with the royalist army, which was surrounding Lisbon.

Joaninha was not there, the old woman was alone.

'What news do you bring, Father?' she exclaimed, the moment she heard him. 'Have you heard anything of him? Has he escaped these calamities, these mortal combats?'

'I know nothing, Sister. It has been impossible to obtain any information from Lisbon for the last three days. The lines are denser and more fortified than ever – everything points to some decisive battle very soon.'

'God be with ...'

'With whom, Sister?'

'With those who are right.'

'Neither of them is. On both sides there is ambition and greed, on both sides immorality, perdition and contempt for God's word. Therefore, it does not matter who wins, neither side will triumph.'

'Alas, my poor child, my Carlos!'

'That's right, Sister Francisca, that's right! Ask God to give the victory to your grandson and to the wickedness he is fighting for. Ask God to let the winners be the declared enemies of his name, the destroyers of his altars, the profaners of his temples. ... Oh, what a fine, great day it will be when Carlos, your Carlos, comes to expel at bayonet-point, from the poor convent of St Francis, the old superior – who shall not run away from him, Sister, from him less than any other ... who, kneeling

before the altar, will bow his head, like the martyrs of old, ready
to fall in the presence of his God at the hands of his . . .'

'Dinis! . . . Father! . . . Father Dinis, what dreadful words
come from your lips! . . . My grandson, my Carlos is not
capable . . . oh, my God! . . .'

'Your grandson detests me . . . and he is . . . he is right.'

'He does not know the truth . . . Carlos is mistaken, he thinks
. . . he only knows part of the truth. And I shall – cost what may
– I shall . . .'

'You will what?'

'I shall set him right, I shall tell him the whole truth. I shall
kneel in his presence, I shall humble myself before my
daughter's child, I shall drag these white hairs and these wrinkles
in the dust at his feet . . . I shall die of shame and remorse before
my child, but he shall know the truth.'

The old woman's mysterious, awful words were spoken with
such vehemence and such unusual vigour that Friar Dinis did not
dare to stop her. He heard her to the end, allowed the force of the
torrent to spend itself and then, raising his stern but steady
voice, said in that cold, firm tone that has such an effect on over-
excited spirits: 'If you should do so, woman, my curse, God's
eternal curse be on your head for ever! . . . Oh, woman, is it not
enough for you that he hates me, is it not enough that your
grandson should cease to love you? . . . Do you want . . . do
you want him to despise us as well?'

The old woman gave a deep moan and, with an old,
remembered gesture, raised her hands to her eyes, as if covering
them so as not to see. Then she said with tears of anguish in her
voice: 'God's will be done!'

XIX

————— ·:· —————

A war of advanced posts. Joaninha in the bivouac. – How
the nightingales in the valley became so disciplined that
they sounded the reveille and the evening roll-call. – Who
the 'maiden of the nightingales' was and why she was given
that name. – A sentry lost and found.

THE old woman spoke these last words with a look of grief
that was so resigned yet so despairing, that the monk was moved
and felt the tears blur his sight.

At that moment Joaninha, who was out walking at some
distance from the house, on the Lisbon road, came running
excitedly, shouting: 'Grandmother, Grandmother!... There
are ever so many people coming! Soldiers and people ... men
and women ... such a lot!'

It was the 11th October retreat.

'God have mercy on us!' said the old woman. 'What can it be,
Father?'

'What else should it be?!' answered Friar Dinis. 'My
foreboding coming true. The battle was decisive, the
constitutionals are winning.'

And indeed the retreating troops and the fleeing populace
started to arrive and all the confusion and grievous spectacle of a
civil war retreat....

Some of the wounded, who could go no farther, stayed at the
house in the valley, left in the charge and tender care of Joaninha;
Friar Dinis took charge of the others and accompanied them to
Santarém.

The constitutional troops were on the heels of the royalists
and a few days later had established their headquarters in
Cartaxo. Dom Miguel was securing his fortification in
Santarém and the old woman's house was the last military
outpost occupied by his army.

Before long all the power and interest of the war centred on that once peaceful and delightful, now desolate and turbulent, valley.

Autumn was in its last days. Nature seemed to take pity on mankind and provide a sad, lugubrious setting for the bloody drama of destruction and misery that was to end there. The last leaves were falling; the sky, black with clouds, poured great torrents of water on to the swampy ground; the floodwaters covered the low-lying land while the high ground was clothed in weeds. Work in the fields came to a halt, cattle and shepherds fled, and soldiers from both camps cut down the age-old olive trees. . . .

Everything was ugly and nasty. Ruin, desolation and death were everywhere around the house in the valley, now turned into fortified military quarters.

And what had happened, in the midst of this disorder, what had happened to our old woman and to our adorable Joaninha?

As soon as the two armies had established their position, Friar Dinis had wanted to take the two women to Santarém, but this was not possible. Entreaties, pleas, direct order: all was in vain. For the first time in her life, that timid, weak, irresolute woman found it in her to be firm and self-willed. 'Here I was born,' she said, 'here I have lived and here I shall die. What does it matter how? . . . My life's short moments of happiness and long hours of grief have been spent here. Where should I go to live or die other than here? I know this house by heart, these trees know me, these places are the last I saw, the only ones I can remember. How should I, now that I am old and blind, get to know other places and be able to live there? . . .'

'What about Joaninha, at her age . . . among the soldiery?' the friar hinted.

'Joaninha,' she replied, 'Joaninha is a child, yet she is more sensible, more courageous, healthier and stronger than most men, let alone women. We shall stay here, Father, we shall stay here and be better off than in Santarém. God will protect us. . . .'

Friar Dinis gave in: the same vague, uncertain hope that heartened the old woman and held her there so firmly was no stranger to the monk's heart. She did not dare so much as mention this hope, but it was apparent that she nursed it in a hidden corner of her soul. . . . Her grandson, the child of her beloved daughter, would find his way to the house where he was born. . . . He would come this way and sooner or later. . . . The old woman, I repeat, did not even mention this hope but it was apparent that she had it – Friar Dinis noticed it, and either because he shared it or because he did not dare oppose reasons that he was not offered, he gave in and said no more.

His main fear was the licentious freedom of military customs, but would Joaninha be any less exposed if she took refuge in a military stronghold such as Santarém now was?

In a short time it became clear that her grandmother was right. Joaninha's frank, innocent dignity and the old woman's sober appearance and serene, kindly melancholy made them so respected by the soldiers that, with the efficient co-operation of the post's commander, a good, worthy gentleman from Trás-os-Montes, they were as safe and undisturbed, in the small part of the house they had reserved for themselves, as was possible in such circumstances. Friar Dinis came to the valley regularly, every Friday, and their other habits were not interrupted.

And gradually, the battles, the skirmishes, the sound and the sight of shooting, the sight of blood, the groans of the wounded, the contorted faces of the dead – war, in short, in all its forms, with all the excitement, all the terrors and all the hopes that go with it – became a familiar, everyday thing to them. . . .

Man accustoms himself to everything, he gets used to any condition, and there is no sort of life, however strange, that does not become natural in time and through the repetition of certain actions.

And yet, from Carlos, not another word. . . . Poor old woman!

Months went by in this way. Winter ran its course and the almond trees began to adorn themselves with their pure white flowers of hope. One after another, the plants started coming back to life, the trees sprouting buds; soon afterwards the birds came trilling their love songs in the branches. . . . Almost unnoticed, the month of April was upon us and we were in the middle of a beautiful spring.

The war seemed to be spent, the combatants' ardour broken; rumours of attempted negotiations circulated everywhere.

In our valley the sentries of the opposing camps, accustomed to seeing each other every day, began to look at one another without hatred. They started by swapping coarse wartime taunts and ended by talking to one another in an almost friendly manner. It was often interesting to listen to them, the ordinary soldiers, holding forth on the lofty matters of state that divided the kingdom and had kept it in turmoil for many long years. I wonder if the ministers in their offices dealt with them any better?!

Joaninha, who had gradually become accustomed to that life of danger and uncertainty, was getting braver by the day and inured to war. Everything adapted to the situation, even the nightingales had returned to the bay trees by the house and, as if they had been trained, obeyed the reveille and the evening roll-call, which they accompanied with their lively, vibrant song.

At such hours Joaninha was always at her window – that old, graceful Renaissance window to which we took a fancy, dear reader, before we came to know her. There she was seen by the look-outs of both armies: they got used to seeing her there at sunrise and sunset and there, silent and motionless, she would listen for hours on end to the meandering warbles of her nightingales, perhaps rapt in still more meandering thoughts. . . .

That is why they gave her the name 'maiden of the nightingales', by which she was known in both camps, a suggestive and poetic name with which the soldiers of both flags greeted her!

And on both sides they respected and adored the maiden of the nightingales. It seemed to be laid down by tacit agreement among them all that that sweet, angelic figure should be allowed to move about freely in the midst of opposing weapons, like the prized domestic pigeon which no hunter thinks of shooting.

Wartime habits are not as lax as is believed, there are more delicate feelings in a soldier's spirit and less roughness in his appearance than is thought. The uniform is, of course, vain and conceited, and convinced of its attractiveness, but it is only brutal in its first approach.

Joaninha bandaged the wounded, cared for the sick, had words of comfort for all of them, and in everything she said and did was so self-possessed, so sweetly serious and so gracefully dignified that, while they all loved her very much, they respected her even more.

Trusting in this respect and general esteem, Joaninha had started, day by day, to extend her excursions in the valley. Of late she had taken to going, towards the end of the afternoon, as far as a small thicket of poplars and olive trees some way to the south, near the spot where the most outlying of the constitutional look-outs were posted at night.

One day, almost at sunset, on a peaceful, hot afternoon, either because she fell asleep or because she was lost in thought, the fact is that the nightingales had been warbling for a long time in the bay trees near her window and Joaninha had not returned.

Look-outs had been posted on both sides and all the usual arrangements for the night had been made.

The constitutional officer who was placing his sentries had arrived that same afternoon from Lisbon with reinforcements. He marched off with his detachment and went along arranging them in suitable positions, until he eventually came close to the clump of trees.

'Silence!' he said. 'Halt! There is somebody there.'

'There's nobody,' answered a soldier, who was one of the veterans at the post, 'nobody that matters – it's the maiden of the nightingales. I reckon she must have fallen asleep in her usual spot.'

'The maiden of the nightingales?! What song is that you are singing me?'

The soldier told him the popular explanation of the name, pointed to the house in the valley and went on exalting Joaninha's virtues and merits. . . .

The officer did not let him finish.

'Back to the rearguard, and quiet!'

He quickly went on to post the two remaining sentries some way off and entered the small clump of trees alone.

It was Joaninha who was there and she was indeed fast asleep.

XX

——— ·:· ———

Joaninha asleep. – The *demi-jour*★ of a *coquette*★. – The poetry of the *Flos Sanctorum*. – How the nightingales always accompanied the maid who bore their name and how well one of them sang in the bivouac. – A hastily sketched portrait, to satisfy the kind lady readers. – Thoughts on the lamentable bad taste of those who govern us in withdrawing military honours from the Portuguese army's most elegant and national uniform. – Concerning the similarity of the author of the present work and a medieval painter. – How embraces, however close, and kisses, unending though they may seem, always have to come to an end.

ON a sort of rustic seat made of greenery, carpeted with grasses and wild camomile, Joaninha, half leaning, half lying, slept profoundly.

The dim light of dusk, filtering through the branches of the trees, cast a feeble glow on the girl's expressive features, while the graceful lines of her body appeared with voluptuous languor against the vague, misty background of the earth's vapours, the shadowy indistinctness of outline enhancing the charm of the picture and allowing an excited imagination to survey the whole harmonious gamut of female attractions.

It was an idealized version of the Parisian coquette's *demi-jour*: it was artless and uncalculated and nature herself had prepared it in her leafy *boudoir*★, scented by the perfumed breeze from the meadows.

As in the poetic, popular legends of one of the most poetic books ever written, the *Flos Sanctorum*, in which a dear bird, chosen by destiny, always accompanies the kindly saint of its devotion, Joaninha was not without her tender-hearted companion. From the densest part of the branches which formed a canopy over that couch of greenery came a torrent of melodies, wavering and undulating like a forest in the wind, strong, wild and beautifully irregular and inventive, like the crude verses of a wild mountain poet. It was a nightingale, one of her beloved nightingales from the valley, which had stayed to watch over and attend on its protector, the maiden who bore its name.

At the approach of the soldiers and the short, whispered dialogue reported in the previous chapter, the sweet bird's lovely song had stopped for a few moments. But when the officer, after posting his sentries some way off, came back on tiptoe and cautiously made his way under the trees, the nightingale had already taken up its song again and this time did not interrupt it, but rather intensified its trills and warbles, then lowered its high-pitched tune to such sorrowful, heartfelt sighs that you could only suppose they were the prelude to the tenderest, most touching love scene ever witnessed in this valley.

The officer. . . . But my kind lady readers naturally wish to know whom they are dealing with and demand, at the very least, a rapid outline sketch of the new actor I am about to bring on stage.

The ladies are right: it is a novelist's duty and one he cannot neglect.

The officer was young, perhaps not thirty years old, although his familiarity with the arms of war, the rigours of changing climates and the visible stamp of suffering he bore on his face had already impressed the stronger lines of manhood on those features that should still have the roundness of youth.

He was of average height, slim in build but with the strong, broad chest a man needs for his heart to beat freely; the stalwart elegance of his military bearing was perfectly visible under his ample, thick military overcoat, a sort of English *greatcoat*★ which the imitation of British fashions had made a familiar sight in our bivouacs. He wore it open and slung back from his shoulders, as the night was not cold, and beneath it could be seen the elegant, tight-fitting, grey uniform of a light infantryman, enlivened by its characteristic black frogs and red trimmings . . .

Such a soldierly uniform, so national, so dear to our memory it was, that these people, who degrade everything that was noble, popular and respected in this country, banned it from the army . . . perhaps because it was too Portuguese! They relegated it to the excise men, they made it the uniform of the Customs officers!

I could not resist this thought. I ask my charming reader's forgiveness for interrupting my portrait.

But, when I am painting, when I am drawing and colouring in my characters, I am like those medieval painters who worked into their pictures distichs with maxims, ribbons embroidered with moral judgements and conceits . . . perhaps because they were unable to make the gestures and attitudes expressive enough to speak for themselves and the pen served to illustrate and supplement the brush. . . . Perhaps; and perhaps it is for the same reason that I slip into the same fault . . .

Maybe, but with me it is irreparable, I cannot paint any other way.

Back to our portrait.

His eyes, which were grey and not very large, but extremely bright and lively, displayed the talent, the volubility, perhaps the thoughtlessness, but also the upright simplicity of a frank, loyal and generous character, quick to anger and quick to forgive, incapable of taking offence lightly, but unable to forget a real insult.

His mouth was small and haughty, which was however not a sign of arrogance, still less of vanity, but a conscious smile of his undisputed and unquestionable superiority.

His face was pale rather than dark and looked long, because of the long black beard he wore in the style of the time. His hair too was black; his forehead high and broad.

When he was silent and serious, his countenance could be said to be hard, but the slightest excitement, the merest smile, made it cheerful and sunny, because volubility and seriousness were the twin poles of that unusual, not easily understood character.

Out of such a classical bust, shaped altogether according to the models of ancient art, a sculptor could make a philosopher, a poet, a statesman or a man of the world, depending on the slight changes of expression he gave it.

Now, at this moment, as he entered the small clump of trees, it was enlivened by a quick, restless look of interest, which was, however, broken, contained and, as it were, *checked* by a hidden fear, a painful, secret thought that coloured then receded from his cheek, like the old, faded colour of a material that has been re-dyed, that is now different, but has not ceased entirely to be what it was before . . .

So a sad November day is cheered by a fleeting, unexpected ray of sunlight breaking through the mist in some part of the sky . . .

Such was, as he stood before the sleeping Joaninha, the – I'll not say youth, because he did not look like one – the singular man on whom the name, the story and the circumstances of the maiden seemed to have made such an impression.

'Joaninha!' he muttered, as soon as he saw her in the still sufficient glow of the twilight. 'Joaninha!' he said again, restraining the violence of his outburst. 'It is she, undoubtedly. But how different! . . . Who would believe it? How charming! How beautiful! Can it be possible that the child who two years ago . . .'

As he said this, with an almost instinctive gesture, he took her sleeping hand and raised it to his lips.

Joaninha started and woke up.

'Carlos, Carlos!' she stammered, with her eyes still half closed. 'Carlos, my cousin . . . my brother! It wasn't true, tell me it wasn't true. It was a dream, wasn't it, Carlos?'

And she opened her eyes little by little, wider and wider, until they were wide with amazement and fixed them on him, wide open with wonder and joy.

'It was, it was,' she went on, 'it was a dream, it was a bad dream I had. You didn't die. . . . Speak to your Joana, your sister, tell her you are alive, that your are not his ghost. . . . No, you are not, for I feel your hand warm in my hot one, I feel it tremble together with mine . . . Carlos! My Carlos! Tell me, speak to me. Are you really alive and well? And are you . . . are you my Carlos? Yourself, not a dream any more, is it you? . . .'

'Were you really dreaming? Dreaming of me, Joana? . . .'

'I was, I always do when I sleep. . . . And most of the time when I am awake . . . I was dreaming about the same as I think about all the time . . . you.'

'Joana . . . cousin . . . my sister!'

And he fell into her arms, and they held each other in a long, long embrace, with a long, unending kiss . . . long, long and unending like the first kiss of a pair of lovers. . . .

The embrace was relaxed and the kiss eventually came to an end, because heaven's reflections on earth are limited and imperfect, like the imperfect creatures that inhabit it.

Otherwise . . . the angels would envy life on earth.

Joaninha, recovering from that virtual paroxysm, opened and closed her eyes, to make sure if she were fully awake. She touched her cousin's face, chest and arms, then felt herself as if she doubted her own existence, all the time speaking incoherent, disconnected phrases: 'It is Carlos . . . Carlos. It wasn't true. It is my cousin. . . . My grandmother had the same dream, but it wasn't true. Friar Dinis didn't say so, nor did anyone else. It was Grandmother and me who dreamed it. But he is here alive . . . alive! He is ours, all ours again. . . . But how did you come here, Carlos? How did I come to be here with you? . . . And alone, the two of us alone here, at this late hour! This oughtn't to be. . . . Heavens! What will people say? Oh, my goodness! Well, I don't care, let them say what they will, but it oughtn't to be. Come, Carlos, let us go to her, let us go to our grandmother! . . . There's nothing wrong in it. . . . My cousin! . . . A cousin I was brought up with! But those who don't know, they might say. . . . Come, Carlos. Oh, Grandmother will die of happiness, poor dear! . . . Of course, I shall go on ahead to warn her, and to prepare her . . . I shall start telling her a bit at a time. . . . Follow me, Carlos, and let us go. But – oh, my goodness! – it isn't necessary, what for? She is blind, poor dear, did you know?'

'Blind! What are you saying? My grandmother is blind?!'

'You didn't know, then? Ah, of course you didn't. There are so many things you don't know, my dear! But I shall tell you everything, everything. Listen, she went blind when. . . . But let us not talk about these sad things that are in the past. Once she feels you near her, it will be the same as getting back her sight. She has often told me that, and I am sure it is true. But listen, one day we shall talk freely, just the two of us, alone. I have so much to say. . . . You can't imagine. . . . Now let us go, Carlos.'

With these words, she took him by the hand and walked out into the open valley, by now feebly lit by myriads of stars that sparkled in the blue sky.

XXI

——— ·:· ———

Who goes there? – Concerning how, when there are two parties to a dispute, the third party does not always enjoy himself. – Carlos and Joaninha in a sort of *pacifist*★ situation, which is the falsest and most dangerous of situations.

THE stars were shining in a clear, blue sky. A mild spring breeze whispered softly. In the empty solitude and vast silence of the valley the gentle murmur of Joaninha's sweet voice could be distinctly heard and the shape of her figure was clearly visible, together with that of her companion, whom she led by the hand and who followed her automatically, apparently without a will of his own, obeying the power of a superior and irresistible magnetism. They were walking between the look-outs of the two encampments without seeing them or thinking where they must be ... and simultaneously, from both sides, the curt, strident voice of the sentries called out: 'Who goes there?'

They both shuddered instinctively at the sudden sound of war and alarm, which called them back to the forgotten reality of the place, the hour and the situation in which they found themselves.... They had woken with a start from that enchanted dream which had carried them to the beloved Eden of their childhood. They found themselves in a cruel, desolate land and they saw the flaming sword of civil war that pursued and divided them, that expelled them for ever from the paradise of delights in which they had been born....

What a picture they made, these two! Out in that bare, open valley, in the light of the sparkling stars, between two lines of black shapes, broken here and there by the chance gleam of a fleeting reflection glinting on a bayonet or a rifle – what an image they were of the truest, most sacred natural feelings, always exposed and sacrificed in the midst of the stupid, barbarous struggles and of the conflict of false principles in which what men called *society* writhes unceasingly.

Joaninha clung to her cousin, he stopped suddenly and his hand went for his sword-handle.

'Who goes there?' the sentries bawled a second time.

'Do you hear, Joana?' said Carlos, in a low, sorrowful voice. 'Do you hear those shouts? It is the cry of war that is ordering us to part. It is the jealous, watchful clamour of the parties, which will not tolerate our being together, which separates brother from sister, father from son! . . .'

'Who goes there?' shouted the sentries louder still, and they heard that dull, short click which is so faint yet makes such a powerful impression on the bravest souls. . . . It was the sound of the rifles being cocked.

It was a supreme moment, danger was imminent and by now inevitable. . . . They could both be killed there, pierced by the bullets of the two hostile camps.

Like those who, trusting their innocence and tolerance, think that they can pass among civil disorders without taking part and for that very reason are distrusted by all and are in everybody's sights, the two cousins were in the falsest, most dangerous position there is in a revolution.

Joaninha realized the danger that threatened them and, with that speed of decision which in women is readier and surer on great occasions, she said to Carlos: 'Speak to your men, make yourself known and make for safety. We shall meet again tomorrow. I shall let you know. Farewell!'

'What about you? . . . The royalist sentries? . . .'

'Don't worry about me. Everybody on this side knows me.'

She took a few steps in the direction of the house and raised her voice: 'Joaninha! It's me, comrades, it's me!'

At once rifle-butts were heard clattering on the ground and the contented laughter of the soldiers, who recognized the dear, welcome voice of Joaninha . . . the 'maiden of the nightingales'.

'You see, Carlos? . . . Farewell! Until tomorrow!' she whispered.

'Until tomorrow if . . .'

'If?! . . . You mean you . . .'

'Listen. Don't tell your grandmother that you have seen me or that I am here. It is necessary, essential, I demand it of you . . .'

'Will you tell me tomorrow?'
'Yes.'
'I promise, then. I shall say nothing. . . . But, oh Carlos! . . .'
'Farewell!'
Carlos took two steps in the direction of his look-outs. Joaninha ran in the opposite direction. But he stopped and did not take his eyes off that graceful figure gliding like a shadow along the valley's skyline, until it disappeared completely.

And he still stood stock still.

Suddenly there were one, two, three flashes, like lightning . . . and the detonations that followed and the whistle of the bullets coming after. . . . It was the constitutionalist sentries who were firing on their captain, whom they did not recognize and whose silence and stillness made him suspect.

One of the bullets actually wounded him slightly in the left arm.

'All right, comrades!' yelled Carlos, walking quickly towards them and raising the full, strong voice that was well known in the ranks. 'All right! You have done your duty. One of you bind my arm with this handkerchief.'

'Carlos!' a high-pitched voice, quivering with fear, shouted across the space. 'Carlos! Say something, answer me, did anything happen to you?'

'Nothing, nothing! Don't worry.'

Silence fell once more. Carlos retired to his quarters in a nearby cottage. The soldiers looked at one another and smiled.

One of them, who was more opinionated, said to the others: 'Our captain doesn't waste time. He only arrived today and we are at it again, hey?'

'Our captain is from these parts. Didn't you know?'

'Hum! I get it. And it's lasted so long? The feller's got a way with him!'

'Quiet! I'll tell you the whole story just now. She's his cousin.'

'Ah, a cousin! Well, there's nothing to be said, then.'

'It's the one they call . . .'

'The "maiden of the nightingales"? She's crazy, she is.'

'He likes them like that, he's crazy himself.'

'What about that nun in São Gonçalo on Terceira Island?'

'Crazy.'

'And the English *Lady*★ who. . . ?'

'Raving mad, she was! I wouldn't be surprised if I saw her fall out of the sky, one day, like a bomb. And she wouldn't half go bang!'

'You bet! Particularly if she met the cousin! . . .'

'But is she his cousin or his sister?'

'It's such a mix-up the family relationship of these people in the house in the valley! . . . The things they say hereabouts, I can't make head nor tail of it! . . . And there's a monk mixed up in it, of course . . .'

'Oh, there's a monk in the story?'

'Yes, and some monk! A real apostolic![1] And so ugly, so thin! He turns up in these parts occasionally. I caught sight of him the other day – what a shot that would have been! I'm almost sorry I didn't . . .'

'That'll do! Today we nearly killed our captain, a close shave. Now if you go shooting his uncle, or father, or whatever he is . . .'

'A monk?!'

'Isn't a monk a man too?'

'No, he's not.'

'All right, that's enough talk for today. But if you want to know what I think, we're in for some tough fighting very soon.'

'Let it come, this is getting boring.'

They lit their cigarettes and smoked.

Good God! As calmly and unthinkingly as that, men light up a civil war like this one, that churns up and disorders all natural ideas and feelings.

XXII

———— ·:· ————

An early morning note from cousin to cousin. – They
deceive the poor old woman. – A night with little sleep. –
Concerning Carlos's conversation with his pillow. –
Joaninha as she was when he went away and Joaninha as he
found her on his return. – Love has its obligations,
unhappy word. – The woman he loved, and whether he
still loved her. – The author quizzes his benevolent readers.
He declares that he does not talk to hypocrites. – Who shall
throw the first stone? – Two different ways in which a
thought occurs.

THE next day, soon after daybreak, a civilian who claimed to
be carrying an important message for the commander of the
advanced post, was brought to Carlos's presence and handed
him a letter: it was from Joaninha.

Faithful to her promise, she had said nothing about their
meeting of the previous evening, said the letter. And that her
grandmother was ill and distressed, so that to cheer her up and
comfort her, she had given her news of her cousin as though she
had had it from someone who had seen and been with him. That
she had calmed down and was more contented, but that her state
of anxiety could not continue. That the poor old woman's health
was declining from day to day; that her life was slipping away;
that not to tell her the truth would kill her.... Joaninha
ended with a thousand affectionate and fond thoughts, and finally
fixed the same place as the previous evening for them to meet again
and to agree on what was to be done. Precautions had been taken
and the commander of the enemy post had given his consent so
that the interview could be held with the maximum of security.

Carlos had not slept all night. An extraordinary excitement
had set his blood in a turmoil and disturbed his nerves. He had
particularly wanted to come to that post. He did expect and hope
that while there he would learn more about his family, see them

perhaps, sooner or later, meet one of them . . . and of all of them the one he most hoped and wanted to see, to be sure, was that sweet, innocent child with whom he had lived as brother and sister since childhood.

But he had left behind a child, a child playing at picking daisies and running after butterflies in the valley . . . a child who loved him very much, certainly, whose sweet image had never left him in his lengthy wanderings, whom he had never ceased to think of with fondness, whom he had never forgotten for one moment, in the happiest or the busiest, the most difficult or most dangerous moments of his life.

But she was a child! The image was that of a child.

It is true. In battle, in the presence of death, in the long siege of Oporto, amid the scourges of cholera and hunger, in times of highest hope, in the discouragement of the gloomiest days, the sweet image of Joaninha, of the Joaninha he used to carry in his arms and put on his shoulders to reach birds' nests in summer; whom he lifted over the swampy patches in the valley in winter – that dear image never left him.

Never! . . . Neither when love's pangs nor love's triumphs – much more forgetful! – seemed to monopolize all his senses and his heart's every feeling.

The nostalgic remembrance of Joaninha, sweetly impressed upon the purest, most virtuous fibres of his soul, shone through all the shadows that darkened it and burned brighter than any flame that lighted it.

A still, clear light, as serene as a torch in the hand of an angel kneeling, innocently and piously, before the throne of the Almighty!

But, on the very day he arrived in the valley, almost the very hour, his heart full of that light, now more live and intense because of the nearness of its source, at that very hour to find, in that lonely spot, among those trees, in the faint, bewitching light of dusk . . . who, in the name of heaven?! No longer the same Joaninha of three years before, not the image he carried in his heart, just as he had taken it away with him, but a sweet, beautiful young woman, a complete, fully grown woman, who had nevertheless lost none of the attraction, the charm, the sweet, delightful fragrance of childish innocence she had when he left her.

He did not expect, nor was he prepared for, the impression he received: it was a surprise, a shock, a confused upset of all his ideas and feelings.

Just what was the real impression he received, he could not explain even to himself: it was of a totally new kind, a kind unique in the history of his experiences, it was unknown to him, it made him feel ill at ease and he was almost afraid to analyse it.

Could it be the first sign of love?

But he had been in love, really and truly in love ... and believed he still was, and he should be in love – by all that is sacred and holy in the duties of the heart, he was obliged still to be in love.

Oh, love's obligations, love's obligations! What more are you, what more indeed but obligations?!...

Carlos did not think like this, he did not believe it to be so. He was loyal and sincere, and had given his heart to the woman who loved him, who had given him so much proof of her love and devotion, who believed in his faithfulness, who existed for him alone – a beautiful young woman, extremely gifted and charming, a woman of superior intelligence and breeding, who had despised crowds of noble, wealthy, powerful suitors to stoop to him, to surrender herself to a poor, despised foreign fugitive.

Who was this woman?

How and where had he come into possession of this jewel, this talisman which made him feel so sure of himself that he saw nothing more in his charming cousin than...

Than what?

The innocent child he had left behind?

But that is not true. Joaninha had made a different impression on him, whatever it was.

What was it then?

And above all, who was this other woman he loved?

And did he still love her?

He did.

And Joaninha?

Joaninha was ... I do not know myself what Joaninha was for him, what he felt towards her at that moment.

What she had been to him, I have explained adequately, dear, benevolent reader. What she will be to him.... Can you, sincere and honest reader – I am not talking to the hypocrites –, can you tell me what place there will be in your heart tomorrow for the woman whom today you merely find beautiful, or charming, or likeable?

Can you answer to me for the part that will be taken in your life tomorrow by the image of the girl you are today observing simply with an artist's eye, taking note, as you would in a charming painting, of the delicate outline, the pure profile, the frank, lively expression?

And when that fatal tomorrow comes, if it should come, you shall answer me also as to the place that will be kept in your heart by that other image which was there before and which, in contact with this new one, I can see from here growing pale, fading. . . . All I can see now are its vague outlines. . . . Now it is just a shadow of what it was. . . . Alas, what will it be tomorrow?

Kind, benevolent reader, dear, indulgent reader, do not be too quick to judge my poor Carlos, and remember that stone which the Son of God said was to be cast by the first one to consider himself innocent. . . . The adulteress went on her way in peace, no one stoned her.

Well, it is true. Carlos had loved, loved intensely, and still loved the woman to whom he had given his promise and was determined to remain faithful. And that woman was beautiful, noble, wealthy and admired; she held a high position in society . . . and had sacrificed everything for him, an unknown exile.

And Carlos was sure that no woman would love him as she did, that the long ash-blonde tresses, the languid doe eyes, the stately, regal appearance, the superbly white complexion, the intelligence, the talent, the elegance of Georgina. . . . Her name was Georgina, and that is all, my inquisitive lady readers, that the discreet chronicler of this most true story can tell you for the time being. Ask him no more, I beg you. Carlos was sure, as I was saying, that all those qualities, her boundless love and her unreserved trust, neither could nor would have a rival.

Yet that kiss and that embrace of Joaninha's. . . . Oh, what had it done to him? What had he felt? How had his talisman kept guard over his heart and soul? . . .

No. Carlos was sure of himself, sure of his old love and

mindful of all that he owed her. And this was what he thought about all that night, which he spent sleeplessly.

Joaninha's image appeared from time to time, like a fleeting ray of magical light, in the midst of those other visions of the past that his thoughts evoked in him. Alas, the latter were evoked by his thoughts, while the former came spontaneously: it was repelled, but it kept coming back . . .

There is a marked difference in these two ways in which things come into our minds.

Morning came at last. Carlos breathed the fresh, keen dawn air and felt a different man.

When Joaninha's letter arrived, he read it and reflected on it without agitation. Certain and sure of himself, he decided to keep the appointment made for that afternoon.

XXIII

———— ∴ ————

Many vague, incongruous thoughts continue to occur to Carlos. – A dance of fairies and sprites. – Friar Dinis, the family's evil genius. – 'We shall see' is the great solution for great difficulties. – Carlos as romantic poet. – Green eyes. – A challenge to all the *moyen-âge*★ poets of our time.

THERE is nothing like taking a decision.

But it has to be taken *and* carried out, otherwise, if the matter is difficult and complicated, doubts that have already been settled gradually begin to get entangled again, to get embroiled ... fresh ones appear, as yet unconsidered sides of the problem show themselves. And then, if the delay is long, by the time the decision taken is eventually carried out, on most occasions it is no longer in consequence of reason and conviction but out of caprice, as a point of honour, sheer obstinacy.

Carlos had decided to keep the appointment arranged for the day's end. But the day was long, time just would not go by. All his ruminations of the night swarmed back into his mind; all the images that had flitted through his imagination revived, came to life and began to dance in his spirit that dance of fairies and sprites which is the delight and torment of those waking dreamers who go around, whom the learned university calls *nervous*, the language of novels *sensitive*, and as the popular expression has it, *crazy*.

Carlos was all this. Why should I deny it?

Among the images that whirled round in his mind, there now came one ... perhaps the one he saw most distinctly of all: his grandmother, whom he had loved so much and in whose motherly heart he knew full well he held the first place, the biggest share, that grandmother who had been such a loving mother to him! Poor old woman, now decrepit and blind. ... Blind, poor thing! How and why had she gone blind?

There was a mystery there, which Joaninha had mentioned

but did not explain.

Behind the patient, humble figure of that grieving, unfortunate woman, appeared a harsh, austere shape, a man covered from head to foot in an armour of ascetic insensitivity, a man who seemed to be the evil genius of that old woman and her whole family, the accomplice and the castigator of a great crime, a mysterious, terrifying creature.

That man was Friar Dinis, a man he wanted to hate, thought he did hate, but one on whose behalf a mystic, secret voice cried out in the depths of his spirit, a voice which said: 'It may all be true, but you cannot hate this man.'

Yes, but over Friar Dinis there hung a tremendous accusation which had made him, Carlos, quit his parents' home! An awful accusation which also involved the poor old woman, that grandmother who adored him and whom he, even if she was guilty as he supposed her to be, could not stop loving....

And did Joaninha know anything of these awful secrets?

He hoped to God she did not.

Did she perhaps suspect something? . . . What?

And was he going to poison the thoughts, profane the ears and corrupt the lips of that innocent child with the disclosure of such horrors?

Should he tell her of his family's dishonour? Should he explain the reason why he had fled his parents' house?

Should he? . . .

No. If Joaninha had any suspicions, he should rather destroy them; if she did know anything, deny it.

He would lie, he would swear falsely if necessary.

And should he not go and see his grandmother, not enter the family home in order to comfort the unhappy woman who was kept alive solely by the hope of seeing her daughter's child?

No, never.... He had passed over that threshold which he believed to be contaminated, dishonoured, blood-stained and defiled with shame and disgrace, passed over it and shaken the dust from his shoes, promising God and his own honour never to cross it again.

But what should he tell Joaninha, then? How could he explain to her such odd and apparently cruel, ungrateful behaviour?

For the meantime the material obstacles of the war would serve as an excuse; afterwards time would give counsel.

We shall see! is the great decision we take in life's difficult moments, whenever we are able to postpone them.

Carlos said: '*We shall see!*'

He made all the arrangements to ensure being safe and undisturbed in the spot where he was to meet his cousin, and the remainder of the day, restless but pleased, he busied himself with his military duties, tired his body so as to rest his spirit, and to some extent and for a number of hours he succeeded.

But an April day is endless, interminable. And the last hours seemed the longest of all. There never were such long hours! Carlos could invent nothing more to do: he started thinking.

What else could he do?

He thought about this, he thought about that. . . . The ideas came and went. His imagination, which had been curbed for so long, took the bit between its teeth and galloped off full tilt into space. . . .

Golden ringlets, jet-black tresses, peaches and cream complexions like angels, pale, transparent and diaphanous ones like enchanted princesses, black eyes, blue eyes, green eyes – Joaninha's eyes, of course –, all these features, blurred and confused but supremely beautiful, all of them, passed before his eyes and they all bewitched him. The unfortunate fellow – why should I not speak the truth? – the unfortunate fellow was a poet.

Steady on! Don't send the lad packing just like that. . . . A poet, let us be clear about it, not because he wrote verses – of that vice he was not guilty – but he had that delicate feeling for art, that sixth sense for what is *beautiful* and *ideal*, which are possessed only by certain privileged organisms that give rise to poets and artists.

Here is a fragment of his poetic aspirations. As my amiable lady readers can see, they have neither metre nor rhyme . . . nor reason. . . . But then they are not verses:

> Green eyes!! . . .
> Joaninha has green eyes
> Heaven's pure light shines not in them as in blue eyes.
> Nor yet the flames and fumes of passion as in black eyes.
> But the meadow's lush verdure, the wood's coolness and liveliness, the sea's transparent swell . . .
> All this is in those green eyes.

Joaninha, why are your eyes green?

In Georgina's blue eyes burns the serene, modest glow and tranquil light of a tried and tested love that has given its all, given all it had to give.

Georgina's blue eyes speak a single word of love, always the same and always beautiful: *I love you, I am yours!*

In Soledade's restless black eyes I never read any words but these: *Love me, you are mine!*

Joaninha's eyes are a vast book, written in moving characters whose infinite combinations are beyond my comprehension.

What are your eyes saying, Joaninha?

What language do they speak?

Oh, why do you have to have green eyes, Joaninha?

The lily and the jasmin are white; red the rose; the rosemary blue...

The violet purple and the jonquil gold.

But all nature's colours come from one alone, green.

Green is the origin and first type of all beauty.

The other colours make up green; in green is the whole, the unity of created beauty.

The eyes of the first man must have been green.

The sky is blue...

The night is black...

The earth and the sea are green...

The night is black, but beautiful. Your eyes, Soledade, were black and beautiful as the night.

The stars that shine in the depths of night are beautiful, but who does not sigh for day at the end of a long night?

And for the stars to disappear, to go away, at last!...

Comes the day. ... The sky is blue and beautiful, but one's eyes weary of looking at it.

Oh, the sky is blue like your eyes, Georgina!...

But the earth is green and the eyes find it restful, never tiring of the infinite variety of its pleasant hues.

The sea is green and rises and falls. ... But oh, it is as sad as the earth is joyful.

Life is made up of joys and sadness...

Green is sad and joyful, like the joys of life itself!

Joaninha, Joaninha, why do you have green eyes?...

It is clear that our battlefront intellectual, the soldier who used the word *crazy* about the thinker of such bizarre thoughts, was right and knew what he was talking about.

Unfortunately, these most sublime poetic thoughts did not express themselves in words. By a miraculous process of mental photography it was possible to obtain only the fragment I have transcribed.

What an honour and glory for the romantic school if we were able to obtain the complete collection!

One would give it an incisive, exciting, *shattering* preface...

It could be given a vaporous, phosphorescent title ... for example: *Mute Echoes of the Heart*, or *Reflections of a Soul*, or *Invisible Hymns*, or *Poetic Nightmares*, or something similar, which one couldn't tell what it was and made no sense.

Then let some frock-coated, round-hatted minstrel, some Renaissance troubadour with a Joinville waistcoat, come here and challenge my Carlos on points of vague, extravagant, vaporous, nebulous romanticism!

And see which of them was capable of writing less logically (less grammatically, for sure), and with the more triumphant disrespect for the absurd, restricting rules of that idiotic classical school which never produced anything but Homer and Virgil, Sophocles and Horace, Camoens and Tasso, Corneille and Racine, Pole and Molière, and a few dozen more equally obscure names!

XXIV

———— ∴ ————

A new Genesis. – The social Adam, most unlike the natural
Adam. – Carlos always the one, according to his good
instincts, but always the other by virtue of his evil
thoughts. – How Joaninha welcomed her cousin with open
arms and what else took place between them. – Sorrow,
part pain, part pleasure.

GOD fashioned man and set him in a paradise of delights;
society refashioned him and set him in a hell of follies.

Man – not the one made by God, but the counterfeit man
forged by society, which has compressed and moulded in its
iron casts that handful of clay which had adapted itself to the
divine image in the earthly paradise – man, misshapen as we
know him, is the absurdest, most preposterous and incongruous
animal to inhabit the earth.

Born king of all creation, he has lost his majesty; he is a
disinherited, outlawed prince who today wanders, a fugitive
among his former estates; haughty still and conceited with his
past memories; low, base and wretched in his present adversity.

From these two wholly and constantly opposed forms of
behaviour, quite enough in themselves to make him ridiculous,
society, in its false wisdom, has created a fantastical, irrational,
impossible system, a compound of the most crack-brained rules
and a mishmash of the most jarring contradictions. And having
hollowed out this perfect model of its pretentious art, it placed
man inside it, disfigured and distorted him, made him into that
absurd, preposterous creature, sickly, fragile and infirm, and set
him in the midst of the fantastic Eden it had created – a perfect
inferno of follies –, saying to him in distorted, blasphemous
imitation of the Creator's words: 'Thou shalt eat of no tree in the
garden. But of the tree of the knowledge of good and evil, of that
alone shalt thou eat if thou wantest to live.'

An indigestion of knowledge, which his poor belly could not

break down, and the conceit and self-importance it produced – such was the result of that commandment which, unlike the other, man did not disobey: such is his usual state.

And when his memories of his earlier existence awaken in him the desire to abandon his present one, inspiring him with a longing to return to the ways of God and nature, society, armed with its irons, descends upon him and binds him, crushes and disfigures him again, squeezing him on the harrowing rack of its moulds.

He must either die or become a monster of depravity.

★   ★   ★

Few sons of the social Adam had so many reminiscences of that other earlier homeland and tended so much to resemble the original type that had issued from the Almighty's hands; few strove so hard to shake off the oppressive embrace of social constraints and redeem himself in nature's blessed freedom as did our Carlos.

But the best and most generous of men in the eyes of society is still weak, false and petty.

What is more, his spirit's every noble urge and lofty design had cost him harsh punishment, severe unjust admonishments, from that great, hypocritical, lying, venal judge – society.

Carlos was much like other men. . . . Good and sincere in the first impulse of his exceptional nature, reflection brought him down to the ordinary level of weakness, hypocrisy and untruthfulness.

He was of the best, but he was a man.

His thoughts, his meditations, all that night and the following day, at the very hour when he was to meet the object that occupied his mind, if not his heart too, all partook of that restless, morbid instability of his social being, in which the faint reflection of his natural being flickered but accidentally.

Doubt, uncertainty, vanity and deceit unhinged and devastated the fine make-up of that soul.

Thus he came to Joaninha, who was waiting for him with open arms, who embraced him, who kissed him without the slightest false coyness of feigned modesty, and who, with the laughter of joy in her heart and on her lips, said to him: 'Well, my dear Carlos, let us sit down, close to one another, and have a talk. We have much to talk about. Give me your hand. Here, in mine. . . . How cold your hand is today! And yesterday it was so hot! . . . Oh, now it is getting so, so hot . . . much too hot! Are you feverish?'

'No.'

'No, you're not, you look healthy enough. And you are so big and strong, as I always imagined a man should be, as I always saw you in my dreams! Because it is strange, Carlos, when I dreamed about you I didn't see you as you were when you went away from here, thin, sad and ill. I saw you as you are now, strong, healthy, cheerful. But you're not cheerful today like you were yesterday, no, you're not. . . . What is the matter?'

'Nothing, dear Joaninha, there's nothing the matter. I was thinking . . .'

'What about? Tell me.'

'I was thinking how different our dreams were – because I dreamed about you as well.'

'You did, Carlos? And what were your dreams like? How did you see me in your dreams?'

'Quite the opposite of how you saw me. I saw you as that little Joaninha, that playful, mischievous little girl skipping through these fields, jumping over ditches, climbing trees. That Joaninha I used to carry in my arms or on my back, and who made me behave as foolishly and childishly as she herself, although I was fifteen years older. I saw you laughing, singing . . .'

'A man's dreams! Who can believe them? Why I have never laughed or played again since the day you went away. . . . And what a day, Carlos! . . . And all those that followed it! There has never been a single day of happiness in this house. Oh! Let me tell you. Friar Dinis. . . . You know I don't like him!'

'You don't?'

'Not a bit. I loathe him. And, God forgive me, I think my dislike of him is unjust.'

'Why?'

'Because he is truly fond of you. Carlos, a father's love and devotion for his child are not greater than his for you.'

'God forgive him!'

'God forgive who . . . and forgive what? His love for you?'

'No but . . .'

'I know what you mean, and you're right.'

'I'm right?!'

'Yes. He is in need of God's forgiveness for a great sin.'

'What are you saying, Joana?! And how do you know?'

'I know. I know the whole story.'

'You?!'

'Me. I know it was his fault my grandmother went blind, our good, kind grandmother, Carlos! ... It was he who made her go blind with the tears he made those poor eyes weep until they wearied of crying and the light went out of them for ever. My sweet grandmother! And why, o God, why?!'

'Why?'

'For your sake, because of the guilty feelings he filled her head with, that you were a bad Christian, that you were not God-fearing, that there was no salvation for you ... you, Carlos! See just how blind that unhappy monk is.'

'Unhappy indeed!'

'But you know he means it in good faith and says it out of the great love he has for you, a love that I cannot understand. The same with my grandmother, who shakes before him. And yet he is fond of her, I am sure he would give his life for her ... for all of us. Not so much for me, but for you and for her he would, for sure. But his love is the sort that vexes and torments. I could almost say the sort that kills.'

'It does, it does!'

'He will surely kill our grandmother. Always frightening her, making her feel guilty! That God of his is a God of terror, of vengeance, of punishment, without pity. Oh, what a man! Everything is sin and wickedness to him ... I can't stand him.'

Carlos took a deep breath, as if relieved of a great weight, while he listened to his cousin's conclusions, which made clear to him her total ignorance of the family's awful secrets.

'And with you,' he said in a more relaxed tone of voice, 'how does he get along with you, how does he treat you?'

'He doesn't interfere with me, he rarely talks to me. But oh, if he knew that I was here with you – goodness me! – what my poor grandmother would have to hear from him! Just as well today is not Friday, otherwise I wouldn't be here.'

'Why? Does he still come every Friday?'

'Always the same. Tomorrow we shall have him with us, for our sins, tomorrow is Friday.'

'Shall I not see you here tomorrow, then?'

'Not here, you can be sure. But come, that's why I came to-day, to talk about that . . . and to see you, to talk to you, to be with my own Carlos . . . and, at the same time, to arrange how to do things. When shall you go and see Grandmother? . . . Our mother, because she is our mother, Carlos, neither you nor I have ever known any other. When may I tell her that your are here? The poor old dear is so ill! She has not left her bed for a fortnight.'

'My poor, poor mother! . . . Oh, if it were not for! . . . Never mind, Joaninha, one of these days I shall go. Just now it is not possible, you must see that. How should I pass the royalist sentries and go to an enemy post? My life . . . well, that is of little importance, but my honour would be at risk. I should almost certainly lose it and perhaps . . .'

'No, Master Carlos, that excuse will not do. It's nigh on a year we have had the war at our door and we know how things are and how to do things. The commander of our post is a man of honour, a perfect gentleman. If I tell him who you are and what you are coming for, he knows how ill my grandmother is and he is very fond of her. He will undoubtedly give us permission for you to come with absolute safety. Do you think he doesn't know that I am here with you? I told him so myself, though I didn't explain who you are. I told him that you are a relative of ours, that you had news of other members of the family and that I had to speak to you. He made no objections, he is a splendid person, good, really good.'

'Is he young, this commander?'

'Young, him? Poor man! He's at least fifty, and I think he has as many children. But why do you ask? And you raised your eyebrows, the way you used to before when you were angry! What was that for, Carlos?'

'Nothing, silly, I just asked.'

'Maybe, but don't ever frown at me like that again, because you look just like . . . I never saw such a likeness . . .'

'Like who?'

'Like Friar Dinis.'

'Me, like him?!'

'Exactly, when you make that face. Look, you're doing it again. Come on! Laugh and be happy, if you want to look like me, and everyone says we are so alike.'

137

'Sweet, innocent child!'

And he kissed her hand, which he was holding in his own. He kissed it once, then again and again, a mixture of tenderness and a vague sort of sadness welling up from deep in his heart with a strange sorrow, part pain, part pleasure, which they both felt and which brought tears to their eyes.

XXV

————— ∴ —————

Happiness in excess also causes dismay and unease. – The astounding contradictions of human nature. – How Joaninha's green eyes clouded over and lost all their sparkle. – The heart of a woman in love always divines the truth.

CARLOS continued to hold Joaninha's hand in his, and his eyes, glistening with tears, were riveted on hers, from whose transparent, diaphanous green depths shone rays of ineffable tenderness.

To describe all that he felt is impossible, so conflicting were his thoughts, such the turmoil and confusion that agitated all his senses.

For a long time neither of them uttered a word, but their silence spoke volumes.

Eventually Joaninha came back to her initial concern and said to her cousin: 'Listen, Carlos, tomorrow is Friday. As I told you, Friar Dinis is coming. If there is the slightest difficulty with the commander, he won't refuse him anything . . .'

'For heaven's sake, Joaninha, for your and Grandmother's sake, not a word to the monk about my being here! Him, oh, I have sworn never to see him again. And if my grandmother . . .'

'All right, I shan't tell him a thing. But when can I tell Grandmother and when will you go and see her?'

'Not just yet. I need permission from Lisbon, or at least from headquarters, to do something that all the rules of war forbid, that in present circumstances and in a war of this sort is quite prohibited. Without permission – and you know that my decisions cannot be altered –, without permission I cannot go. In any case, Friar Dinis had better not so much as think!'

'And how long, how many days must go by?'

'How do I know? A week, a fortnight perhaps, maybe more.'

'And my poor grandmother, poor dear thing, eating her heart out...'

'You comfort her, Joaninha. Tell her that you've had news of me, that I am well, that I have everything I need and that I hope to see you all very soon.'

'And can I ... can I, I shall see you every day, shall I not, Carlos?'

'Tomorrow is Friday...'

'Tomorrow is a black day ... I wouldn't want to, even. Not tomorrow. I know that. But, except for tomorrow, Carlos dear, oh, every day!'

'Yes, sweet angel, yes.'

'You promise?'

'I swear it.'

'Whatever happens?'

'Whatever.... Except for one thing.... But that is not ... not possible.'

'What is it, Carlos? What can it be, what can happen to prevent you?'

Carlos shuddered, hesitated, blushed, went pale, wanted to tell her the truth but did not dare.

Why? And what truth was this? I shall not be the one to disclose it, since he did not speak it: as a discreet and faithful narrator, I shall imitate my hero's discretion.

Was it discretion, then?

No, it was really something else.

Was it a secret thought?

No.

Was it an evil intention, a premeditated deceit, was it?

No, not that either.

What was it, then?

It was the doubt, it was the weakness, it was the vanity, the well-meaning, forced lie, the necessary falsehood of social man.

Carlos lied and said: 'Only if I am expressly forbidden ... by my superiors.'

But this was not what he feared. This was not the one sovereign motive he feared might one day suddenly sever the sweet bonds of companionship to which he had so quickly accustomed himself and which he already thought of as a necessary, essential part of his life. No it was not. Carlos had lied. . . .

Joaninha looked him straight in the face. . . . Carlos blushed again. She blanched. . . . Then blushed in her turn.

'Carlos, you wouldn't lie to me . . .'

'Joaninha!'

'You are my Carlos. . . . You love me just as you did before . . .'

'I am, oh I am! And I love you.'

'Like before?'

'More.'

'I tell you, Carlos, I've never loved and never shall love any man but you.'

'Joana!'

'Carlos!'

They were about to fall into one another's arms. That simple confession of innocence was about to be accepted, but by whom and how, great heavens?! Those precious words, those sweet words which a less artful woman finds so difficult to say; which, suspected, discovered and heard long before by the heart, spoken a thousand times by the eyes, no man can rest or consider himself happy, secure in his happiness, until he hears them pronounced by the lips; those heavenly words which explain the past and answer for the future, which are the last, irrevocable sentence in a lengthy suit made up of anxious moments, of uncertainties and alarms, Joaninha had pronounced those last, fatal words, *I love you*, as naturally, as sincerely, as easily and un-hesitatingly as if they were – and they assuredly were – as if they had always been the one thought, the constant fixed idea of her life.

Happiness in excess can also cause dismay and unease. A moment before, Carlos would have given his life to hear those words; a moment afterwards – oh, astounding contradiction of our dual nature! –, a moment afterwards, he would have given his life not to have heard them. At one moment he was about to throw himself into the arms of the innocent creature who held them open in an angelic ecstasy of the most passionate love; the next moment, he shuddered and was horrified by his happiness.

'Joana!' he exclaimed. 'Joana, my dearest, are you sure I am worthy. . . . Are you sure you should? . . .'

141

'I'm sure. Since I understood anything, I have never thought differently. From when you went away, I began to understand my thoughts ... I told my grandmother and she...'

'And she?...'

'She blessed me, called me her beloved daughter, embraced me, kissed me and told me that was the first happy, joyful hour she had had for many years.'

Carlos gave no answer and looked at Joaninha with an indescribable expression of fondness and sorrow. The radiant happiness that shone upon her countenance – which at that moment had all the beauty with which a true love illuminates even the least attractive features –, the radiance of her happiness began to fade and grow dim. The transparent limpidity of those green eyes clouded over: neither the bright sparkle of the aquamarine nor the deep glow of emerald lit them now. They had the dull, deadened gleam, the matt, stony smoothness of one of those opaque, lustreless gems used by artists to set in the necklaces of ancient statues.

'Goodbye, Joana!' said Carlos, distressed and worried.

'Goodbye, Carlos!' she replied automatically.

'I shall see you the day after tomorrow.'

'Of course.'

'The day after tomorrow I shall tell you...'

'Don't tell me.'

'Why?'

'Because you don't have to, I know already.'

'You know?'

'Yes.'

'What?'

'What you haven't the courage to tell me, Carlos, but my heart has divined. You don't love me, Carlos.'

'I don't love you?! Me?! ... Great God, I don't love her!...'

'No. You love another woman.'

'Me! Joana, oh, if only you knew...'

'I know everything.'

'You do not.'

'I do. You love another woman, another woman who loves you, whom you cannot and must not abandon, and who I...'

'You?'

'I know is beautiful, gifted and graced with elegance and

charm, because . . . because you, dear Carlos, because your love could not be given for less.'

'Joana, Joaninha!'

'Don't say anything, don't say anything today. . . . Today, above all, don't say anything. Tomorrow . . .'

'Tomorrow is Friday.'

'Just as well! I shall have more time to think, to consider, before I see you again. Goodbye, Carlos!'

'Just one word, Joana. Do you think I could deceive you?'

'No, I'm sure you wouldn't.'

'Until tomorrow. . . . The day after tomorrow.'

'Goodbye!'

They embraced, half-heartedly this time, and exchanged a shy, chaste kiss. Their lips were cold, their hands trembled and their anxious hearts throbbed, beating so strongly that they could hear them.

They went their respective ways. The night was as clear and tranquil as the previous one: the stars shone as brilliantly in the blue sky, the silence, majesty and beauty of Nature were the same. . . . Only they were changed . . . changed, so changed and different from what they had been!

The arrangements had been made with care. The two of them reached their destinations without mishap.

XXVI

—————— ⋰ ——————

How to read the authors of antiquity, and the moderns too. – Horace on the Via Sacra. – Duarte Nunes, iconoclastic historian. – Police and steamboats. – The vandals of the blessed regime that governs us. – Shakespeare read in England by the fireside, with a glass of *old sack*★ on the writing-desk. – Whether Sir John Falstaff was a greater man than Sancho Panza. – A great, important archaeological discovery concerning St James, St George and Sir John Falstaff. – Proof of the latter's visit to Portugal. – The enthusiastic Briton at the Tomb of Héloise and Abelard in the Père-Lachaise. – Bentham and Camoens. – The author goes to his window and an amazing poetic *mirage* produced by some stanzas of *The Lusiads*. – Finally: how the journey to Santarém proceeded and what is to happen to Joaninha.

IF I go to Rome one day, I shall enter the eternal city with my Livy and my Tacitus in the pockets of my travelling coat. There, seated among those immortal ruins, I know that I shall understand their history better, because the texts of the great writers will be illustrated for me by the artistic monuments which saw them write and which in some cases recall, in others actually witnessed the memorable events, the progress and decadence of that remarkable civilization.

And Juvenal and Horace? My Horace, my faithful old friend Horace! . . . It must be a pleasure fit for a king to walk along the Via Sacra reading that delightful satire, the ninth of Book One, I believe:

> *Ibam forte sacra via, sicut meus est mos,*
> *Nescio quid meditans nugarum . . .*[1]

It must be a greater pleasure still, much greater, than kissing the

144

Pope's foot. It seems that way to me, but, as I've never been to Rome. . . .

Nor is it necessary. One needs only to pick up the beautiful chronicle of King Fernando, the one Duarte Nunes disfigured least.[2]

Duarte Nunes was an iconoclastic reformer of our ancient chronicles. He lopped away all the images and scraped off all the poetry of those venerable, delightful Portuguese sagas. In historical terms they were little more than sagas, it is true, but as sagas they were beautiful. And Duarte Nunes, who was a poor pedant of a grammarian without taste or imagination, went to work on the delicately carved Gothic filigree and tracery of those monuments and shattered them, leaving only the historical facts, which amounted to little and even that uncertain, and believed he had repaired a history, when he had merely destroyed a poem. We lost a *Nibelungenlied*[3] when we could have had one and we didn't get a history because that was no way to make history.

Well, as I say, let anyone take a copy of the beautiful chronicle of King Fernando; let him obey the law by contributing his shilling to the profit and glory of the laudable company that has exclusive rights to these steam-driven scrap-heaps which ply up and down the river; let him board one of the said scrap-heaps which, apart from the filth and stench, offer no danger except the falling apart of that whole creaking contraption which in any civilized country, where the police did something more than spend their time inventing conspiracies, would long have been condemned to plod to Lamas[4] at its own speed. However, there are no others here, nor will there be in the near future, thanks to the great amount of attention now said to be given to the country's material interests. So let him take his seat, suffer what I myself suffered, get to Santarém, rest, then set to reading the chronicle. He shall see if it is not quite different, see if in the presence of those precious remains, mutilated and defaced though they be by successive waves of barbarians – in a word, spoiled by the worst and most vandalous of all vandals, the administrative and municipal authorities of the blessed regime which governs us; if even so he does not behold before his eyes the men, the scenes of times gone by, if he does not hear the stones speak, the inscriptions shout aloud, the statues rise from the tombs and all the colour and poetry of those marvellous ages revive and come to life before him!

I have experienced it many times, it is infallible. I had never understood Shakespeare until I read him in Warwick, on the banks of the Avon, beneath an aged oak, in the light of that dull white sun in Albion's cloudy sky ... or at night, with my feet on the *fender*★,[5] the kettle boiling on the hearth and on the writing-desk the old crystal of a fine cutglass goblet glinting at me, reflecting the amber rays and soft, fragrant glow of *old sack*★,[6] while the fire and the heavy, polished copper candlesticks cast on the old panelled ceiling and on the dark oak wainscot that lines the room, those strong, flickering shadows with which old women invent visions and souls from the other world, and poets – poets like Shakespeare – create the shade of Banquo, the witches of *Macbeth* and even the rotund belly and great dangling sword of my particular friend, Sir John Falstaff, the inventor of 'legitimate consequences', the founder of the great school of pigheaded reformists, of pugnacious poltroons who save their homeland with fustian and who are unbearable once they have a protector.

Oh, Falstaff, Falstaff! I do not know if you are a greater man than Sancho Panza. I think not. But you have a bigger belly. You have more room in your belly. When our forefathers repudiated St James as a Castilian dog and invoked St George,[7] you, Falstaff, came in his retinue from England and settled here: here you stayed and became the patriarch of this vast progeny of Falstaffs who are around us.

This important moment in our history, the dismissal of St James and the coming of St George of England with Sir John Falstaff as his figurehead, this great archaeological discovery which explains so many modern things, how did I make it? By going to the actual sites and studying the old models there, which is my creed.

In everything and for everything, that is how it is. One day an Englishman came to Paris, a legitimate, raw Englishman, unsullied by continental corruption: nankeen trousers, heavy shoes, carroty hair, hat tipped back on the back of his head. Being a keen admirer of Héloise and Abelard, he went to the Père-Lachaise,[8] came to the lovers' tomb, took a small book out of his pocket and began to read those Paracletan letters which have turned many a less eccentric head than that of my pure-blooded Englishman. Which he is not: he became so inflamed that he started running around like a mad thing, yelling for a cathedral canon to come to his assistance because he wanted to identify himself with his model, to purify his passion, in sum to be a complete, or incomplete, Abelard.

I am not susceptible to such enthusiasm, especially since I resigned as a poet and stooped to prose. But this is what happened to me the other day. I had been busy reading my Bentham, because he is, when all is said and done, a great man, that Quaker, and he has written great books. My head was tired, I picked up my Camoens and went over to the window. My windows are now the foremost in Lisbon, they overlook the whole expanse of the Tagus. It was one of those brilliant winter mornings such as you find only in Lisbon. I opened *The Lusiads* at random, chanced upon canto IV and began to read those lovely stanzas that begin: 'At last, in Lisbon's noble harbour. . . .'9 Gradually my blood stirred inside me, I felt the arteries throb in my temples. . . . The letters flew from the page, I raised my eyes and found myself looking at the pitiful galley, the *Vasco da Gama*, which sits there as a monumental caricature of our naval glory. . . . Yet I saw none of that: I saw the Tagus, I saw the Portuguese flag fluttering in the morning breeze, the Tower of Belém in the distance . . . and I dreamed, I dreamed that I was Portuguese, that Portugal was Portugal again.

Such was the power that the prestige of the scene gave to the images evoked by those lines of poetry.

At that moment, the galley salutes some approaching gigs. . . . It was the navy minister who was going aboard.

I shut my book, lit a cigar and went to attend to my camellias. I couldn't bear the sight of the printed word for three days.

But what is to be had from all this, what has it all to do with my travels, or for the Vale de Santarém episode over which we have dawdled for so many chapters?

It has a lot to do with it: it goes to show that when history is read or narrated in the actual places where it took place, it has a different charm, a different strength; and it helps me to give you the reason, kind reader, why I, in these travels of mine, stayed in that valley hearing from my travelling companion and writing down for your benefit the fascinating story of the maiden of the nightingales, the green-eyed maid, our good Joaninha.

Yes, here I have been, lying on the ground, with the mules grazing the grass, the drovers sitting around smoking peacefully and the last hours of a long, hot July afternoon coming to a close and being cooled by the breeze that precedes evening.

But enough of the valley, it is late. Hey there! Bring the mules and let us get up. Spur on to Santarém, where a fine, congenial dinner awaits us in the illustrious palace of Dom Afonso Henriques[10] – and not just the 'beef and laughter' of Friar Bartolomeu dos Mártires,[11] but a real, hospitable dinner, much less austere and much more cheerful.

'Why? Is the story of Carlos and Joaninha finished?' my gracious lady reader might ask.

'No, madam,' replies the author, highly flattered with the query. 'No, madam. The story has not finished, one could almost say it is just beginning, but there has been a change of scene. Let us go to Santarém, since the second act takes place there.'

XXVII

———— ·:· ————

Arrival at Santarém. – The olive groves of Santarém. – Fora de Vila. – A symmetry that is not for the eyes. – The way of measuring the verses of the Bible. – The pedantic architecture of the seventeenth century. – We enter the Alcáçova.

THE day was in its last hours when we reached the foot of the steep slope that leads to the height of Santarém. The small number of people, the poorly cultivated gardens and orchards, the ruined houses, all pointed to our being in the outskirts of a great population centre that was neglected and in decline. However, the noble town still possesses the most beautiful of its adornments and suburban glories, they have not completely destroyed that: its olive groves. The olive groves of Santarém – whose proverbial abundance and beauty is one of our most widely held and cherished popular beliefs! – the olive groves of Santarém are still there! My heart recognized them and rejoiced to see them. I greeted in them the patriarchal symbol of our ancient existence. In those aged trunks crowned with verdure I seemed to see, as in Tasso's enchanted forests, the time-honoured images of our forbears; and in the rustle of the leaves, stirred at intervals by the wind, I seemed to hear the mournful sigh of their laments for the shameful degeneration of their descendants. . . .

Disfigured like the others, profaned like all of them, the olive groves of Santarém are still a monument.

The Mediterranean peoples unfortunately do not profess with the same respect and austerity that veneration of woodland which is so sacred for the nations of the North. The olive groves of Santarém are an exception: the cult of trees is rare among us.

We ascended the steep slope at a steady trot – I excited and impatient at finding myself face to face with that profusion of monuments and ruins which I had pictured in my imagination

149

and which I was by turns afraid and eager to compare with the reality.

We finally reached the summit. The majestic entrance to the great town is before me. My imagination did not deceive me. . . . What a grand, magnificent sight!

Fora de Vila is a public square, vast, irregular and rambling like a romantic poem. At first sight, at that late hour and in poor light, the effect is wonderful and sublime. Palaces, convents and churches solemnly and gloomily occupy their old places, ranged erratically all around that enormous square, where the eyes cannot see the symmetry we can feel inside us. It is like the rhythm and metre of the Bible's long verses, which are not measured in feet or syllables, yet their accent falls unerringly in the spirit and in the *inner ear* with a remarkable regularity.

And all deserted, all silent, mute, dead! One thinks one is entering the great metropolis of an extinct people, of a nation that was powerful and famous but disappeared off the face of the earth and left only the monument of its gigantic constructions.

On the left, the huge convent of Sítio, or of Jesus, then the convent das Donas, followed by that of St Dominic, famous for the tomb of our Portuguese Faust – with no disrespect to the memory of the Blessed Friar Gil,[1] who became a great saint, it is true, but was first a great sorcerer. Opposite, the ancient nunnery of Santa Clara and next to it the low Gothic arches of St Francis, about whose last superior, the austere Friar Dinis, I have told you so much, dear reader, and have as much again to tell you! On the right, the great Philippine[2] construction, a perfect example of the massive, pedantic, reactionary architecture of the seventeenth century, the college, a generous, fine type of its kind and, as far as its kind can be, of Jesuit buildings. . . .

There is no soul, no genius, no spirit in those ponderous masses, which have neither elegance nor simplicity; but there is a certain imposing grandeur, a bonded solidity, a calculated symmetry, proportions that are cold but well based and methodically blocked out, revealing the thought of the century and of the institution that was so characteristic of it.

It is not the sturdy beliefs of the Middle Ages that rise in the pointed ogival arch; nor is it the flowery laxness of the fifteenth and sixteenth centuries, already wavering between the

Byzantine and the classical, between the mystical ideals of Christianity on the wane and the material symbols of a reviving paganism. No: here the *Renaissance* triumphed, only to degenerate. There is the Inquisition, the Jesuits, the Philips, the Catholic reaction, building temples *so that* people shall believe and pray, not *because* people believe and pray.

Before that, monastery and cathedral, hermitage and convent were the expression of a popular belief; thereafter they became the formula of government ideology.

There they are – behold them – facing one another, the monuments of the two religions, expressive and eloquent every one, translating more straightforwardly than books, manuscripts or traditions the beliefs of the ages that erected them and left them engraved there, not realizing what they were doing.

Lower down, at the foot of that slope, that black pile, is the still superb remains of the once enormous palace of the counts of Unhão.

We skirted the square and made our way into Marvila on the north side. We are inside the walls of old Santarém. The entrance is so magnificent, but everything inside is now so wretched, most of the houses old without being ancient, the streets Moorish without being Arabic, lacking the slightest vestige of their origin except for their narrowness and want of cleanliness.

The churches, however, almost all of them, the walls and the ramparts, some of the doors and a few private houses retain sufficient of the old appearance and make one forget the vulgarity of the rest.

We walked along the gloomy, seedy Rua Direita, which is the centre of such meagre trade as there still is here, a few poorly stocked shops with scarcely any customers. Here is the curious Torre das Cabaças[3] and the old church of São João do Alporão. Tomorrow we shall see all this at our leisure. Now to the Alcáçova.

We have entered the gate of the ancient citadel. What an astonishing, misshapen confusion of rubble, of stones, of mounds of each and debris! There are no streets, no paths: it is just a labyrinth of dirty, ugly ruins. Our destination, our friend's house, is right next to the famous, historical church of Santa Maria da Alcáçova. It will not be easy to find in such a jumble.

XXVIII

———— ∵ ————

After much searching the author eventually discovers the church of Santa Maria de Alcáçova. – Disappearance of the national style of architecture. – The earthquake of 1755, the Marquis of Pombal and the fountain of the Passeio Público in Lisbon. – The leader of the Portuguese Progressive Party in Dom Afonso Henriques's fortress. – A delightful view of the environs of Santarém observed from a window of the Alcáçova early in the morning. – The author is overwhelmed by vague, poetic, fantastical ideas, like a dream. – The introduction to *Faust*. – Difficulty of translating German poetry into our romance dialects.

AFTER much searching among dilapidated old houses and heaps of rubble, we eventually found the church of Santa Maria de Alcáçova. *We* found it is not accurate: I at least, for my part, would never have found it, nor would I believe that was it when they pointed it out to me. The royal collegiate church of Afonso Henriques, the virtual cathedral of the first town of the realm, one of the foremost, most ancient and most historic temples in Portugal, this?... This insignificant, nondescript Capuchin church? This miserable, ridiculous pile of bricks, with no architecture, no taste, designed, erected and built by the village bricklayer and his apprentice?! Impossible.

Yet it was, that was it. The old chapel royal, the venerable church of Alcáçova, went through successive repairs and transformations until it came to this wretched condition.

Taste has been so perverted here in Portugal, especially since the middle of the last century: the damage caused by the great earthquake interrupted the thread of all our national architectural traditions to such an extent that in Europe, perhaps in the whole world, you will probably not find another country where, alongside such fine old monuments as we have, there are such mean, ridiculous, absurd public and private buildings as almost all those which have been put up in Portugal in the last century.

It is in the repairs to and rebuilding of the ancient churches that this dreadful style, this absence of any sort of style, of any art, is most offensive and most scandalous.

Take the classical gable placed atop the Renaissance façade of the Conceição Velha in Lisbon. Or the plaster repair-work that obscures the elegant flutes of the Gothic columns of our cathedral.

It is not possible to go lower in architectural terms than we have done, when, after the Marquis of Pombal *translated* for us, in low, vulgar prose, the rococo of Louis XV, which at least in the original was showy, scalloped, fanciful and gallant like a madrigal, this bastard, hybrid style progressively degenerated and gave itself classical airs, until in our own time it has gone as far as the fountain of Passeio Público.[1]

But let us leave all this and the church of the Alcáçova too. Let us go into the palace of Dom Afonso Henriques.

It must be here right next to this plasterwork ruin of a chapel. How does one get in?

Through this low, narrow opening, cut, obviously a few years ago, into what looks like a garden or courtyard wall.

Yes, this is it. Let us dismount.

We were received with open arms by our good, trusty friend, the present owner and inhabitant of the royal fortress, Senhor M.P.[2]

What a remarkable coincidence! That the illustrious, respected leader of the Progressive Party in Portugal, the man with the most sincere democratic convictions and who allies them most sincerely to his respect for and attachment to the trappings of monarchy, this man from the Minho, from the cradle of the dynasty and of the nation, should have taken up residence in the fortress of our first king, conquered by his sword in one of the most famous deeds of that age of prodigious feats!

We went into the small cloister-shaped garden that links the old royal dwelling to its chapel. So it was, no doubt, in earlier times: the east wall of the church forms the wall of one side of the courtyard, but contact was stopped probably when the Crown transferred the palace and separated it for ever from the church.

Planted with old orange trees, its walls lined with lemon trees and vines, that small enclosure, despite the quantity of flower-beds and brick flowerpots with which it is Moorishly crowded, is pleasant and charming to look at.

Our friend introduced us to his wife, a lady of kind, sober demeanour; we kissed his charming children and went to attend to our ablutions, which, after such a day's travel, were indispensable before we could sit down to table.

The palace of Afonso Henriques is like his chapel: not the slightest, faintest trace of its former origin. One knows that this is it from the properly verified, unquestionable topography of the palaces, and from that alone. . . .

But what do I care, at this moment, for the antiquities, the ruins and the demolitions, when I feel myself being demolished inside by an exasperating, destructive hunger, a vandalous, insatiable hunger?!

Let us dine.

We ate, we talked, we drank tea, we talked more and ate more. Visitors came, we talked politics, we talked literature, we talked above all about Santarém, about its ruins, about its former grandeur, about its present misfortune. Finally we went to bed.

I have never slept so marvellously well in my life. I awoke next morning to the unrelenting, insistent clanging of the bells of the Alcáçova. I leaped out of bed, went to the window and looked out upon the loveliest, most majestic and, at the same time, most delightful picture I have ever set eyes on.

At the end of a broad, pleasant, tranquil valley lies the placid bed of the Tagus, whose gleaming, russet sand is covered with water only near its banks, over which lean, fresh and green still, the willows that adorn and protect them. Beyond the river, standing in the fertile river mud of those alluvial lands, the lush olive groves of Alpiarça and Almeirim. Farther away, the town of Dom Manuel with its heath and its vineyards. On this side of the river, the vast plain known as the Rossio,[3] sprinkled with houses, villages, gardens, clumps of wild trees, orchards. Closer to the foot of the hill on whose peak I am standing is the picturesque part of the town called the Ribeira, its houses and churches looking so charming from here, its cross to the memory of St Iria and the romantic memories of its armourer.

While my eyes wandered over this vast, lovely sight, my

imagination grew wings and flew away to the infinite space of the ideal regions. Recollections of all times and all manner of thoughts flocked into my mind and seemed to hold me in a dream in which the most contradictory and incongruous images follow one another.

But they were all melancholy, all sad memories, none of them offering hope!...

They bring to mind those lines of Goethe, those sublime, inimitable lines from the introduction to *Faust*:

> Once more you hover near me, forms and faces
> Seen long ago with troubled youthful gaze.
> And shall I this time hold you, limn the traces
> Fugitive still, of those enchanted days?
> You closer press: then take your powers and places,
> Command me, rising from the murk and haze;
> Deep stirs my heart, awakened, touched to song,
> As from a spell that flashes from your throng.
>
> You bear the glass of days that were glad-hearted;
> Dear memories, beloved shades arise;
> Like an old legendary echo started,
> Come friendship and first love before my eyes.
> Old sorrow stirs, the wounds again have started,
> Life's labyrinth before my vision lies,
> Disclosing dear ones who, by fortune cheated,
> Passed on their way, of love and light defeated.[4]

I do not have the courage to set down here the rest of my inept translation: it is faithful, but has no other merit. Who can translate such lines as these, who shall transfer them from so boundless and free a language into our narrow, severe romance dialects?

XXIX

---- ·:· ----

Life's pleasures. – Imagination and feeling. – Poets who
died young and poets who died old. – How these travels are
written. – A book of stone. – A child playing with it. –
Ruins and repairs. – The author's hobby-horse in matters
artistic and literary. – St Iria, or Irene, and Santarém. – The
Ballad of Santa Iria. – How many saints of that name are
there in Portugal?

THIS day-dreaming, this poetic musing in the presence of the
sublime spectacles of nature, is one of the greatest pleasures God
has granted to certain kinds of temperament. It is delightful to
experience such pleasure ... but which of life's pleasures does
not depend principally on a powerful stimulating acid? Take it
away, what you are left with is prosaic and dull; leave it and it
eventually ulcerates the organism. The pleasure is more intense
because the action of the stimulus is felt more, but the ulceration
increases, the heart becomes raw flesh ... pleasure becomes
torment.

Unhapppy the man who has reached this state!

Happy the man who, like Goethe, can regulate the dose of
opium he wishes to take, who is sparing with his senses and his
life and economizes the faculties of his soul! In such men,
however, it is the imagination that prevails, not feeling. Byron,
Schiller, Camoens, Tasso, all died young: the heart killed them.
Homer and Goethe, Sophocles and Voltaire died of old age: they
were sustained by the imagination which does not consume life,
because it does not expend sensibility.

To imagine is to dream: life sleeps and rests the while. To feel
is to live actively: it tires and consumes life.

This is what I was thinking – for I was not thinking about
anything, just musing, while those lines from *Faust* were in my
memory and that moving view of the Tagus and its banks before
my eyes.

This is what I was thinking, this is what I write down: this is what I had in my mind and this is what goes down on paper, because I cannot write otherwise.

I am very sorry, dear reader, if you expected something else of my *Travels*, if I unintentionally fail to keep promises you thought to see in the title, but which I certainly did not make. Perhaps you wished me to count the leagues of the highway milestone by milestone? The height and breadth of the buildings palm by palm? Their foundation dates number by number? To summarize the history of every stone, of every ruin?

Go to Father Vasconcelos:[1] there you shall find everything about Santarém, truth and fabrication, in massive folio and large print. I cannot write books of that sort, and even if I could, I have other things to do.

I am sorry about only one thing: of being so clumsy with a pencil, otherwise, with a couple of strokes, I could tell you much more, and better, than I can with all these words, which, after all, say so little and depict so badly.

Santarém is a book of stone in which is inscribed the most interesting and poetic part of our chronicles. Rich in illuminations, in cut-outs, in floral pieces, in illustrations, in superb arabesques and tracery, it was the most beautiful, most precious book in Portugal. Bound in green and silver enamel by the Tagus and its banks, fastened with bronze clasps by its strong Gothic walls, this magnificent book should have lasted for ever, until the hand of the Creator stretched forth to erase the memory of His creature.

But this Nineveh was not destroyed; this Pompeii was not submerged by any gigantic catastrophe. The people whose history is in the book still exists. But this people fell into childish ways: they were given the book to play with and they tore it, mutilated it, pulled out its pages one by one and made kites and dolls and paper hats with them.

One cannot describe otherwise what this so-called government, or administration, has been doing and allowing to be done in Santarém for more than a century.

Time's ruins are sad but beautiful; those brought about by revolutions bear the solemn stamp of history. But the mindless depredations and the even more mindless reparations inflicted by ignorance, the mean repairs made by a parasitic art, desecrate, they take away any prestige.

This is the general impression made on me by this place. Let us have lunch, for I hear we are being called to eat, and we shall see afterwards if I am wrong.

At lunch the conversation naturally turned upon the most obvious subject: Santarém. Dom Afonso Henriques and his warriors; the Blessed Friar Gil and the Holy Miracle; the Armourer and the Constable; King Fernando and Queen Leonor; Camoens banished here; Friar Luís de Sousa born here; Pedro Álvares Cabral; the D'Ocem brothers – nearly all the major figures of our history paraded before us.[2] St Iria too, the godmother and patron saint of this place, whose name eclipsed Roman and Celtic names here.

Anyone who has a hobby-horse slips it in everywhere. My hobby-horse in matters of art and literature connected to our peninsula is popular ballads and romances. There is one about St Iria.

Why is it that the St Iria of popular poetry is so different from the St Iria of monastic legends?

Here is the ballad, in the revised version I have made by collating many versions from different provinces with the Bordas-d'Água, or Ribatejo, version, which is, for the most part, the one that should be followed:

I sat at my window embroid'ring my cushion,
of gold was my needle, my thimble of silver,

a horseman rode by and asked us for shelter,
my father refused him: how sad it made me!

'Night is upon us, the road is deserted!
Father mine, of our house let it never be said

that a traveller on horseback asking for shelter
at nightfall should find our door to him closed.'

I begged and I pleaded; he scarcely could bear it!
But so did I plead that at last he gave in.

I opened the door and he entered with pleasure;
I showed him the hearth and he sat him straight down.

I put water before him, his hands he did wash,
I gave him a towel to dry himself on.

Few were his words, for he scarcely addressed me,
but always I felt that his eyes were upon me.

When I lifted my eyes, as soon as I raised them,
his own beauteous eyes he kept fixed on the floor.

I set food before him, he ate it and well,
I prepared him a bed, he lay down to sleep.

I gave him good-night, not a word he did answer:
such an ill-mannered guest I never did know!

Near midnight it was and I hardly breathing,
I felt myself lifted, my mouth being covered . . .

I was borne off on horseback in somebody's arms,
galloping, galloping, onwards and madly.

Even with eyes closed I knew who 'twas bore me,
I kept silent and wept, but he uttered no word.

Farther on, far away, only then he did ask me
by what name I was known in the home we had left.

'They called me Iria, the Lady Iria,
but now I'm Iria the sick at heart.'

On and on, through the night, ever onward we travelled;
when dawn came he tried to force me to love him . . .

Hour followed hour as with me he struggled;
neither pleading nor force could persuade me!

He drew out his sword . . . and there he did kill me;
he opened a grave and he buried me there.

––––––––

Seven years have have gone by, when a horseman comes riding;
on a hillside a beautiful shrine he did see.

'What shrine is that yonder, with so many pilgrims?'
'It is Santa Iria's who a martyr did die.'

'Oh, Santa Iria, my first ever loved one,

forgive me I beg and your pilgrim I'll be.'

'I shall never forgive you, you murderous robber,
who cut off my head as if I were a lamb.'[3]

Either there were two saints with the same name, who both
had adventurous lives and left a long, deep-rooted memory of
their beauty and martyrdom – which I can hardly imagine – or
the monks' account has a good deal of fable of their sole
invention, which the people refused to believe; otherwise the
simplicity of this oral tradition is hard to explain.

The poetic narrative of the popular ballad is as simple and
natural as the version authorized by ecclesiastical records is
complicated and full of wondrous occurrences.

It is a serious matter. It shall wait for a new chapter.

XXX

———— ∵ ————

The story of St Iria, according to the chroniclers and
according to the popular ballad.

THE miraculous St Iria – St Irene, who gave her name to
Santarém – who was a maiden of noble rank, born in what was
formerly Nabantia[1] and a nun in the mixed Benedictine convent
administered by the saintly Abbot Celio, flourished about the
middle of the seventh century. The young Britaldo, son of the
the Count or Consul Castinaldo, who governed those lands, fell
passionately in love with her and, failing to break down her
virtue, fell ill with a disease which no physician was able to
identify, let alone cure.

It is a known fact that even the saintliest woman is not
distressed by having men die for love of her, and always has
some feeling for those who become her victims.

St Iria decided to comfort poor Britaldo and, since her great
virtue allowed her to go no further, determined to try to cure
him of his mad passion and convert him. One fine morning she
left the convent – nuns did not yet observe such strict and
absolute confinement – and went to the lovesick Britaldo's
house.

She comforted him as a woman and scolded him as a saint.
Finally, placing her lovely, blessed hands on his head, she cured
him in an instant of his physical ailment and, if she did not cure
his spiritual suffering as well, at least she stilled it, for it seemed
to have ceased.

But, as the Devil, having once got into a man's body, seems
not to leave it except to install himself in another, no sooner did
the enemy abandon poor Britaldo than he straight away went
and ensconced himself in no less a personage than the monk
Remigio, who was the fair Iria's superior and spiritual director.

The friar is consumed with lust and, gaining nothing with
pleas and lamentations, swore revenge. However, he

161

dissimulated: he pretended to have mended his ways and, when she least expected it, gave her a beverage of his own diabolical concoction which, as soon as the saint had drunk it, immediately produced in her the most obvious signs of maternity, which went on increasing.

The report of the damsel's presumed condition spreads; she is showered with insults and slander by those who, before, had most respected her. And Britaldo, deeming himself put to scorn by the hypocrisy of that scheming woman, instead of dismissing her from his memory, feels all his old passion revive, pure no longer and much more fervent.

Such are the mysteries of the heart of man! So base! say the ascetic. So enigmatic! say I along with the more tolerant.

Fresh approaches, promises and threats by the furious lover. . . . The saint resists them all, strong in her virtue.

The pious damsel was in the habit of going, every night, to a secret cave situated near the boundary wall, by the River Nabão, so as to be more alone with God and pour out her soul to Him at will. Britaldo found out, watched for an opportunity and had her stabbed to death there by one of his servants, whose name has been preserved by the legend to bear witness to its truth: he was called Banam.

Banam! It is a good melodrama name.

When the innocent creature was dead, Banam removed her habit and threw her body into the river, which quickly carried it to the the swirling waters of the Zêzere, into which it flows; from there to the Tagus, which, in front of the ancient Scalabicastrum,[2] laid her to rest in its golden sands, to the greater glory of the saint and to the everlasting honour of this most noble town which now bears her name.

But, while the saint's body was drifting down-river, Celio, the abbot of the convent, had a revelation which uncovered the truth and miracles of the event; and, communicating it forthwith to the monks and to the people of Nabantia, he set out with them, bearing a cross, and walked the length of the fields of Golegã until they reached the Ribeira of Santarém. There, he blessed the waters of the river and they obligingly flowed back, revealing the sepulchre, which was of rare alabaster, wondrously carved by the hands of angels.

They came close to the tomb, opened it, saw and touched the

saint's body, but could not remove it, for all their efforts. They realized that it was a miracle and, contenting themselves with taking relics of the hair and tunic, they all returned to their own place.

The waters came together again and flowed as before, and never once opened up until six and a half centuries later, when the good queen St Isabel, wife of King Dinis, offered such fervent prayers at the riverside, begging the saint to appear to her, that the river opened again, like the Red Sea obeying the voice of Moses, or so say the pious chroniclers, and disclosed the blessed sepulchre.

The Queen walked into the river without wetting her feet, followed by her royal spouse and all his court, but for all her prayers and all the human strength expended by the others, they were unable to open the tomb: they broke all their tools, it was impossible. Realizing that a superhuman power was preventing it being opened, the King immediately ordered a lofty column to be erected over the tomb, so high that the river could not cover it even when its floodwaters were at their highest.

The river waited, with the utmost patience, for the stonemasons to finish and, when it saw that it could carry on flowing, gave a warning, they all retired, the waters flowed together once more and the column stood out over and above them.

Three and a half centuries went by and, in the year 1644, the Santarém town council had the said column or pedestal, which was only of brick, rebuilt of carved ashlar and the saint's image placed on top.

It is still there, though rather badly treated. I saw it there with these sinner's eyes this very month of July 1843. But, with neither miracle nor prayers, the river had long before retreated to a small part of its bed and the column was altogether on dry land, as it is all the year round until the floodwaters rise.

Such is, very faithfully summarized, the story of St Iria as told in the books.

The tale told in the ballads is, as we saw, very different and much simpler: it is told in a few words. The saint is at her parents' home; an unknown knight, whom they shelter one night, gets up at the dead of night, carries off the innocent, unsuspecting maiden, makes off at full speed on his horse and, arriving at a heath a goodly distance away, attempts to ravish her. The saint resists, he kills her. Years afterwards, the wicked knight is passing the place, sees a beautiful shrine erected on the very spot where he committed his crime, asks to which saint it is consecrated and is told it is St Iria's. He falls on his knees and begs the saint's forgiveness, but she throws his sin in his face and curses him.

And there the story ends.

Could it be the people who forgot part of their traditions or was it the monks who added things in their records? Because the monastic legend is really beautiful and full of poetry and romance, things which the people do not ordinarily despise.

The phenomenon is difficult to explain and extremely interesting to the less run-of-the-mill observer who wishes to study men, nations and eras where they reveal themselves and allow themselves to be known most openly, in common beliefs such as these, these old curiosities ignored by the lofty philosophy of the ignorant.

The extreme simplicity of the romance, or ballad, of St Iria and the fact that, of all those that are preserved in the memory of our people, it is the most widely known and most uniformly repeated in all parts of the kingdom, with few variations in the words and none in the context, lead me to believe that it must be one of the oldest compositions, not only in our language, but in the whole peninsula. The words do not have a very old flavour: it is one of those almost primordial poems that tradition has kept on handing down and simultaneously translating, imperceptibly, from parents to children. Nor, to be sure, is it one of those that descended from the palace to the cottage and escaped from town to country, as is the case with many others: this one evidently came from popular gatherings, from rustic religious festivities, and has existed there until the present.

The poem's metric form is what the scholarly expression used in the Iberian peninsula has called 'ballad in *endechas*'.[3] For this, though not for the more common octosyllabic form, I follow the theory of the clever German philologist, Depping,[4] to whom our peninsular literature is so indebted, and I believe that they are really twelve-syllable lines, the couplets thus consisting of just two lines each, as the word obviously means. When they sing it, the people do not divide the lines into hemistiches, as is done by those who write them down, whereas in ballads in the more usual metre the popular sung form distinctly divides each eight-syllable member in two.

I could be wrong, but I suspect that the four final couplets, in which the rhyme changes completely, must be a later addition to the original. However, these eight lines, with slight variations, appear everywhere.

XXXI

––––––– .∴. –––––––

Quomodo sedet sola civitas. – Santarém. – Portugal in verse
and prose. – Exquisite workmanship of some doors and
windows in the Mozarabic style. – A bust of Dom Afonso
Henriques. – The African sage-brush. – The 'Porta do Sol'.
– The walls of Santarém. – Back to the story of Friar Dinis
and the green-eyed maid.

IT was past ten o'clock in the morning when we set out to begin
the lengthy stations-of-the-cross visit to the relics, temples and
monuments that are what is now left of Santarém.

There is no throb of present-day life here at all: today it is only
a book that registers what went before. Between the marvellous
history of the past that all these stones commemorate and the
horrendous prophecies for the future that seem to be engraved
upon them in mysterious characters, there is nothing else: the
present does not exist, or it is as if it did not, so small, so petty,
so insignificant, so out of proportion it seems in relation to all
this.

It makes you feel like chanting along with the inspired poet of
Jerusalem: *Quomodo sedet sola civitas!*[1] Portugal is, always was, a
nation of miracles, of poetry. Her prestige has been destroyed; we
shall see how she lives in *prose*. Lands do not die, nor families or
races, but nations cease to exist. On with it, then, if that is what
you want. I have no more scruples.

We passed by the church of the Alcáçova, which we found to
be already closed, and keeping to our left we walked through
what now looks like a path between two farms, but which was
evidently, in other eras, the most fashionable[2] street of this
courtly town. Here, almost side by side with the church, are
some doors and windows exhibiting the most delicate
Mozarabic workmanship and artistry that I can recall having
seen.

And by the way: why should we not adopt, in this peninsula

of ours, the term *Mozarabic* to describe and classify this architectural genre which is peculiar to us, a style in which one can feel a relaxation of the severe Christian concepts of medieval architecture in contact with the example of the sensual customs of the Moors and their luxurious, redundant elegance?

To which enchanted palace did these superbly wrought doors belong? Which beauties leaned over these tracery windows to watch the chosen one of their hearts ride past? So beautiful they are, so elegant still, these crumbling stones, barely propped up by the rough, dry wall beneath them, that they naturally awaken in the dullest imagination all the dreams of fairies and troubadours that poetry has created from the mysteries of the Middle Ages.

A little farther on, in a poor, ugly, broken niche, there is what is supposed to be a bust of Dom Afonso Henriques, which the local ciceroni claim is very ancient. It did not have that effect on me.

We came to the Porta do Sol[3] and sat down to enjoy the majestic view. It is majestic but sad. The bluff that plunges down to the river is barren and almost bare: it is covered, like the sparsely populated nape of an old man, with just a few tufts of ash-grey growth of a low-growing bush, half frutex, half grass, which people here call *salgadeira* [sage-brush] and which, according to tradition, came from Africa to bind the soil on these slopes and precipices. The plant's appearance and habits are really African and oriental, there is nothing European about it. But this last, most westerly part of our peninsula is, geologically speaking, so African already, so little like Europe, that the transplantation may not have been necessary and perhaps the popular memory retained the notion that the Moors used the plant for this purpose.

They say this Porta do Sol is where the executions were carried out in former times. The site was well chosen, there is nothing sadder and more melancholy. Nearby there is a square turret belonging to the city walls, which at that point form an angle where they follow a north–south direction. On this side the fortifications and sections of wall are very little damaged, and from the belvedere which we climbed up to one can form a perfect idea of what an old walled city was like.

Could it have been here, said I to myself, that our Friar Dinis,

167

whom I have been missing, the old superior of the convent of St Francis, came to weep his last dirge over the ruins of the old monarchy? Was it here, in this melancholy, desolate place that his last tears flowed? Could he, who no longer wept, have found someone here to give his eyes the founts of water that his heart pleaded for, so as to unburden itself of the sorrows that tormented him in the barren wilderness of his desolate old age?

These ideas were passing through my mind when the historian who detained us in the valley for so many chapters, recounting the events of Joaninha and her family, said to us: 'Let us sit down here in the shade made by this wall and finish the story of the maiden of the nightingales. In the afternoon, we shall go to the Ribeira to honour the memory of the Armourer. Tomorrow morning the plan is for us to go and visit the Graça Church, the Santo Milagre and the convents of St Dominic and St Francis. Let us conclude our story today.'

'Agreed!' we replied.

We shall start on a new chapter, then, dear reader, and now you need not fear my dread digressions, nor the interruptions to which I am given. Will the story of our Joaninha continue straight and fluent until we finish it, for good or bad? Previously, a novel or a drama in which no one dies was considered unexciting; nowadays, there is a certain aversion for the tragic and funereal, which is perfectly suited to the century of material comfort we live in.

Well, dear, benevolent reader, I am subject to no school for beginnings or ends, and I shall relate the story as it happened.

Listen.

XXXII

--- ·:· ---

We return to the story of Joaninha. – Preparations for war.
– Death – Carlos wounded and taken prisoner. – The
hospital. – The nurse. – Georgina.

'LISTEN!' said I to my benevolent reader at the end of the last
chapter. But it is not enough just to listen: you must be so kind as
to recall what you heard in chapter XXV and the situation in
which we left the two cousins, Carlos and Joaninha.

In this preposterous, unclassifiable book of my *Travels*, the
thread of the stories and observations does not so much break as
become intertwined, and in such a manner that, I am fully
aware, much patience is needed to unravel and trace it in such an
entangled skein.

Let us proceed with patience, then, dear reader; I shall do my
best to be brief and as direct as possible.

Remember how, on a clear, serene, starry night, those two
took leave of one another in the middle of the valley: how sad,
uncertain and unhappy was their farewell and how very different
they were from before.

That same night, the ordered confusion of an important troop
movement reigned in the constitutionalists' quarters. The long
apathy of many months was followed by an unexpected flurry of
activity. Preparations were being made for the bloody battles of
Pernes and Almoster which, though not immediately decisive,
did so much to hasten the end of the struggle.[1]

Carlos found orders to present himself at headquarters; he left
immediately. His brain, occupied with quite different thoughts,
so bewildered and foreign to himself, followed his body
automatically. He went, arrived, received the instructions he
was given and returned more satisfied, more tranquil.

It was a matter of death. True agony of mind is unknown to
the man who has yet to bless the death he saw before him, who
has yet to summon death as the sole remedy for his misfortune,

or, more desperate still, as the only way out of his tragic circumstances.

Such moments are rare in life, it is true; but when they occur, it is no exaggeration to say 'rather death, much rather death than this'.

Ah, and if the death one visualizes is one of honour and glory! If enthusiasm, pulling vigorously on the nerve-strings, makes them vibrate with those secret, mysterious notes that grip a man's heart and raise it to the heights of sublime renunciation of self and of everything that is petty, base and mean in his nature – oh, then death surely appears as a triumph, a blessing!

Carlos was oblivious of everything except his sword, which he sharpened with scrupulous care, and his good, trusty English pistols, which he cleaned with minute precision, loading and priming them with all the fondness of an artist savouring the pleasure of putting the final touches to a favourite piece of work.

What little of the night remained was taken up in this; the march began before daybreak. And the first rays of the sun were greeted by rifle-volleys and the thunder of cannons.

The fighting was prolonged and bloody, as with brothers who hate each other with all the hatred that was once love, the cruellest hatred that exists in nature!

Daylight was falling, when, among the many stretchers with wounded that were brought into a hospital in Santarém, there was one, riddled with bullets and covered in blood who, both from the remains of his uniform and from a well-known, by now characteristic look about him, could be clearly seen to belong to the constitutional army.

Many and dangerous were this man's wounds. They laid him on a sort of bunk with some straw on it and, when his turn came, he was examined and bandaged like the rest. He gave no sign of suffering; he kept his eyes closed, his pulse was strong, but not irregular with fever; he uttered not a word, let out not a groan and complied with everything that was said and done to him, except for releasing from his left hand, which he pressed against his chest, whatever it was he held in it and that hung from his neck on a thin black ribbon.

They left him like that for a long time; he fell asleep. His sleep was short, but he slept deeply. When he woke up, he found himself no longer in the vast caravanserai of that chaotic hospital, but in a small airy room, clean and almost comfortable, for all the world like a convent cell except for the good bed in which the sick man lay and the remarkable elegance of the nurse who cared for him.

The room was, indeed, a cell in the convent of St Francis in Santarém; the patient our friend Carlos; and the nurse who was caring for him, a beautiful woman, not above normal height, though not a fraction less, wrapped in the abundant folds of a long silk robe, of exactly the colour which, in the language of the Rue Vivienne, is called *scabieuse*; her head was adorned with Brussels lace and with black and scarlet ribbons, which heightened the delicacy of the lace, the infinite charm of the long fair coils of her hair, and the symmetrical purity of a perfect, classical, oval face, with little mobility of expression, but extremely beautiful, in a way that a face can be beautiful when it reflects little of the soul and when the serene languor of a pair of blue eyes tempers and moderates a strength of feeling which is perhaps no less profound, but certainly less expansive.

Kneeling by Carlos's bed, with his right hand between her two, her eyes dry, but fixed on the soldier's drooping lids, that woman was like a statue of grief and anguish. By an inner door, which led into a sort of dark alcove, his arms folded and thrust inside his sleeves, a hood over his head, stood an old monk, tall but bent with the burden of years or of sufferings.

The monk was watching the patient and the nurse, but evidently did not wish to be seen in this occupation, because, at the slightest tremor of the patient, he backed hastily, and as if in alarm, into his chamber.

A single wax candle lighted this scene, casting dark shadows over it, and giving it an air of solemnity that was quite magic and sublime.

Carlos continued to grasp in his left hand, with the same determination, the reliquary or talisman, or whatever it was that he would not release from his heart. The beautiful nurse occasionally kissed that tenacious hand, which trembled at each kiss, soft and gentle though the light touch of those delicate lips was.

His other hand was in her hands, but it was totally insensitive.

The silence was sepulchral: all that could be heard was the sick man's faint, irregular breathing.

Suddenly, Carlos opened his eyelids slightly and exclaimed in English: '*Oh Georgina, Georgina, I love you still*'★.

Two tears – two of those pearls which are produced in the heart with such pain and sometimes fall from the eyes with so much pleasure – sprang from the lady's heavenly blue eyes and gently ran down her cheeks, which were white with a mortal pallor.

Carlos awoke completely, opened his eyes and directed them fixedly at the woman's angelic countenance.

He stayed that way for some minutes. She said nothing, either by word of mouth or by gesture: only her tears spoke to him, flowing very, very gently, like a continuous, natural spring that flows without effort or stimulus, down an easy, natural slope.

'Where am I, Georgina?'

'In my arms.'

'What happened to me?'

'That you cannot be happy away from them, you know that.'

'Of course I know ... I should know.'

'You should. Now you shall find out. The past ...'

'The past? Which?'

'The past no longer exists.'

'And the future?'

'I do not believe in the future.'

'Why?'

'Because you told me not to.'

'Me?! ... I'm a ...'

'A man.'

'Oh!'

'That's enough, now rest. We'll talk tomorrow.'

'I am wounded badly, and now it hurts. ... It didn't hurt before.'

'You are wounded, but out of danger, and I am here. Sleep.'

'I cannot. What house is this?'

'The convent of St Francis in Santarém.'

'Heaven forbid!'

'You are a prisoner. Get well and I shall free you.'

'You? And you here, how?'

'I came to fetch you and this was how I found you.'

'Georgina!'

'What are you holding so tightly in your left hand?'

'Look: the locket with your hair.'

'You still love me, then?'

'Of course! Like the first . . .'

'Don't lie Carlos. . . . And go to sleep.'

'Oh, my God, my God! Georgina here, I in this condition and. . . . And my family?'

'Your family is safe.'

'Where?'

'Right here, in Santarém.'

'I want . . . I don't want. . . . Oh, yes, I want to die. God have pity on me!'

'Calm yourself, Carlos.'

But Carlos could not calm himself: he fell silent because the torrent of conflicting thoughts and the unexpected nature of his situation choked his voice, and the exhaustion of his strength paralysed his body movements. But his restless, agitated spirit whirled inside in a mad frenzy. It was incredible what he was going through.

With the aid of tranquillizing draughts the attack diminished, he spent a more peaceful night and by morning the patient did not give cause for concern to the physician who came to visit him.

He was forbidden to speak and Georgina had the courage to resist him, to refuse to answer him every time he attempted to disobey the instructions on which his life depended . . . his and hers, because the unhappy woman loved him . . . oh, she loved him as one loves only once in this life.

Days, weeks went by. Carlos was better, he was safe. Georgina was able to tell him one day: 'Carlos, my dear, you are out of danger. I am going to restore you to your family.'

'My family?!'

'Your family. Your grandmother, your cousin . . .'

'Joaninha! Oh, Joaninha! . . .'

'Your grandmother, who has also been close to death, but is finally safe, does not know you are here. We have kept it from your cousin too.'

'Ah!'

'Yes. We agreed not to tell either of them until we could be sure you would get well. However, today you shall see them. And I . . .'

'You?'

'I have nothing more to do here.'

'Georgina!'

'Carlos!'

'You don't love me any more?'

'No.'

This was followed by a heavy, oppressive silence, like the calm that precedes great storms. Georgina's face was impassive. Carlos laboured under the weight of a horrible, indescribable feeling of oppression.

XXXIII

─────── .∴. ───────

Carlos and Georgina: an exchange of views. – I no longer love you! Dreadful words. – True love is not blind. – Monk in the affair again. *Ecce iterum Crispinus*:[1] Friar Dinis is here with us.

'YOU no longer love me, you, Georgina?!' exclaimed Carlos, after a long difficult struggle with himself. 'You no longer love me, Georgina? Do I no longer mean anything to you in this life? That blind, delirious, infinite love that welled out of your heart and you poured in torrents into my soul, that love which I came to believe was the greatest, the most sincere, perhaps the only true woman's love there yet existed in the world, has that love come to an end, Georgina? Has the celestial fount from which it flowed dried up in your breast? Not even the memories of our past happiness, or the remembrance of the cruel predicaments it cost us, of the tremendous sacrifices you made for me, can nothing awaken in your soul an echo, however faint, of the old harmony of our lives – of our life, Georgina, because the two beings of our existence became fused in one! Oh, why did I live to see this day? And you, what extreme cruelty inspired you to save a life you had condemned, had sacrificed, when you separated it from your own?'

'Carlos,' answered Georgina, with the cool but tender compassion that drove him to despair. 'Carlos, do not overtax your as yet poor state of health. The emotional strain you are inflicting on yourself might be prejudicial. Keep calm. You are deluding yourself and unintentionally trying to delude me too. Control yourself, Carlos, let us take our time and examine our situation, which is undoubtedly not pleasant for either of us, but which is bearable, if we have the sense to face the whole problem without fear and to come to a frank, honest understanding of exactly what is involved. Listen to me, Carlos. You loved me a great deal...'

175

'Oh, so much, so very much! No man...'

'Few men, it is true, have loved as you did.... Who knows, perhaps no man. I do not wish to lose this last illusion.... I have no other.... Perhaps no man loved as you loved me, or ... believed you loved me. I ... oh, I loved you.... Almighty God be my witness! I loved you in the blindness of my soul and the simplicity of my heart, with such total self-abandonment and so complete a renunciation of my own self as I honestly believe are due only to God, a love which a creature may only dedicate legitimately to his Creator. I have been well punished, I deserved it.'

'Georgina, Georgina!'

'Let me go on. I too want to unburden myself now. Listen to me, you are under an obligation to listen to me. If I gave you proof of my love, that you must know. If, from the moment I loved you, one word, one gesture, a single thought, just one, and the faintest spark of imagination gainsaid my absolute, exclusive dedication of my whole self ... tell me.'

'No, my love. No, my life. No, you are an angel, you are...'

'I am a woman who loved you as I do not think people love ordinarily.'

'Surely not.'

'We were happy, it is true, and I believe that few lovers were as happy as we were, for the short time that it lasted. You left for your island. You had to leave, I realized it and resigned myself. Your letters comforted me, those letters burning with passion, written – oh, surely! – written with the purest blood of your heart. I never doubted what they told me. One does not lie like that, you did not lie then. It is not true that love is blind. Ordinary love may be, but love like mine, real love, has the eyes of a lynx. I could see clearly that I was loved. You never wrote swearing your faithfulness, but I knew, I could see that you were faithful to me. Months, years went by like that. On the island and in Oporto you were the same. I suffered a great deal, but I comforted myself, I lived on hope ... a sad way of living, but sweet sorrow! Finally, you came to Lisbon, then here ... and your letters, which were no less tender nor less passionate...'

'Well, I never stopped, for a single moment....'

176

With an emphatic gesture of gentle, but resolute denial, Georgina placed her hand over poor Carlos's mouth, as if to prevent him saying something blasphemous. He seized it with both of his and kissed it over and over again, carried away in a frenzy, in a paroxysm of tears and sobs that would have broken the most indifferent heart. The lady was moved, the unchanging sternness of her lovely face faltered, she lowered her immense eyelids; but if a more rebellious tear came to her eyes, it rapidly flowed back into her heart, because when she raised them again and fixed them calmly on her lover's, those clear eyes, divine and severe as those of an offended angel, were dry.

She went on: 'Your letters, which were no less tender nor less passionate, nevertheless began to be less natural, somewhat exaggerated. . . . They were evidently less genuine. I sensed it, I saw it and I thought I should die. A family of my acquaintance was travelling to Portugal at that time. I came with them. As soon as I arrived, I sought and obtained the means of moving between the two opposing camps safely – my heart warned me that it would be necessary. And so it was. I arrived in the valley on the day you were leaving for that fatal action which nearly cost you your life. I found you a prisoner and nearly dead in the hospital for the wounded. At your side was a monk . . .'

'A monk! My God, could it be him?'

'It was.'

'So you know?'

'Yes. I told him who I was and what you meant to me . . .'

'You told . . . him?'

'I did. I do not know if I did right or wrong. I only know I didn't care what I was doing. I saw afterwards that I had not been mistaken in placing my trust in him. We brought you to this convent, treated you and managed to save your life. . . . And while this concern relieved me of others, I was . . . I was happy. Your people . . . your family from the valley also came to Santarém – your grandmother and your cousin, Carlos . . .'

'Joaninha! Is Joaninha here?'

'Yes, she is. Keep quiet and, as I told you before, you shall see her presently.'

'I? What for? I don't want . . .'

'But I do. You shall see her. Now you know that I know everything.'

177

'Everything what, Georgina?'

'Do you want me to repeat it? I shall. That you love your cousin, and that she adores you. And, believe me, Carlos, I love her already as if we were sisters. Now do you understand why I don't love you? Now do you understand that everything is over between us and I see in you, can only see in you, the betrothed, the husband of the innocent creature I have taken under my protection and to whom I swear you shall belong.'

'You swear falsely.'

'How so? Do you want more victims? Are you not satisfied with destroying me? I, at least, am not of your blood. But that decrepit old woman who is your grandmother and has truly been your mother twice over, because she brought you up – that innocent girl who loves you in the simplicity of her heart . . . and this poor old monk . . .'

'Oh, he has to be here, I can see. The evil genius of my family is involved in this. A curse on you, monk!'

The unhappy Carlos had barely pronounced these words when the door of the inner chamber was opened wide and before him stood the rigid, ascetic figure of Friar Dinis.

XXXIV

—— ·:· ——

Carlos, Georgina and Friar Dinis. – The peripeteia of the drama.

CARLOS was half sitting, half lying on a *chaise-longue*; Georgina standing, with her arms folded, in a calm thoughtful posture. The bright rays of a hot May sun beat against the narrow panes of the small window that was the room's only source of light; it was protected from excessive brightness by a long, full curtain.

Carlos suddenly took hold of the curtain and pulled it back to allow more light into the room. A brilliant shaft of sunlight fell directly on the monk's ravaged face and reflected from his sunken eyes what seemed like a flash of divine wrath, which made the two lovers shiver.

It was, however, no more than a flash: it vanished and faded away immediately. The eyes were left looking deathly, mute, staring, glassy, like those of a man who has just expired and whose lids have not been closed.

Even so, those eyes had the magnetic power to mesmerize others, not allowing them even to blink.

Bent, leaning on a rough staff, his light grey hat under his arm, the monk took a few quavering steps to where they were, painfully dragging his loose sandals, which made a dull, defeated sound and caused – I know not why or how – those who heard them to shudder.

He stopped a short distance from them and, forcing a thin, feeble, yet vibrant, solemn voice from the depths of his bosom, said to Carlos: 'You cursed me, my boy, and I am here to forgive you. No, it is I who beg your forgiveness. Carlos, you detest me with all the violence of your soul, with all the strength of your heart, and I am here to tell you that I love you, that I wish only to give my life for you, that deep down inside me there wells up this infinite love that has no equal, begging your mercy, beseeching you in the name of God and of nature, begging you, for all that is sacred in heaven and worthy of respect on earth, to lift that curse, my son, from the head of a dying man.'

These words were spoken in such a voice, they were pronounced from within the soul so vehemently, that it was not his lips that formed them: they it was that burst through the lips and found their way out.

The soldier appeared to be half conscious, bewildered and uncomprehending of what he heard. Georgina, so far impassive, harsh and unshakeable with her lover, felt moved now by the old man's anguish. Because the suffering that came through those sombre words and exuded from that cadaverous face would have made the stones weep.

At the same time, a dull noise, a vague, muffled tumult of a thousand sounds, which seemed to recede, coming together, returning, approaching and disappearing, then scattering only to come together again, finally dispersing yet again, resounded distantly around the town, swelling in the squares, compressed in the streets and sending muted echoes to that remote and lonely convent cell, like the sea heard in the distance receding from the shore with that melancholy murmur which comes before an equinoctial storm.

'Do you hear that babble of noise, Carlos? It is your cause that has triumphed. It is the cause of these mad fools that has failed, and the cause of God who has let Himself be defeated. The hour has come, the words of Balthazar have been written, confusion and death reign alone, sovereign lords, on the face of the earth. I want to go and die where there is a God – forgive me this blasphemy, Lord! – where His name is not profaned and cursed. In the shelter of a rock, under a tree, it shall be, in some lonely place on these moors, where at least no one will tear my shroud and defile it in my last moments, because I am a monk, a monk, a monk . . . the accursed monk! But I want to die a monk, and a monk I shall die. Ah, if only I had lived as one!'

'But what was it, what happened?'

'The remainder of the royalist army is at this moment evacuating Santarém. They are fleeing to the Alentejo. The constitutionals defeated them at Asseiceira and it is all over for us. For me, Carlos, there is just one word needed. Will you say it?'

'Me?'

'Yes, you Carlos. Take back the dreadful words you uttered, and in God's name, my son, forgive your...'

Carlos's breast was in turmoil, racked by a great struggle. Horror, pity, hatred and affection came and went alternately from his heart to his cheeks and back from his face to his breast. An involuntary cry burst from his lips at the height of this conflict: 'Monk, monk! And who murdered my father, who blinded my grandmother and who covered my ... my whole family with ignominy?'

'You are right, Carlos, it was I. I did all that – kill me. But ah, kill me, kill me with your hands, do not curse me. Kill me, kill me. It is surely divine justice that it should be so. Oh yes, my God ... at his hands, Lord! So be it, Thy will be done....'

The monk fell prone on the ground and with his hands clasped and outstretched to the young man, cried out beseechingly: 'Kill me, kill me! There is little life left here. You need only put your foot on my neck – go on, crush the poisonous reptile which bit your family and caused his own misfortune and the ruin of everyone who loved him. Yes, Carlos, may you be the one to carry out God's wrath. Kill me. All these years of penance and remorse have done nothing. Kill me. Deliver me from myself and from the wrath of God that pursues me.'

XXXV

———— ∴ ————

Family reunion. – The mysteries explained. – The heart of woman. – Parricide. – Carlos finally kisses Friar Dinis's hand and embraces his poor grandmother.

GEORGINA said to Carlos: 'Give this man your hand, help him up and speak the words of forgiveness he is begging of you.'

Carlos made an eloquent gesture of horror and repulsion. Georgina knelt down by the monk, took his hands in hers and stroked them gently; she then lifted his face, leaned it against her and gradually soothed him. The old man looked like a pampered, unhappy child cuddling into the arms of its mother: now he muttered only an occasional sob, and these became less and less frequent.

They were both kneeling, the monk and the lady; the old man could hardly hold up and she supported his listless body in her arms, clasped to her bosom. And Georgina said, with that irresistible tone of voice which the daughters of Eve inherited from their original mother, who had been taught it before by the angels or learned it later from the serpent – a tone of voice that is the final, most decisive of woman's seductive charms – she said: 'This man is going to die, Carlos. And will you let him die like this, *my Carlos?*'

All his hatred, all his insults fell silent and vanished at those words from the suppliant angel. He had not heard her say *my Carlos* like that for a long time; he was unable to resist: he stretched out his arms to the monk, fell on his knees at his side and a single embrace united all three.

As in the eternal group of Laocoön, the old man and the two young people felt themselves crushed by the serpents of the same suffering and sank together under the same anguish.

They stayed like that for a long time, and all that could be heard among them was an occasional sob and that faint sigh of tears which one hears with the heart rather than with the ears.

Eventually the monk said, with a voice so timid and feeble as to be scarcely audible: 'Carlos, my Carlos, forgive too . . . oh, forgive the memory of your unhappy mother!'

The young man started convulsively, like a corpse on a galvanic pile. On his feet, rigid, trembling, he cried out with a thunderous voice: 'Devil! You devil in human shape, what have you made me remember? What you said just now was right, you monster! You should only die at my hands. And you shall!'

He flung himself at an enormous holywood candlestick that lay on the floor near him, a terrible herculean club, enough to cleave heads of iron let alone the monk's shrivelled skull! He heaved it in the air with both hands; the old man stretched out his head towards him as if eager to die . . . Georgina involuntarily closed her eyes, and a great, dreadful crime was about to be committed. . . .

Two piercing cries, two shouts of terror and despair, the sort that come from human mouths only in situations of life and death, suddenly rang out in the chamber: a doddering old woman, more dead than alive, dragged along by a child little more than sixteen years old, was standing in front of Carlos and the two of them were covering the frail, sagging figure of his victim with their fragile bodies.

'My son, my son!' the old woman wrenched from her breast with a hoarse cry. 'He is your father, my boy. This man is your father, Carlos.'

The weighty candlestick fell from the young man's nerveless hands and rolled along the floor with a dull, heavy sound. Carlos crashed senseless to the ground. With one bound, Georgina was at his side and helped him back on to the *chaise-longue*. He was bathed in blood from a wound in his neck which had burst open with the violence of the emotion. The two old people went and knelt by his side. The two young women worked to bring him to his senses and staunch the blood. Their cambric handkerchiefs and the lace from their necks and heads were all made into bandages and compresses. The bleeding eventually stopped.

Wonders of the female heart! Generosity that makes one forgive and forget their innumerable faults! The two women both loved this man. This man was not worthy of such love. No, by heaven! The monster loved them both: and that is the whole story. And they, who knew it, who resented it and who considered him worthy of a thousand deaths, vied with one another in their care and anxiety to save him.

We men are not capable of so much.

And therefore we are so full of admiration.

And are so ready to forgive.

And so happy to forget.

But we are unable to love so much, true's true. . . .

We love *better*, that we do; *so much*, no.

The young man was still in a swoon. Friar Dinis and the old lady were praying. Georgina and Joaninha – you will have realized that it is Joaninha – looked at one another, reddened, but remained motionless. The Englishwoman held out her hand to the sweet child, gave an involuntary shudder, but spoke firmly: 'I have given my word, Joaninha! I no longer love him, I promise.'

'I love him more and more, Georgina. He is so unhappy!'

'Will you swear to me that you will not leave him, that you will always watch over him and save him from himself, his own worst enemy?'

'I swear it!'

'Goodbye, then, Joaninha! I am out of place here. I have already heard things I should not hear. Your family secrets are not my affair. This man's heart is not mine, nor do I want it. It is a big, generous heart, Joaninha, but. . . . Do not let yourself be ruled by it, if you want to keep him. Goodbye! Santarém has been abandoned by the royalists. I am going to Lisbon. Comfort your dear grandmother and this poor old man. He is not so guilty, I am sure. . . '

'Oh no! Carlos believes that he murdered his father and it is not true. My grandmother has told me everything.'

'Not true!' murmured Carlos, without opening his eyes. 'It is not true? Then it wasn't he who killed my father?'

'No, my boy!' the old woman cried out. 'No, my boy, this unhappy man is your father.'

'And my mother?'

'Your mother . . . and I were two unhappy creatures. What more do you want to know? Your mother loved this man . . .'

'Oh!' said Carlos. 'Oh!' And he looked with eyes wide with amazement at his grandmother and the monk, who lowered

184

theirs to the ground and stood like two criminals in the presence of an unbending judge.

'But this man who is . . . who you want to have me believe is my . . . my father . . . God in heaven! He killed the other.'

'It was self-defence, it was to save my miserable life. . . . Oh, if only I had not! And for what? What did I want to live for? For this!'

'And my uncle, Joaninha's father? Did he have to die as well?'

'The two of them joined together to murder me and ambushed me on the heath. I did not recognize them – it was night and pitch black. I defended myself not knowing against whom and had the misfortune to save my life at the cost of theirs. My son, my son, may you never have to feel what I felt when, gathering up the bodies one by one to throw them in the river, I recognized my victims. . . . It was winter, the floodwaters covered the valley and were still rising. When they abated and the partly decomposed bodies were found, no one discovered how they had died. It was supposed they had drowned. No one ever knew the truth, except for me and your unhappy mother, whom I told as my punishment, whom I saw die of grief and remorse, who expired in my arms, weeping for him and cursing me. Should that not have been punishment enough, my son? No, it was not. This coarse habit which has chafed my body all these years, these scourgings which have lacerated it, fasts, vigils, prayers have so far gained nothing from God. His wrath will not leave me, His anger will follow me to my grave. . . . Perhaps it will pursue me beyond the grave!'

There was an awful silence at this point; no one breathed. The monk continued: 'I did not consider myself sufficiently punished with your mother's death agony, the most horrible, desperate agony I have yet witnessed – oh, my God! I had the cruel courage to explain to your grandmother the dreadful circumstances of her death and to make clear to her all the heinousness and hideousness of my crime. I tore her heart to pieces and saw her eyes run with blood and water until she became blind. What more do you want? I thought I might die without having to go through this final penance. God willed otherwise. Here I kneel repentant at your feet, my son. Here is the murderer of your mother, of her husband, of your uncle . . .

the destroyer and the dishonour of your whole family. Do with me what you will ... I am your father...'

'My father! God have mercy on me!'

'Mercy and forgiveness, my son, for your father!'

Carlos got up slowly, went to the old man, took him bodily in his arms, made him sit in the chair he himself had just left and, kneeling before him, kissed his hand in silence. Next, he went and embraced his grandmother, who fondled him eagerly with her quavering hand and said in a whisper: 'Now I can, now I can die. Now I can die because I have embraced him, because I have felt him close to me, my son, the son of my darling daughter...'

Carlos did not utter another word. A string had broken in his heart and either it had destroyed his emotion or prevented him expressing it. He left the cell, motioning that he would come straight back; but they waited for him in vain.... He did not return.

Three days later a letter came from him, from near Évora, where he was with the constitutional army.

XXXVI

——— ∴ ———

Joaninha's story not yet complete. – Carlos's heart on trial.
– Immorality – A faulty disposition is not immoral. –
Horror, horror, damnation! – A baron who does not
belong to the Linnaean family of barons. – The Atamarma
Gate. – A senatus consultum in Santarém. – Our Lady of the
Victory 'leased'. – A dirge for Santarém.

'So, is that the end of Joaninha's story?'

'No, not quite.'

'Is there much more?'

'Not really.'

'Whatever it is, let us finish, because everyone is impatient to
know how it all ended – what the monk did, what happened to
the Englishwoman, what was the destiny of Joaninha and her
grandmother, and if poor Carlos . . .'

'So you are concerned for Carlos, an immoral, unprincipled,
heartless man who paid suit – paying suit is nothing –, who
loved two women at the same time? Horror, horror! as the
romantic dramatists say. Horror and damnation!'

'Horror it may be, horror it probably is . . . yes, horror it is
without a doubt. And damnation the poor fellow certainly got.
But immorality?! Immorality is deceiving, lying and betraying,
and he did none of these. It is a great misfortune to have a heart
like his, but don't come telling me it is a proof of not having a
heart. I say he had too much heart, which is a serious defect, a
pathological, abnormal condition. Physically it leads to death
and morally it can also destroy the emotions. I quite believe it,
but it is a common ailment and one which many people learn to
live with, until one day . . .'

'One day, the organ, which has been growing progressively
larger, can no longer function, the circulation ceases and with it
life itself. It must be a horrible death!'

'You mean physically?'

'Yes, physically. But it is much the same in moral terms. And if that is Carlos's defect...'

'Feeling too much?'

'No, having felt too much – because the heart, as a moral organ, only grows to such an extent owing to the great excess and violence of feelings that have worn it out and weakened it. If that is Carlos's defect, his disease, I can tell you I know the end of the story without hearing it.'

'What was it, then?'

'One fine day he lapsed into complete indifference and became what they call a sceptic. His heart ceased to beat with any generous feeling and he turned politician or speculator.'

'Maybe.'

'But which of the two was it – member of parliament or baron? We want to know.'

'So you shall.'

'We want to know now.'

'What if he were both?'

'Oh, horror, horror, hell and damnation! Red-hot irons, black, red, blue devils, multicoloured devils! In that case all romanticism's heavy artillery should rain down on that monster, that...'

'That what? Because, when a man's heart is used up...'

'I don't believe that. As if a person's heart gets used up!'

There was laughter all round at the expense of the poor unbeliever and we got up to go and visit the Santo Milagre,[1] as it was the appointed time and the prior was waiting for us.

The end of the story of the green-eyed maid tomorrow.

On the way we met our old friend the Baron of P.[2] – a baron of a different genus, not a member of the Linnaean family which I have tried to classify in this work for the enlightenment of our century – an honourable gentleman, a rarity nowadays, typical of our old provincial nobility, with all their old-world dignity and courtesy, which distinguishes them so sharply from the ill-mannered vulgarity of your improvised notables. . . .

He was looking for us in order to act as our guide. We followed him.

On the way we continued to note some of the more interesting things in that extremely interesting town, where one cannot walk a step without one's thoughts or imagination finding something to occupy them. Veering a little to our right we found ourselves at the famous Atamarma Gate.[3]

Dom Afonso Henriques entered the city here; here he made that daring surprise attack that won him Santarém and put a final end to Arab rule in this country.

The enlightened town councillors of Santarém have, from time to time, had the noble and generous idea of demolishing this gate – Afonso Henriques's triumphal arch, Portugal's noblest monument!

The idea is worthy of the age.

Fortunately, it seems there has not been money for the demolition and the senatus consultum of the worthy senator priests could not yet be carried out.

Not that I believe this to be the genuine Moorish arch through which Dom Afonso's warriors entered; what I do think is that successive alterations to this gateway to the old town, repair-work, restorations and preservation, have brought it to what it is today, and even in its present condition it is a respectable monument that only barbarians would think of dishonouring and destroying.

It is topped by a shrine to Our Lady of the Victory. Tradition has it that it was built and dedicated to the Virgin by the heroic founder of the monarchy and of Portugal's independence. This is one of the many points on which faith in traditions should be respected and believed in without close examination, because the critics gain nothing by raising doubts and national pride loses a great deal by admitting them.

Let her be, the Virgin of the Victory over Afonso Henriques's arch. Let us bow down like good Portuguese in adoration of the symbol of Christian faith and patriotism raised by the bloody hands of the victor!

But was it or was it not he who built this shrine? There are no documents; contemporary historians remain silent; history must be exact and truthful. . . .

Yes, it must. And the great important facts that mark an age and are landmarks in a nation's history, I too shall reject them ruthlessly if they lack the indispensable corroboration. Now, who is likely to preserve the, as it were, episodic circumstances of a known and proven feat of magnitude if not poets and popular traditions, and the greatest poet of them all, that great keeper of traditions, the people?

I believe in Santarém's Lady of the Victory and in many other saints whom popular religious belief keeps in so many niches, chapels and crosses throughout Portugal to record memories for which no other account was made, nothing written down, for which there is no other document and which the monkish reporters thought unnecessary to write down in their books of hours, books black or red, because they considered it to be better written and preserved in the books of stone where it was.

Poor fellows! They failed to reckon with the improvers, restorers and demolishers from later civilizations who, in order to put things in order, first remove everything from its place.

The Santarém town council, unable to demolish the arch, opted for a compromise which I am prepared to bet no one can guess. They leased the shrine on top of it, altar, saints and all; and it was leased out for a number of years, goodness knows why or what for – the fact is, it was.

Last year (1842), however, there began to appear a religious reaction which the speculators immediately decided to turn to their personal gain by making their percentage in the market of sectarian sharp dealings. But they are wasting their time, thank goodness! As I say, this reaction in people's ideas came about and the shrine of the Lady of the Victory, atop the arch, goodness knows why or what for, was *de-leased* and restored to popular worship.

We climbed up to look at the inside of the shrine. It is a poor, ridiculous restoration with neither the solemnity of old things nor any modern elegance.

It disappointed me sadly. Let us move on to the Santo Milagre quickly, because I want to make my peace with Santarém and it is starting to get difficult.

But the injustice is mine – what fault does the poor town have?!

'Oh, Santarém, Santarém! They abandoned you, murdered you and now they spit on your corpse.

Santarém, Santarém, lift up your head crowned with towers and monasteries, with palaces and temples!

See yourself mirrored in the Tagus, princess among our towns, and you will see how beautiful you were, how great, how rich and powerful among all Portuguese cities.

Raise yourself, giant skeleton of our greatness, and see

yourself in the mirror of the Tagus. You will see how great and strong they are even now, these disjointed bones they left you.

Raise yourself, death's skeleton, lift your sickle, shake off the worms that defile you, crush the reptiles that ravage you, the vile toads that smear you with their spittle, the poisonous lizards that insolently parade on your dishonoured tomb.

Raise yourself, Santarém, and tell ungrateful Portugal to leave you in peace, at least, among your ruins, to bleach your glorious bones; to leave you the ashes of your captains, of your men of letters and great men in their marble urns, consecrated by time and past reverence.

Tell her not to let the bricks of your temples be sold, not to let them make barns and stables of your churches, not to order soldiers to play ball with the skulls of your kings and billiards with the shin-bones of your saints.

They have taken away your magistrates, your teachers, your seminaries ... everything except the rubble and the debris, the rubbish and dungheaps that they allowed to accumulate in your streets and spread over your squares.

Santarém, noble Santarém, Liberty is the enemy of neither heavenly nor earthly religion. Without them it cannot live: it decays, it putrefies and destroys itself in its own delirium.

The religion of Christ is the mother of Liberty, the religion of Patriotism, her companion. Anyone who fails to respect the temples, the monuments, of each of them is a poor friend of Liberty, he dishonours her, deserts her and delivers her over to the derision and hatred of the people.

★　　★　　★

Let us move on to the Santo Milagre.

XXXXVII

———— ∴ ————

The Graça and its fine Gothic façade. – The tomb of Pedro
Álvares Cabral. – Another baron, not one of those of
renown. – The church of the Santo Milagre. – Some fine
Mozarabic medallions. – Concerning how, with the arrival
of the prior and the judge, the author had a view of the
Divine Miracle, and the solemnities involved. – The
monument to Her Supreme Highness the Princess Infanta
Dona Maria de Assunção. – The house where the miracle
occurred converted into a chapel in the Philippine style. –
The man in boots and his connection with Santarém's Santo
Milagre. – A remarkable and amusing piece of cleverness
on the part of the Rossio regency. – Haroun Alraschid and
the theory of fun-loving governments, the best possible
governments. – The Santarém palladium returns home
from Lisbon.

W E bent our way to the left and passed in front of the elegant,
reticulated Gothic frontispiece of the Graça Church. The
absence of some parish official, or other insignificant personage
of equal importance, who has the keys to the church and
convent, caused us to give up hope of visiting the tomb of Pedro
Álvares Cabral, who is buried there, as well as other beautiful,
interesting antiquities of no less value.

We pursued our way to the house of the Baron of A., another
illegitimate one because he is not numbered among the knights
of renown,

> Who, without sailing beyond Taprobana,
> In Portugal's ancient land did build
> A new realm which they raised so high.[1]

We found him ready to accompany us and to preside, in his
capacity as judge of the fraternity, over the great ceremony of
the exhibition and display of the Divine Miracle.

We went down together to the church, which is nearby.

The church itself is small and in the worst modern taste inside and out. There is nothing remarkable about it except four or five carved stone medallions, with male and female busts in relief, which obviously belonged to the old building and are now encrusted in the crude brickwork of the nave.

The busts are carved in the most exquisite Gothic style, in high relief and designed with an honesty not to be found in much later sculptures.

They are possibly relics of the original church of the Divine Miracle and have been preserved during successive rebuildings. A blessing on the scrupulous person who saved them from the latest *improvement* made to the unfortunate, unattractive temple – which was not many years ago, to be sure.

I refer to the carving of the heads as Gothic because it is the common, incorrect expression used by everybody. As I have already remarked elsewhere, it would be more exact to say Mozarabic.

The prior arrived, the judge gave his instructions, a number of brothers came with torches, which they handed out to each of us, and we moved in procession to the lateral door of the high altar, from which one ascends a fairly wide, comfortable staircase, to a sort of recess parallel to the top of the throne, where Santarém's great palladium is always kept.

We ascended, accompanied by the prior in surplice and stole. Once at the top, we knelt round him and he mounted some steps, opened a sort of sacrarium door with a golden key hanging from his neck, then he knelt, got up and shook incense, knelt again, recited some Bible verses, to which the sacristan made the response, and finally took from its repository a sort of ampulla made of gold, an antique, though not earlier than the sixteenth or at most fifteenth century.

After we had bowed our heads to receive the blessing which the priest gave us with the relic, we were allowed to get to our feet and move closer to see and examine it.

Among some crystals, by now quite old and dull, one can actually discern a small, dark-yellow object, which is piously believed to be the remainder of the consecrated particle which the Jewess stole for her spells.

I do not need to relate the story of the Divine Miracle of

Santarém, as everyone knows it. The good prior, a plump, well-preserved, ex-Trinitarian monk, did not excuse us its merest detail, and we had to hear it with the utmost seriousness.

When the ampulla had been locked away with the same solemnities, we began to chat to the prior.

In that same recess, close by the holy relic, were kept for some five or six years, if I remember rightly what the good priest told us, the mortal remains of the Infanta Dona Maria de Assunção, who had passed away in Santarém during the last months of the occupation of the town by the royalist forces. Her body, embalmed incorrectly and with poor quality fluids, was placed in a tin-plate coffin. In a short while the putrefaction destroyed and burst the tin and a terrible stench of decay befouled the church. They put up with it for years; from time to time representations were made to the government but no solution could be obtained. Until the prior eventually declared that if they did not have someone take charge of the poor princess's sad remains, he would be obliged to put them underground, whereupon they replied that he should do as he saw fit. He saw fit to bury them in the nave of the church, which he did, on the side where the Epistle is read, which is to say on the right.

And there lies, under a plain tombstone, with neither identification nor epitaph, Her Royal Highness the Princess Dona Maria, daughter of His Supreme Majesty King John VI, King of Portugal, Emperor of Brazil and of the conquest and navigation etc. etc.

Such is the world, its splendours and glories!

The visit to the Divine Miracle is not complete unless one goes to see the house where it occurred. It was preserved for some centuries with great veneration and in 1600-odd it was transformed into a chapel. Now it is abandoned, it rains inside and there is only an ill-fitting door to protect it against animals getting inside. A great pity and great neglect, because the little chapel is elegant and attractive, wrought in good marble, in the best seventeenth-century style, late Renaissance well on into classical: it is a perfect example of the Philippine style which prevailed throughout the peninsula in that period.

The story of the Divine Miracle of Santarém has been frequently linked to the history of Portugal. Even in this century, at the time of the War of Independence,[2] it came to be associated with one of the most important events, as well as with the strangest and most amusing adventure that is remembered in Lisbon.

I refer to none other than the *man in boots*. And may I be forgiven my apparent irreverence by my pious lady readers, who know full well that I am not one to make fun of serious, holy matters. But the fact is that the history of the Divine Miracle is connected to the famous story of the *man in boots*.

The contemporary reader and posterity, for whose enlightenment I am mainly writing this learned book, should know, then, that because of Masena's invasion, Santarém's famous palladium was sent by order for safe keeping in Lisbon, where it was kept for some years, in fact long after the complete withdrawal of the French.

When there was no longer any danger of the invading army stealing or, which was more likely, defiling the holy relic, the people and council of Santarém began to reclaim it, and the council and people of Lisbon to show very little wish to return it to them. It was a contention such as between Alba and Rome and caused a serious problem to the circumspect Numas[3] of the Rossio regency.

Few predicaments as serious as this faced that unhappy government, which suffered so many and came so badly out of most of them.

Not this one, however, which it dodged with the most admirable and unexpected strategy, worthy of adorning the marvellous spectacles of the great Haroun Alraschid or of some other good-humoured prince, one of those rare, happy men who in happy times played at being king and poked fun at their people, but made them laugh too.

Well, gentlemen, the regency of these lands found itself in a tight spot over the restoration of the Divine Miracle, which in all justice should be made to Santarém, but which Lisbon was refusing and threatening to obstruct. It was feared there would be popular disturbances.

I do not know who had the idea, but the rascal had good taste, and the government had the good taste to accept it and act on it. For the day on which the Divine Miracle was to leave Lisbon, sailing up the Tagus, with the expected solemnity and ecclesiastical pomp, they advertised on billboards that a fellow would cross the river, from Lisbon to Almada, in cork boots, which would keep him upright and dry, allowing him to sail on foot with no boat, sail or wind to assist him.

The hoax was a huge one, but it was swallowed all the quicker and more completely. On the appointed day the capital emptied of people, and in boats of different sizes or along the beaches people of all classes swarmed to the place and spent the best part of the day waiting for the *man in boots*.

Meanwhile, with great stealth, the Divine Miracle was embarking on its up-river boat and sailing with wind and tide to the happy shores of Santarém.

Nobody in Lisbon saw it leave and no one had news of it until they learned of its arrival in Santarém and of the great festivities given in its honour by the pious, nostalgic people of the Ribatejo.

The Haroun Alraschids of the Rossio laughed up their sleeves and never did a government laugh so innocently over deceiving the people.

We commemorated the story as it deserved by dining at the Alcáçova, leaving the afternoon to visit the Ribeira in search of traces of its illustrious Armourer.

XXXVIII

———— .·. ————

Dinner in the royal palace of Afonso Henriques. – *Sautés*
and *salmis*. – The author goes down to the Ribeira of
Santarém in search of the Armourer's forge. – The
Constable's sword. – Disappointment. – An elegant salon.
Archaeological ideas evaporate. Fossils. – Everything
better when seen from a distance. – The public ball. – The
soirée with obligatory piano. – Theatre: the prima donna's
cacophonies; incurable syphilis of the translations;
derangement of the originals. – The compulsory ballad, the
underground passage and the cemetery. – Sublime
galimatias of the ridiculous. – Beauty and necessity of the
word *galimatias*. – As to whether one can die of nostalgia. –
Danger of applying the scalpel and the magnifying glass to
the most perfect of human things. – On logic as the most
pernicious incoherence there is.

T HERE awaited us, indeed, at the house of our good host in
the royal palace of Afonso Henriques, a splendid dinner, at
which most of the local gentry were present. I shan't say the
notables, which is an affected word for which I have an
insuperable aversion. The delicacies of the table were in the
genuine Portuguese tradition and no less tasty and exquisite for
being served unadulterated by foreign-sounding *sautés* and
salmis. Particularly outstanding were the products of the two
great rival wine-growing areas, the Ribatejo and the
Ribadouro.[1] The dinner was prolonged and jovial.

We finished late, then got straight on our horses and rode
down to the Ribeira via the Atamarma Gate. It was almost
sundown when we arrived there.

It is the democratic suburb of the noble town and now its
strong point and source of wealth. It reminds one of those
villages which grew up in the shadow of feudal castles and
which, when later freed from their oppressive protection,

flourished and expanded in substance and strength. The castle, meanwhile, is empty and in ruins.

Most of Estremadura's and Beira's trade with the Alentejo passes through here. The inhabitants are busy and hard-working, and preserve the old dignity and independence of their original temperament; it is the only live part of Santarém.

We traversed the suburb in all directions, trying to discover some trace, calculate some spot where we might locate, by the most audacious conjecture, our Armourer's forge with his well-tempered swords and shining, shapely armour – and the youthful Nun'Álvares strolling nearby along the river bank – as the chronicle tells us,[2] excited by the perfection of his work and taking his father's fine old sword to be polished by the rustic prophet who so often predicted his future greatness and saluted him as Constable, Count of Ourém and saviour of his native land.

We could discover nothing for our imagination to so much as fool itself with, nothing to give us, more or less anachronously, a slight basis merely to reconstruct the Gothic dwelling of the famous cutler-prophet, whom history inherited from the romantic chronicles and whom romance now wants back again from history.

There are few private houses in Santarém which can be said to be really old; in the Ribeira there is not one. Successive patching and repatching has anachronized everything. Anachronism is a felicitous expression of Count Raczynski, which he uses correctly to refer to the state of most of our monuments.[3]

While up there in the upper town, or Marvila, in Santarém proper, are the temples, the convents, the outer walls, which still preserve the historical configuration of the town, here there is not even that.

I returned utterly disappointed with the Ribeira – that is, with its bricks and mortar; its inhabitants I like immensely.

Another surprise, of a quite different kind, awaited us that evening in Marvila, in the elegant salon of the Baroness of A., with whom we went to take tea.

To find, in the midst of the ruins and discomfort of the neighbouring buildings, which are deserted and decaying, a house in the full bloom of civilization and life; to see charm and elegance gracefully doing the honours of the house, though it was fully to be expected, is nevertheless surprising at first sight: it was like the touch of a fairy's wand.

In such pleasant and youthful company, all our archaeological thoughts evaporated, despite the presence of two or three fossils who were perhaps there so that we should not be wholly without local colour.

We conversed at length, mainly about Lisbon, about our mutual friends, about the previous winter's parties and about the likelihood of future prospects.

We made disparaging remarks about Portuguese society and praised Paris and London to the skies, probably Peking and Nanking too, and came to the conclusion that even Timbuktu would be better than our wretched country's boring capital. Even so we missed it and, with a few concessions here and there, we eventually decided it wasn't such a bad place after all.

Admirable condition of human nature, that everything seems better and less ugly to us when seen from a distance!

The dullest public ball, with its hateful noise and confusion, where, in order to set eyes on a pleasant, familiar face, one had to weave a way through hundreds of barbarous elbows coming at one from all sides; to be trodden on cruelly by novice dancers, by some newly arrived member of parliament and by the editor of the Galocha's[4] new boots and – worst of all! – to see the absurd toilettes, the fabulous hair-styles, the unbelievable faces and antediluvian figures of so many ugly and ungainly women . . . well, that same ball, when it is no longer more than a memory recollected in the boring surroundings of some tedious provincial town, seems quite different. The lights, the flowers, the music, all the bustle, are recalled with pleasure, while the rest is forgotten and a poor fellow involuntarily finds himself sighing for it.

The most boring soirée, with obligatory piano, sisters' duet, cousins' polka and elderly aunts playing cassino, recollected in the selfsame circumstances, also comes to be remembered as nothing other than a select, intimate gathering, with easy, pleasant conversation . . . oh, society's real pleasures!

As for the theatre, one has but to remember, when in the provinces, the sufferings his ear went through with the prima donna's bawlings, the tenor's cacophonies or the infuriating snores of that sleepy São Carlos[5] orchestra!

The revolting translation of a comedy, riddled with incurable syphilis, at the Rua dos Condes theatre, is softened in the imagination by all the charm of Scribe's style.

And the frenzy of the original of an ultra-romantic drama, crowned with the unfading laurels of the Conservatory, for the eternal gaping of our mouths! At a distance, one applauds it enthusiastically, forgetting that one smoked outside during the whole of the first act, slept all through the second and chatted during the rest, until the unfailing scene with the ballad, the underground passage, the cemetery, or what have you, in which the lady, her hair dishevelled and dressed in a white gown, goes mad in style, the beau, drawing his hand across his forehead, wrenches from deep down in his thorax the compulsory three *ahs!* and swears he will kill his own father should he appear, the support player loses his support, whiskers tears out his whiskers[6] ... and damnation, hell and damnation!... 'Ah, shameful woman! You know not that in this bosom beats a heart, that from this heart come arteries, from these arteries my veins – and in these veins runs blood ... blood, blood! I want blood, because I thirst for something and that thing is blood. ... Ah! So you thought.... Kneel, woman, I want to kill you ... carve you in pieces, massacre you!' And the women kneels and there's nothing for it but to applaud....

And we always applaud.

I am not speaking for myself, because I like this sort of thing: it is the rest who get bored and tired of this hotchpotch all the time, always the same....

What I'm getting at, then, is that in the provinces there is none of this monotony, that one forgets the boring part and that from there one is not even aware of the sublime *galimatias* of the ridiculous.

I beg the illustrious puritans who, by the use of sixteenth-century sublimate, have succeeded in bringing our language to a state of decrepitude in order to cure it of its French infirmities – I beg them to forgive me my *galimatias*, because it is much more Portuguese than anything else. The famous oration *Pro gallo Mathiae* was the origin of this delightful, suggestive word[7] which was certainly engendered in France, but we have more need of it here nowadays than they do anywhere else.

Returning from the philological digression, let us get back to optrics and catoptrics.

Distance is a wonderful thing!

And they say one can die of nostalgia! Nostalgia is life-giving, it is the salvation of much that, at the height of enjoyment and undisputed possession, would perish of inanition or would die of the oppressive disease called excess.

This is why I do not care to dig my scalpel into the most perfect things made by man, or apply my magnifying glass to their firm and delicate works. . . .

Let us carry on using these words we have inherited, without bringing arbitrators into the inheritance, lest it come about that we discover we are poorer than we thought. . . . Let us go on repeating these expressions made up by our forefathers, without analysing them too closely, lest it happen that we see too clearly that we have been lying all our lives. . . .

I hate philosophy and I hate reason, and I sincerely believe that in such a topsy-turvy world as this, a society which is so false, an existence as absurd as this one is made by its laws, customs, institutions and conventions, to affect in words the accuracy, the logic and integrity that does not exist in things themselves, is the worst and most pernicious incoherence there is.

Let us say no more about this, because it is not good for one, and let us end the chapter here.

XXXIX

———— ∴ ————

The author charged with scepticism. – Unlettered moralists. – Logic, the greatest dream of this life. – Difference between a poet and a philosopher. – Horace's heart. – The Jesuit College in Santarém. – Jesuits and Templars. – The natural ally of kings. – 'Not to get beyond the *Gazette*', a more precise modern expression for 'to stay in the ink-well'. – The Blessed Friar Gil and Doctor Faust. – How the author went to the sorcerer saint's tomb and found it empty. – Who could have stolen him?

THE end of the previous chapter is, I know, a terrible document in support of the charge of scepticism that has been brought against me by certain unlettered moralists, at whom I have the audacity to laugh, at them, their indictment and their accusation, at the same time protesting that I shall neither seek redress nor appeal, nor ask for any reversal of the wondrous judgement their most excellent hypocrisies may deign to pronounce against me.

After this solemn declaration, let us proceed.

And as for you, benevolent reader, to whom I wish to give only pleasure, if these fantasies still weary you, I advise you to turn over this obnoxious page, because the reflections in the last chapter are as out of place in my book as most things are in this world. Go to sleep, then, and wake not from the fine ideal of your logic.

It is a discovery of mine, of which I am vain and conceited, this idea that logic and punctuality in life's affairs are much more a dream and an ideal than the most fantastic dream and the most exquisite ideal in poetry.

The reason is that philosophers are much crazier than poets; in addition, they are foolish, which the latter are not.

Let us turn the page indeed, it will be better.

Today it is a beautiful morning, a perfect, clear day. That dry, harsh wind, which is the scourge of Portuguese summers, is still sleeping in Father Aeolus's cave. There is a soft gentle breeze in the air, that exhilarates and revitalizes one. What a waste of a day to spend it seeing ruins! I would I could spend this day in the eternally young heart of nature, under the rejuvenated lushness of the trees, lying on the constantly renewed carpet of green grasses and dappled daisies, in blessed indolence of body and spirit, feeling the slow, regular beat of a heart free and released from all undertakings, a true Horatian heart, *Solutus omni foenore!*[1]

I wish I were back once more in the valley, with Sister Francisca winding her yarn on the doorstep, our Joaninha untangling her skein, and even if the awful spectre of Friar Dinis comes and casts his tragic, gloomy shadow over the idyll of this lovely scene, he cannot destroy all its bucolic charm, do what he will.

We shall return to our valley, dear reader, and there we shall conclude, as is right and proper, the story of the maiden of the nightingales. But now, let us have lunch, for it is late and we must finish our archaeological studies in Marvila and Santarém.

Here we are in the Jesuit College, an enormous, grandiose, magnificent building, fit accommodation for the company royal, which had it built to educate its princely children.

I believe this one and the one in Coimbra were the two main houses the Jesuits had for this purpose in Portugal.

They were the Templars of modern times, the Jesuits. The formidable, almost regal power which the former built for themselves with the sword, the latter founded with doctrine. Wealth, power, influence, both had these, with the applause and acquiescence of all; both lost them the same way.

Extinguished and persecuted, the two orders were revived in mysterious circumstances and became secret societies in order to conspire; both took various names and different disguises in order to do so in greater safety.

Both in vain!

The preponderance of the democratic element, which has been increasing for centuries, puts an end to all such conspiracies. Without it, on their own, the monarchies would have collapsed. Democracy is the natural ally of kings.

The college building is wholly in the Philippine style, as I said before; the church is one of the finest specimens of this style, which is generally dry, harsh and lacking poetry, but is nevertheless grandiose.

Here was housed afterwards, for many years, the patriarchal seminary, whose classes were attended by the young men of the district. Nowadays a different sort of lecture is delivered from the administrative chair. It is the seat of so-called civil government; the subject of the lectures is how to corrupt the nation's morality and defraud the representative system.

All other forms of education were taken away from Santarém. There is talk of a high school and something else that 'didn't get beyond the *Gazette*', a modern Portuguese expression that should take the place of the old, outdated one 'it stayed in the ink-well', for many reasons, particularly because nowadays the only thing that stays in the ink-well is common sense; all the rest gets out, everything. And we have to be thankful when it doesn't get to the printer's reams to be spread abroad.

Santarém is the best situated, most suitable place in Portugal to house a great establishment for public education. Why shouldn't the military academy be here, or the national orphanage, or some other great school? Why all this centralization of education in Lisbon? What justification is there for a privilege granted to the capital at the expense of the provinces?

We left the college and went straight to the convent of St Dominic, one of the oldest monastic establishments in the country and one I very much wanted to visit. I cannot describe my feelings when the rusty key was turned in the church door and the old temple was revealed to our eyes. It had just been used – you will not believe it – as a barn!

The last coating of rotting straw was still stuck to the damp flagstones and gave off a strong, pestilential stench that choked us. We were hardly able to see the tombs of the D'Ocem brothers and so many other interesting monuments that fill the upper part of the church. The lower part, or what is called the body of the church, is a wretched modern anachronism.

Breathing that loathsome air with difficulty, I decided to use my time, for as long as I could bear it, to inspect the main, and most interesting, relic in that defiled church: the chapel and tomb of the great sorcerer and great saint, the Blessed Friar Gil.

Somewhere I called him our Doctor Faust, and he really is. All he needs is a Goethe. *Vixere fortes ante Agamemnona multi*.[2]

There were brave men before Agamemnon and great sorcerers before and after Doctor Faust. But without a Homer or a Goethe one does not achieve the fame and reputation gained by those gentlemen. We need someone to put in verse the splendid struggles, comic and awesome by turns, of our Friar Gil of Santarém and the Devil. What I did in *Dona Branca*[3] is little more than a rough sketch. The great Lusitanian mage only appears episodically there and he needs to be shown as the central character of a substantial plot, a full-length portrait under the spotlight, occupying the centre of the stage.

Then his passionate craving for knowledge, his vast studies, the hidden mysteries of nature he uncovered in order to penetrate the invisible world; the thirst for gold, for pleasure and for power that obsessed him and caused him to fall into the clutches of the evil one; the disgust and surfeit that disillusioned him afterwards; finally his repentance and the regeneration of his soul through penances, prayer and contempt for vain human science – these different phases of such an extraordinary poetic existence would then be shown as they have yet to be seen, because no one has seen them with the eyes of a great moralist and a great poet, such as are needed to observe and understand them.

I remember that I have always perceived this since I was a boy, when they made me read the *História de S. Domingos*,[4] which is so cantankerous and dull at times, despite the marvellous style of our best prose writer. I used to leave the other chapters in order to read and reread just the adventures of the divine sorcerer, which were what interested me.

With all these recollections flowing back into my mind, with the splendid lines from *Faust* recalled to my memory and with the innumerable associations suggested to me by these ideas, I walked straight to the saint's chapel, all excited and as it were touched by his magic wand.

The chapel – what a disappointment! – the Blessed Friar Gil's chapel is a miserable modern *rifacimento*★, on the left side of the church, with no trace of antiquity, no distinctive ornamentation; it is heavy, crude – old, yet not ancient, a real nondescript of bad taste and drabness. Who would have thought it?

The saint's tomb is raised above the altar on an ugly sort of throne. I climbed up over the dirty, dilapidated credence to examine it more closely.

The tomb is of stone, but it is obvious that the stone has been painted recently; it has no ornamental carvings. And it was empty, its lid open and broken!

Who stole my saint?

Who was the accursed villain who dared commit such a sacrilege?

XL

———— ·:· ————

The nuns of Santa Clara. – A nocturnal adventure. –
Whether nuns frighten liberals. – The psalm. – Three
monks. – The Franciscan's address. – The body of the
Blessed Friar Gil. – What is to be done with the nuns? –
Woebetide the government that allows the barons to
devour any more.

IT was night. Confusion, disorder, alarm and anxiety reigned
within the walls of Santarém. Three men arrived at the dead of
night at the old convent of Santa Clara and gave a mysterious,
whispered signal at the door. They were answered from within
by a similar sound and shortly afterwards, noiselessly and with
the most meticulous precautions, the convent door was slowly
opened.

The three men entered and the door was closed after them in
the same cautious manner.

What is going on?

The men carried a sort of chest, which seemed to contain
precious objects of great value, such was the devotion with
which they shielded it.

There is something criminal about this mysterious adventure.
But in these times anything can happen.

It was the year 1834.

Let us enter the convent of the poor nuns of Santa Clara, who
are so distressed and dispirited now that they, like the monks,
are being threatened with dissolution.

It shall not happen: their institutions do not frighten true
liberals, and the others have got the monks' properties to feast
on. They are occupied; the nuns are safe for the time being.

Such was the hope of the three men who, at that late hour of
the night, entered the forbidden precincts of the convent. Let us
follow them, however, for the time has come.

They came to a small chapel in the nuns' cloister, went and

placed on the altar the chest they were carrying and knelt before it in devotion. The low, faint chanting of female voices was soon heard in the distance and shortly afterwards the whole community of the convent nuns, carrying torches, in two files with the abbess in the rear bearing her crosier, processed into the cloister and walked towards the same chapel.

The psalm they were chanting was this:

O God, the heathen are come into thine inheritance; thy holy temple have they defiled; they have laid Jerusalem on heaps.

The dead bodies of thy servants have they given to be meat unto the fowls of the heaven, the flesh of thy saints unto the beasts of the earth.

Their blood have they shed like water round about Jerusalem; and there was none to bury them.

We are become a reproach to our neighbours, a scorn and derision to them that are round about us.

How long, LORD? wilt thou be angry for ever? shall thy jealousy burn like fire?

Pour out thy wrath upon the heathen that have not known thee, and upon the kingdoms that have not called upon thy name.

For they have devoured Jacob, and laid waste his dwelling place.

O remember not against us former iniquities: let thy tender mercies speedily prevent us: for we are brought very low.

Help us, O God of our salvation, for the glory of thy name: and deliver us, and purge away our sins, for thy name's sake.[1]

This was what the poor nuns were singing. They were singing in Latin, which they scarcely understood, but their hearts' instinct told them and their excitable feminine imagination warned them that the time had come when the terrible prophecy of the psalm they were intoning would be carried out before their eyes and would fall on them also.

There were, therefore, tears in the voices that sang those

words; those sounds that came from the soul vibrated there too, with a deep, solemn melancholy.

The three male figures remained on their knees, bowing before the altar.

The psalm came to an end and was followed by a brief interval of silence. Then the three men stood up and, as the long cloaks in which they were enveloped fell open, one could see that the middle one was a thin, old monk, shrunk and bent, who despite the law still wore the black habit of the Franciscans belted with its rope. The other two were Dominicans and wore black and white, being the colours of their equally banned order.

The old Franciscan climbed the altar steps with uncertain feet, kissed the chest that lay on it and, turning towards the community that watched him in religious silence, said with a hollow voice, as if it came from the tomb, and yet was strong and emphatic: 'Sisters, we have come to deliver to you this precious object. God does not wish the bodies of his saints to be exposed to the birds of the air and the beasts of the earth. This is the blessed body of one of the greatest saints produced by this land of Portugal when it was blessed. Now it is cursed and should not preserve its relics. The sons of St Dominic were expelled from their house, as were we, the sons of Francis. We found ourselves, they and us, without roof or shelter, and we have merged our sorrows so as to lament them as brothers, as sons of fathers who loved and helped one another. Together we shall tramp the wilderness and together we shall knock at doors closed against us by ungodliness and indifference to beg for our daily bread, because we are hungry. What does it matter?! Do we not profess, do we not glory in being beggars? What do we live on, always, if not on charity? Weep not, sisters, weep not for us. God who permitted it knows what He does. May He be praised in eternity! We had sins enough for worse! The Lord of justice and chastisement has really treated us mercifully. They took everything away from us, everything! Even these shrouds which we had chosen to wear in life and which not even death dared to steal from us. Secretly, like someone disguising himself for a criminal act, we donned them tonight in order to commit what will be called a theft and was for us a sacred obligation. We went to our brothers' former house and we stole the body of the Blessed Friar Gil. We hand it into your keeping: guard it. As long as these walls remain standing, may they shelter it from the impious acts of these godless, lawless people. They will not dare drive you out of here; perhaps they will starve you.... That cannot happen: God will not permit it. But whatever may be His will, resign yourselves to it, my sisters. He alone knows how He loves us and how He punishes us. Let us praise Him for all things.'

At this point there were laments and fervent prayers, such as are heard only in moments of despair.

The distressed nuns were prostrate on the damp stones of the cloister, on the tombs of their sisters, on what were to be their own graves. The monk, with arms outstretched, pronounced the solemn blessing, tracing with his right hand the sacred symbol of redemption: 'God Almighty bless you, Father, Son and Holy Spirit!'

'Amen!' they responded in chorus and the three outlaws withdrew, leaving their treasure in safe keeping.

That is how the body of the Blessed Friar Gil of Santarém disappeared from his tomb.

No one knew about it. I found out and kept the secret religiously.

Times are different now: the liberals now realize that they must be tolerant and that they need to be religious. There is no danger in telling them where he is.

When Portugal has a government that knows how to govern properly, it will have to make regulations for the nuns and give them security; it will have to make use of them in charitable institutions for the education of the young, the treatment of the sick and the protection of the disabled.

The barons are sniffing around after the few possessions the poor nuns still own.

Woebetide the government that allows the barons to devour any more!

XLI

—————— ∴ ——————

The thief who stole the saint's body discovered by the benevolent reader's shrewd perspicacity. – A major gap in our story. – Why is it not filled? – The black page in *Tristram Shandy*. – Novels and romances, trivial books. – The square in front of St Francis and its acacias. – What can have become of Joaninha? – The heart of northern European women. – Let us leave: I am tired of Santarém and its ruins. – The soldier's trumpet and the trump of doom. – Eheu, Portugal, eheu!

OF course, dear reader, in the old Franciscan who goes stealing saints' bones from their tombs at night and hiding them in a nuns' convent, of course, I say, your natural perspicacity has already recognized our Friar Dinis, monk *par excellence*, monk obdurate, monk intractable.

It was indeed he, without a doubt.

That is how the scene occurred and that is how it was recounted to me. What happened between it and the events with the monk, Carlos, Joaninha, her grandmother and the Englishwoman, I was unable to discover.

It is a major gap in our story, but let it stay that way rather than be filled by the imagination.

Oh, I detest the imagination.

Where the chronicle is silent and popular tradition has nothing to say, I would rather have a whole page of dots, or one completely blank – or all black, like in the estimable story of our particular and worthy friend, Tristram Shandy – than a single line invented by the reporter.

That is all very well for novels and romances, insignificant books that everybody keeps on reading, even those who deny it.

I suspect I read them too, but I always say I don't. . . .

Anyway, let us get back to the monk and to my travels.

With my mind full of him and my memory still ringing with

the remembrance of the dreadful scenes that had taken place, just a few years before, in his old monastery, I finally approached Santarém's royal convent of St Francis.

I paid little attention to the fine square and to the majestic view to be had from it, even less to the sickly acacias that attempt a feeble, puny growth there, probably planted by an unsuitable hand at an unsuitable time, because they are obviously recent: they were put there since the dissolution of the convent. They are a sad but true symbol of the listless, artificial life with which they attempted to animate something that was already dead.

Let us go inside and see if we can discover among the low, pointed arches of the cloister and among the lofty naves of the temple some trace of this house's last superior and of that ill-fated family whose destiny was, in an unfortunate hour, so closely linked to his own.

I find this more interesting, I must confess – oh, much more! – than all these tombs and inscriptions that are scattered around and are the distinguishing feature of what is one of the oldest and most historic buildings in the realm.

But I question it in vain, stone by stone, block by block: the lifeless echo of solitude is the sad reply to my questions. It answers that it knows nothing, that it has forgotten everything, that desolation and neglect reign here and that all remembrance of an earlier condition has been wiped out. . . .

What became of you, Joaninha, and of your love? What has become of that man who dared love you when he loved another? And that other person, where is she? Did she really resign herself? Did she really bury beneath the ice which is supposed to clothe the heart of northern women in a threefold, but false, armour, all the intense inner fire that covertly gnawed away at her heart?

I have no hope of learning anything about this here.

All I was able to discover was that, on the day after the nocturnal scene with the nuns of Santa Clara, Friar Dinis left Santarém for an unknown destination; that on the same day Georgina had also left, taking the Lisbon road, and had taken grandmother and granddaughter in her carriage, the two of them almost lifeless and out of their minds; that there had been no more news of Carlos and that Joaninha had his last letter, the one he had written near Évora, clutched tightly in her shaking hands when she left.

Well, I too want to leave, I want to get away. I am bored with Santarém; I am tired of these never-ending ruins, these interminable, dilapidated remains, the unsightly appearance of these heaps of rubble, the sadness of these empty streets. I am going away.

Nevertheless the convent of St Francis is a fine ruin, worthy of a lengthier examination and a patience I no longer have.

Everything here makes me impatient!

The fine Gothic church has been turned into a military depot; the destructive hand of the soldiery has gone about breaking and flattening these precious monuments, scratching with their bayonets on the most highly polished, best preserved glaze of these ancient burial monuments; they have chipped and spoiled their most delicate carvings. They have lifted the tombstones and, to the sound of the military trumpet, have awoken the dead of centuries, who thought they were hearing the trump of doom....

I am definitely going away, I cannot stay here, I do not want to see this. I am not so much shocked as nauseated, disgusted, furiously angry.

Curses on the hands that have defiled you, Santarém; that have dishonoured you, Portugal; that have demeaned and degraded you, nation that has lost everything, even the landmarks of your history....

Eheu, Portugal, eheu!

XLII

———— ∴ ————

The author protests. – Jangling nerves. – What is needed to make ruins solemn and sublime. – God is as much in the Colosseum as in St Peter's. – The author wants to get away from Santarém. – But how, without seeing King Fernando's tomb? – The condition it is in. – A model of the Byzantine style. – A royal crown on a skull. – The king of spades and the symbol of the Empire. – Those who have never seen a king, think he is made of gold. – Brutalities committed by the soldiery on a king's tomb. – What is to be found in royal graves. – Phrenology. – Public revenge, late but insulting. – Camoens and Duarte Pacheco. – Religion's false shadow. – The materialistic regime of the barons. – Popular prose and poetry. – Synthesis and analysis. – The inner sense. – Whether the author is a demagogue or a Jesuit. – Jesus Christ and the barons.

DO not accuse me of exaggerating what I wrote at the end of the last chapter. What I wrote was felt, in fact I felt much more than I wrote. There might be some inaccuracy in the choice of words, because I really cannot explain what I feel seeing a ruin in that state. My nerves start jangling, they throb in unbearable discord and dissonance. I would rather see these altars exposed to the rains and winds of heaven; I prefer the sun to burn them by day and that at night, in the white light of the moon or the pale gleam of the stars, the owl should hoot and the nightjar murmur over their tumbling archways.

Like that the temple would not seem to be defiled, nor the monument to have lost any of its majesty. I could kneel among the loose stones and the moist grass and lift up my mind to God, my heart to glory and splendour, my spirit to the sublime aspirations of idealism. The material, coarse, onerous things of life would not bother me there.

God, the prime mover of the world; God, Eternal Reason;

God who is love and glory; God the spirit's strength, poetry and nobility – God is as much in the battered ruins of the Colosseum as in St Peter's bronze and marble domes.

But here?!... In the dilapidated wreck of an old convent patched up by the Public Works Department to be used as a soldiers' barracks, there is no spirit of any kind.

I want to get away from here!

What?! Without seeing King Fernando's tomb? Out of the question, of course. Where is it?

In the choir loft.

Let us go up to the choir loft.

Oh, I know not, for loathing, how I shall tell![1]

What a state it is in, the beautiful tomb of the handsome, frivolous king, who was as much inclined to the delights of pleasure as was his father to the austerities of justice!

Oh, nation of barbarians! Oh, what an accursed nation of iconoclasts is this!

The tomb of the second husband of Dona Leonor Teles is a sarcophagus in fine white friable stone, simply and elegantly carved, with greater sobriety of ornamentation than is ordinarily the case with fourteenth-century monuments, but sculpted with a chaste, contained finish quite different from the life of the king they put in there after his death.

One can still make out vestiges of the bright colours with which the reliefs were cut into the white stone: the Byzantine style, of which I know no other example in Portugal. This is – or rather was – a treasure.

Was, because the soldiers' brutality has disfigured it to an incredible degree. These present-day vandals imagined, in their stupid greed, that some great quantity of hidden treasure must be inside it. Maybe they thought they would find the king's skull with the royal crown on it, all encrusted with pearls and rubies, supposedly buried with him. Perhaps they thought they would find, in the grasp of his withered fingers' dried-up bones, that globe of solid gold shown on the king of spades in the filthy pack of cards that soldiers use and which they consider the indisputable, infallible insignia of the Empire supreme. Perhaps they supposed that, even after death, a king must be made of gold.... Anyway, who knows what they thought or imagined? What we do know, because we can see, is that they tried to break open the tomb. First, they attempted to lift the tombstone: they did not succeed because the upper stone is so solidly joined to the body, or coffin, of the tomb that the whole thing seems all of a piece and seamless. But in their determination they broke and crushed the finely carved corner-pieces and the delicate grooves of the edge, yet the cover-stone did not give way; it was as if it had been welded together by the angel of the last judgement with that tremendous seal which shall be broken only on the day the world comes to an end.

The soldiers, in their greed, were not dismayed by the religious nature of the tomb, nor did this almost supernatural resistance of the monument's stone cause them a moment of contrition. One can see that some powerful, mighty old devil went to work at it with crowbar and battering-ram, but that he worked for a long time in vain.

They eventually gave up with the cover and decided to attack, more brutally, but to better effect, the walls of the sarcophagus, which they suspected might be thinner. This was the case and they succeeded in opening a crude hole in the front wall, through which a man's arm can easily enter and explore the inside of the tomb at will.

I did it myself, and putting my arm through this barbarous opening I found soil, dust, a few vertebral bones and two skulls, one a man's, the other a child's.

I do not recall any memory of a young prince being buried there too, as they used to do in earlier times, placing the children's bodies in the same tomb as their parents, relatives or even mere friends of the family.

I confess I experienced a sort of malign pleasure imagining the stupid, long faces of the brutal desecrators when they found in the King's tomb what there is in all tombs, whether of kings or of beggars: bones, earth, ashes, nothing!

For my own part, I was tempted to steal King Fernando's skull. If I believed in phrenology, I believe I would not have resisted. I do not believe in that science, in this case fortunately . . . for my conscience. And I do not know what I should do if the skull turned out to be someone else's. But as he was the 'weak king' who made 'a strong nation weak',[2] his are not the sort of relics one keeps.

Oh, and what if this desecration, this neglect, this affront to the king's tomb, here in his favourite town – King Fernando was a Santarémian by inclination – is the severe judgement of posterity, the public reprisal of the centuries which, late but with added insult, eventually falls on the condemned memory of the bad prince and dishonours his ashes as it had already dishonoured his name?

I should like to believe that nothing of the sort could happen to the tombs of King Dinis, of King Pedro I, of the two Johns, I and II, of ...

Yes, and where is Camoens's tomb? And Duarte Pacheco's, where *was* his? This last is a much more humiliating query....[3]

In Portugal there is no religion of any sort. Even its false shadow, hypocrisy, has disappeared. All that remains is a stupid, idiotic, ignorant, debauched and shameless materialism flaunting its hideous, cynical nudity in the midst of the desecrated ruins of everything that was spiritually uplifting....

A large nation can go on living and wait for better times, even when paralysis of this sort benumbs the life of the spirit in the noblest part of its body. But with a small nation it is impossible: it must die.

Another ten years of barons and their materialist regime and the last sigh of the spirit will inevitably flee from Portugal's dying body.

I firmly believe this.

But I still have better hopes, even so, because the people, the ordinary people, are healthy; it is we who are corrupt, we, the ones who think we know everything and know nothing.

We who are the mean prose of the nation do not understand the poetry of the people; we understand only what directly touches our senses and are strangers to the sublime aspirations of an inner sense that scorns our presumptuous theories, because they are the limited, trivial result of a stunted analysis based on imperfect, insignificant material data. Whereas that inner sense, which the ordinary people have, comes from divine reason and is based on a higher, transcendent synthesis inspired in the great, eternal truths which do not have to be demonstrated because they are felt.

And I who write this, am I a demagogue? No, I am not.

Am I perhaps a fanatic, a Jesuit, a hypocrite? I am not.

What am I, then?

If you do not understand what I am, it is not worth telling you. . . .

Dear reader, forgive me one last reflection at the end of this boring chapter and I promise not to reflect any more.

Jesus Christ, who was a model of patience and tolerance, the only true founder of freedom and equality among men, Jesus Christ suffered, with resignation and humility, all the insults that were thrown at him and his divine mission: he forgave the murderer, the adulteress, the blasphemer and the ungodly. But when he saw the barons lending money in the temple, he was unable to contain himself: he took hold of a whip and thrashed them unmercifully.

XLIII

—— ·:· ——

Departure from Santarém. – Pinacotheca. – Impatience and
nostalgia. – Friday. – An unknown martyr. – The image of
sin. – We are back in the valley. – Sister Francisca and Friar
Dinis. – Penelope's tapestry. – And Joaninha? – Joaninha is
in heaven. – The dead woman winding yarn and waiting to
be buried. – Hope, a Christian virtue. – A letter.

I am truly weary of Santarém; I am leaving.

We bade an affectionate farewell to the good, honest family
who had accommodated us with such kindness and old-
fashioned Portuguese hospitality. We departed.

As soon as I began to breathe the fresh morning air of the olive
groves I felt my spirit released from that tiring pressure one
experiences during a lengthy visit to an antique museum or an
art gallery.

Forgive me not saying 'pinacotheca'. I know it is in fashion
and that the word is adoptable according to the strictest
Horation rules, since it 'falls from the Greek source'[1] direct and
unadulterated. But it sounds so unpleasant to me in Portuguese
that I cannot bear it.

Santarém has wearied my spirit, like everything that makes us
think a lot. Yet I leave with a feeling of nostalgia and I shall never
forget the days I have spent here.

What am I made of, what sort of a person am I, that I cannot
stay long in a place, yet cannot leave it without regret?

I am already feeling sorry at leaving Santarém. Why could we
not have left tomorrow and still spent today here?

And today is a Friday! A bad day to start a journey!

Friday! It was the day of ill omen in our valley, for our poor
old blind woman who lived out her sad life there, with its grief,
remorse and heartbreak, yet with hope in God, resigned to her
martyrdom – an obscure martyrdom, yet stained so by blood
seeping painfully, drop by drop, from a heart torn and devoured

in silence by the invisible vulture of a grief that does not show itself, that has no fits of weeping or sobbing.

It was on Friday that the terrible monk, that suffering woman's living devil, appeared, tremendous and frightening, before her blind eyes, magnified by her imagination to the colossal, gigantic size of a supernatural avenger.

He was the tangible image, visible to her soul, of the great sin that was always against her.

I suppose I need not say that I do not have this superstition about days of ill omen that the unhappy old woman had and which her Joaninha shared. But I confess that, remembering the family's misfortunes and the day together, I did not care to be returning to the vale of Santarém on a Friday.

However, we were in the valley and I could already see from far away those trees and that window which had made such an impression on me, when these thoughts came into my mind and saddened me.

I slackened my pace very slightly, allowing my travelling companions to go on ahead of me and, by the time I was near the house, I had lost sight of them.

Instinctively I stopped in front of the window, stung by an irresistible interest and curiosity. . . . Not a soul thereabouts. I dismounted and went straight up to the house.

As soon as I passed the trees, my eyes hit upon an unexpected sight, which might have been conjured up by magic.

On the same spot, in the same manner, with the same clothes and in the same posture as I described her in the opening chapters of this story, sat our old sister Francisca . . .

She it was and could be no other, sitting in her old chair, winding her interminable skein of yarn, like Penelope weaving her tapestry. The only difference, now, was that the reel did not stop and the yarn went on and on, rolling on and on, with the same uninterrupted rhythm, on to the ball; and that the old woman's arms laboured on slowly, but unceasingly, like automatons, a distressing sight.

Facing her, sitting on a stone, his head bowed and his eyes fixed on a large, old book that rested on his knees, was a gaunt, thin man, shrivelled as a skeleton, livid as a corpse and motionless like a statue. He wore a nondescript black garment, which could have been a priest's soutane or a monk's habit, but unbelted, loose and hanging in broad, full folds from the man's scrawny neck.

He, too, could be none other than Friar Dinis.

I went up to them. Neither of them heard me and he, the only one who could see, did not see me.

Without realizing it, I went on aloud with the train of thought that had been going through my mind and exclaimed: 'And Joaninha?'

'Joaninha is in heaven,' answered, without his starting or raising his eyes from his book, the monk's shade, for he seemed nothing more.

'Joaninha, poor Joaninha! But what happened, how did the unhappy creature die?'

'Joaninha is not unhappy. She went to be an angel in the house of God.'

'And ... and ... Carlos?' I stammered, hesitating because I was afraid of upsetting the monk.

'Carlos?!' he replied, finally raising his eyes and fixing them on me.

Oh, I have never seen eyes like that, nor shall I again!

'Carlos?! ... And who is it asks me? Who is it that knows so much about me and mine? Mine? I have no family, I am alone.'

'Alone?! Isn't there someone else I can see? ...'

'You see this dead woman, who is still here because I killed her, and who is waiting here for the time to come for me to bury her, that is all. I am alone and I wish to be alone. Everyone is dead. What more do you want to know?'

'I have come from Santarém ...'

'Santarém is dead too, and Portugal. Here the only living thing is my sin, which God has not yet forgiven, nor do I have hope ...'

'Our religion made hope a virtue.'

'It did.'

'And in this it is different from the others.'

'But is there still anyone in this land who knows it?'

'There are more than there ever were. At least, there are more who know it better.'

'Maybe. God's judgement is past understanding.'

'And His mercy is infinite.'

'But His wrath is implacable, His justice awful.'

'Mercy is greater.'

'Who taught you all that?'

'The Gospels, my own heart, and my mother who explained both to me.'

'Sit here . . . by my side.'

I sat down. The monk took my hand in his and gazed at me with a look in his eyes that no language can express, no brush could paint.

He stayed like that for a while, as if observing me. I saw what was obviously a tear well up, then I saw it recede and his eyes become dry again. I heard him choke back a sigh that came into his throat; I distinctly felt the shudder that ran through his body, but I noticed that he became perfectly calm afterwards.

Then he said to me, in a voice that was sorrowful but placid, without any harshness: 'Do you know the story of the valley?'

'I know everything up to Carlos's departure for Évora.'

'Here is the letter he wrote.'

He took from his breviary a folded packet, yellow with age, stained, one could see, with many tears, some of them still fresh.

'Read it.'

I read it.

This was Carlos's letter.

XLIV

—— ∴ ——

Letter from Carlos to Joaninha (1).

Évora Monte
May 1834

I am writing to you Joana, my sister, my cousin; to you alone.

I cannot and dare not say anything to any other member of my family.

In any case I no longer know who my family are; my head is bewildered and lost in the aberrations of my heart. I went astray because of it, it has ruined me.... Oh, I am sure that I am doomed.

Doomed for everyone, including you. Do not say no: you are kind enough to say no, but don't. You are kind enough not to think it, but you can't help feeling it is true.

I am finished.

And hopelessly, Joana, because my nature is incorrigible. I have too much nervous energy, too much strength of feeling in my heart. It is these excesses that have destroyed me ... and continue to destroy me!

You do not understand this, Joaninha; assuredly you do not understand me, and it is difficult. You are a woman and women do not understand men. I always suspected it and now I am perfectly sure of it. A woman cannot and should not understand a man. Woebetide the one who realizes it!

And so.... When one has to die, better to know what sort of death one is to die than to expire ignorant of the evil that destroyed us.

You are young and inexperienced, your heart is full of delightful illusions. I am going to shatter them before they grow stronger, otherwise they will cloud your reason and make you a blind slave, for ever, of the worst enemy we have: the heart. I want to tell you my story: from it you shall see what a man is worth. Mark you, there are none better than I, and few as good. Imagine what the rest are like!

You are no longer ignorant of the reason why I fled my home: I knew that it was polluted by a great sin and I supposed it to be defiled by a terrible crime. That man, who is my father, I hated him. Now that I know just who he is – God forgive me! – I hate him even more!

As for my grandmother, I supposed her to be an accomplice to the crime; she was only an accessory to the sin. God forgive her, and well He might and should, since He made her so weak. She was to blame for my poor mother's demise because of her unpardonable collusion.

God can and should, I repeat. . . . But what about me? How can I forgive her the colour I feel in my cheeks when I refer to my mother? She has suffered and gone through a great deal, poor creature! Her penance is a martyrdom, her old age a long Calvary and that man who made her sin a ruthless persecutor. But that is all for God to deal with, it is nothing to do with me.

I am a son. My mother died without forgiving, so I cannot forgive either. And who is going to forgive me? No one, nor do I want them to.

Not you, dear sister, no, you must not. Because I loved you with a heart that was no longer mine; I accepted your love when I was not worthy of it, when I could not call it mine. I betrayed you when I loved you, I lied to you when I told you I loved you; I lied to you, I lied to myself and I was not truthful to anyone.

But wait, listen, let me see if I can pick up the thread of this incredible story of mine – incredible to you, really quite simple for anyone who knows a man's heart.

When I left Portugal, I can say that I had not been in love. Childish fancies, social philandering, affairs started out of vanity or nourished by the senses alone, these are not worthy of the name love.

I had not been in love.

There are three sorts of women in this world: the woman one admires, the woman one desires and the woman one loves.

Beauty, wit, grace, spiritual and physical qualities incite admiration.

Certain physical forms and a certain voluptuousness excite desire.

What causes love is not known; sometimes it is all of these, or more than these, or none of them.

I don't know what it is, but I do know that one can admire a woman and not desire her, and that one can desire one and not love her.

Love is not defined and never will be. True love, because the other things are not love.

I lived just a few months in England, but they were the first time I can say I really lived. I was received, by chance, by destiny – by my star, because I still believe in the stars, though I believe in little else in this world –, I was received into the bosom of an elegant family blessed with everything that can bestow distinction in this world.

I was intrigued by those highly civilized customs but at the same time I found them attractive and easily adapted to them. I became accustomed to idling gently in that mild, artificial hothouse atmosphere, without losing my exotic, foreign nature. I was well liked but I did not deserve it. My true spirit and character were not what they were taken for. I lied: men are always lying. I hate lies. I have never willingly lied and yet my whole life is a lie.

So I lied and I was liked because I lied. Good God! Why did truth come from out of your mouth, Lord, and why did you send it to this world?

There were three young ladies in the family. To say that they were the three graces is a tired banality, so trite that it gives no idea of what they were like. Three angels perhaps; I can say angels with greater accuracy. And when, during our long, solitary walks in those permanently green fields and those hills crowned with copses and carpeted with soft grass, their simple, plain, artlessly worn white dresses fluttered in the afternoon breeze . . . and their long ringlets – one had blonde hair, another brown and the third of an indefinable colour – when those long ringlets fell loose from their twisted coil with the evening dew – and I contemplated all three, in that dim, mysterious light, with adoration and pensive devotion – I would sincerely exclaim: You are three angels from heaven and I have to adore you!

And so I adored those three angels, all three, and I could not adore one without adoring the others.

They were fond of me, I am sure of that and oh, I would have to be a monster not to confess with tears of gratitude and remorse that they unwittingly became accustomed to my company and could no longer do without it.

The most difficult, subtle heights of perfection of their very idiosyncratic and expressive language; the most appreciated excellencies of their favourite authors; the difficult spirit and tone of their society, at once so superior and blasé, yet so complete and so organized as to raise life to perfection and free it of material considerations – all this and an indefinable feeling for the genteel which one only acquires with natural tact, it is true, though not with that alone, all this I learned there, from the friendly lessons which I received all the time quite unawares.

If I have any merit I owe it all to them; if I have deserved any recognition in society, I owe that to them also.

You see how I confess my debt; you shall see how I repaid it.

The perfect tone of English society has invented a word that does not exist in other languages, nor can it until civilization has polished them. *To flirt* is an innocent verb which is conjugated by the two sexes and does not mean to *make love* – an absurd, vulgar word I detest. It doesn't mean to 'court'; it means more than being pleasant, less than philandering, creates no obligations, has no consequences; one can start, finish, stop, postpone, continue or discontinue at will and without commitment.

I *flirted*, we *flirted*, they *flirted*. . . .[1]

There is no pleasanter or more agreeable pastime for the spirit than to *flirt* with a charming, elegant English miss. With two the pleasure is angelical. With three it is divine.

For those who are born to it, it is not dangerous. For me that easy feeling soon degenerated into a deeper emotion.

First, came admiration.

And how I admired them, all three, my gentle charmers!

And they were aware of it, they laughed and enjoyed it, delighted to charm me.

They caused me to feel desire!

I thought I was lost and tried to go away.

They refused to let me and made fun of me, of my hot Spanish blood and the violence of my feelings. . . .

In a short while I was passionately in love with one of them. I was very fond of the other two, but love, really to love, soul, as I thought, and heart, I would swear, it was the second, Laura, the loveliest, noblest, most elegant and splendid figure of a woman I think God ever modelled in a moment of genuine artistic inspiration, which He deigned to feel towards the lump of clay He had in His hands when He made her.

XLV

—————— ∴ ——————

Carlos's letter to Joaninha: continuation (2).

LAURA was neither tall nor short; she was well built but not fat, and slim without being thin. Her eyes were of a limpid, pure, velvety hazel; large and vivacious, they looked so regal when they flashed with anger, and so soft when her anger subsided, that it is difficult to decide when they were more beautiful. Her hair was almost the same colour, but had, in addition, a golden shimmer which gleamed, or rather sparkled in the sun, though only occasionally, not all the time, nor in every position of her head, which was small, shaped in the most classical mould of ancient statuary, resting on a truly noble neck, which was in perfect harmony with the line of her shoulders.

Her waist was small and slender, though not exaggeratedly so, and one could see that it was so by nature, without the least artifice. Her foot did not have the fabulously minute dimension common in our peninsula; it was well proportioned like that of the Venus of Medici.

I have seen many more beautiful women, some more adorable, but none so fascinating.

Her face, oval and perfectly symmetrical, pale; only her lips were red like the reddest rose.

The effect of her overall appearance is not possible to describe. Her mouth, which was small and delicate, did not often smile, but when it did, oh! . . .

To see her at a ball, dressed all in white, with a belt of black beads – an invariable toilette for her from a certain date – with no other adornment or flowers, only a long string of pearls spilling about her neck – was to see something loftier and more sublime than just a woman.

Such was Laura. Laura, whom I loved with all the love I had. It was not much, I know that now, but at the time it seemed infinite.

I told her. I told her one day, when we were out walking alone and after we had walked for hours, oblivious of time, without exchanging a word. We were thinking, I about her, I don't know what she was thinking.

About me perhaps?

She was, but she didn't tell me.

And she heard me out without a word, without once looking at me, without removing the hand that I was holding, that I kissed, that felt cold and moist in mine, which were burning.

It was late, we made for home. At the door she told me: 'Don't come in!' And I saw her face was wet with tears. I tried to follow her, but she made an imperious gesture which disconcerted me. For the first time, after so long, I went alone, sadly and gloomily, to my lonely quarters, where I spent the night.

Towards dawn I decided to go to bed. I did not sleep.

The next day I received a letter from Julia: this was the name of the eldest, most compassionate and affectionate of the three sisters.

The note seemed unimportant; there was nothing unusual in the expressions; she asked me to lunch with her. She said nothing about her sisters.

I sensed that my hour had come; I thought I was going to be expelled from that innocent Eden in which I had lived. Julia's handwriting, a pretty, perfect, natural hand, looked to me like a collection of terrible, cabbalistic signs, carrying the secret of my condemnation. I dressed and went. I found myself alone with Julia in the elegant *parlour*★ which was for her exclusive use.

It was a small study, decorated only with a few *étagères*★ with books and music, a harp and an easel.

On the easel was a sketch for my portrait; on the music-stand a French romance for which I had composed lyrics in Portuguese. . . .

The urn was hissing on the table. Julia was making tea and appeared not to be paying attention to anything else.

I have to describe little Julia to you – Juliet, as we called her, her two sisters and I, who vied with each other as to which of us loved her most.

Oh, what sadness and what everlasting regret when I remember those times of fraternal companionship!

Julia was small, very dainty, really like a child in her face and figure, and in the expression and manner of her whole enchanting, diminutive person.

No Englishwoman, since the time of Queen Bess, had so dainty a foot and *ankle*★. None, since King Alfred, attended so elegantly to the elegant occupations of a British interior – a delightful genre picture without parallel.

Lady Julia R. was the smallest and prettiest British subject I think has ever existed. In the moonlight, out in her park, flitting among the few eccentrics who exposed themselves to fresh air during the short English summer, she could easily be taken for the beautiful queen of the fairies, bringing to life Shakespeare's wonderful vision in *A Midsummer Night's Dream*.

Her eyes, which were sky-blue, always moist and gentle; her hair, a light silky brown, worn in loose curls around her head and falling down on to her shoulders and into her face, so that it was a constant struggle to keep it out of her eyes; a graceful body, a mouth made for kisses, small teeth, very white and close together, a small, slender, pale hand – all this made Julia an ideal type of goodness, simplicity and angelic innocence.

And she was an angel . . . oh yes, indeed!

I watched her for a long time in silence; she gave me an occasional sad smile, but said nothing. Eventually we ate and the table was cleared. She told her maid: 'Phoebe, I shall be alone with Carlos and I want to be alone. Not at home for anyone.'

'Yes, madam.' Indispensable answer of an English servant to everything.

And we were left completely alone.

XLVI

———— ·:· ————

Carlos's letter to Joaninha: continuation (3).

J ULIA eventually looked up at me with those moist eyes of hers, which were shaded by the longest, silkiest lashes I have ever seen in a woman, and said: 'Carlos, I am sad. You must comfort me. Say something that will comfort me. Speak to me.'

'What can I say?'

'You are a gentleman, Carlos. Tell me that you are and lift this burden of fear from me.'

'Do you doubt it, Julia?'

'No, I do not. We are all very fond of you here – much too much, I'm afraid. How could we doubt you?'

'Oh, Julia, forgive me!' I burst out, throwing myself at her feet, taking both her hands in mine and kissing them over and over again in an absolute paroxysm of remorse. 'Forgive me, Julia. I know I have done wrong and I promise...'

'Do not promise anything, except that you will be a gentleman. That I know and feel you can do.'

'I swear it for ... for her sake.'

'Her?! ... She loves you, Carlos. It is better to speak the truth at once and face all the consequences of a difficult situation than delude ourselves and still not avoid them. Laura loves you, but she must not and cannot love you. If she were free, I do not know what I would say ... what I would do. ... But I am not the one concerned,' she went on quickly and agitatedly, 'I am not involved, Carlos, it is she. Laura cannot love you, she is engaged. She is leaving for India three months from now.'

'For India?!'

'Yes, it is true, as you shall see. Her fiancé is a captain in the India Company and she will leave when they marry.'

I felt my heart dying inside my breast: it was the first time I really felt the pangs of love.... It was the first sincere love in my life and it was also the first time I was going through the agonizing pains of love.

I who had always made fun of such pains, who relegated them from reality to the world of novels, I!... Oh, what poet or novelist ever succeeded in depicting suffering such as I experienced at that moment?

I don't know what I did or what I said. All I remember is feeling Julia's tears fall on to my cheek and mingle with my own, which flowed abundantly. I looked up at her and the expression I saw in her eyes. ... Oh, how can I ever forget it?

All the loving kindness and compassion of the female heart's infinite store poured from those heavenly eyes to comfort me. Nothing was left in them except a profound, disconsolate, mortal sadness!...

At that moment a vague thought, an insane idea, or rather a confused, obscure premonition crossed my mind – or was it my heart?... What if Julia?... But that is not possible.

'Julia! Julia!' I cried out. 'I want to see her. I must see her just once. Do not deny me this last favour. I know I must, I need to, have to keep away from her. But first I must tell her...'

'What?...'

'That I love her as I never loved before and as I shall never love again...'

'Oh, Carlos!'

'That I shall always, always....'

Julia stood up without a word and, giving me a look of ineffable compassion, quickly left the room.

I was left alone. I do not know what I thought or if I thought. My head felt stunned, my heart exhausted – my mind was in a state of depression bordering on stupidity. If someone had pointed a pistol at my breast I should not have raised an arm to push it away ... I no longer felt pain or desire. I felt as if I was starting to die and I thought that dying would not be difficult.

I do not know how long I stayed like that, not very long. I was aware that the door was being opened, but I did not have the strength to look up. Until I felt a dear, sweet hand in mine. ... It was Julia ... and Laura too – God in heaven! – who were both at my side.

Julia held my hand in hers and Laura, leaning on her sister's shoulder, looked down on me with those eyes whose usual severity had given way to such sweet tenderness and such heavenly compassion that I swear to God at that moment I firmly believed I had before me two of his angels, come down on the wings of divine pity to bring me all the forgiveness, bring my soul all the mercy of heaven.

How shall I tell you, Joana, dearest Joaninha, how shall I tell you who love me and whom I love, because I do love you and, God punish me as he must, I love you blindly with this abominablc, infamous heart He has given me – how shall I tell you, and for what purpose, the words we spoke, the pledges I made, the vows that were sworn, the promises that were exchanged?

Julia went over to the window – an indulgent chaperone who did not watch us and feigned not to hear us. The day went by that way, a long June day that seemed too short and swift to us. It was dark when we went to have dinner.

Laura came to table in travelling clothes: she was leaving that night for Wales, where she had a friend with whom she was to stay until the terrible day and to prepare for it, as she told me, far away from me, in the bosom of friendship.

That meal can be imagined. We did not even pretend to eat. When we rose from table, we found the coach at the door, with the coachman up front and the servant by the carriage door. We got in, the three sisters and I.

It was two miles to the inn, where the mail coach stopped and where Laura was to meet it. We travelled them without any of us uttering a word.

A big beautiful moon moved, with its cold, melancholy light, through a cloudless sky. It was one of those superb, rare nights of the short British summer.

The crunch of the sand under the tread of the coach wheels on the smooth alleys of the park; the low branches of the trees, which we brushed against as we passed; the tame deer, which stood up to watch us; the pheasants, which got up in their low flight from thicket to thicket at the sound of the whip, which the coachman used more to restrain than to incite the horses – these were all impressions which held for me an inexplicable sadness I had never felt before. My soul went out to it all; I felt my happiness leave me for ever and it was I who was throwing it away and would be left alone and abandoned, an outcast in life's desert.

I had not the strength to blaspheme, to curse God, otherwise I would have done it.

I would. Although my life has been tormented by more grievous, deathly agony, on no other occasion have I felt so ready to deny God and to cease believing in Him.

It may have been a result of His inexhaustible pity, which resolved to come to my soul's aid before it damned itself; it must have been, at that very moment I distinctly saw before my soul's eyes the only image that could call it back from the abyss: it was yours, Joana! It was my Joaninha, little and innocent; that little angel child, so fresh, gay and sweet, whom I had left playing in our valley: our rustic valley, so rough and unsophisticated! Oh, how strongly I was hit by the nostalgia I felt for it in the midst of those perfect, well-behaved beauties of British culture! The green rays of our eyes, sparkling like emeralds, came across space and began to shine among those other fires that blinded me. The wild rock-rose and the bristly gorse of our heathland wafted to me from afar their rustic perfume which overwhelmed the sweet, pleasant, grassy smell of these evergreen lawns that surrounded me. The coarse, dry, whitish leaves of our olive trees seemed to shine at me among the serried masses of the luxurious northern vegetation, promising me peace for my heart and announcing to me the end of the conflict in which it was being torn to shreds by passion.

And you, Joana, you poor, innocent, hapless child, you appeared to me in the midst of all this, stretching out to me your sweet loving arms, as on the day when I said goodbye to you in that bitter-sweet vale of my tears and laughter, where I was to live the few moments of real happiness in my life and where the real torments of my soul were destined to cut it short and destroy it for ever. . . .

Oh, of what stuff is a man made and how is he fashioned? Why and what does he live for? What have I, and all of us, come into this world for?

Sitting there on the silk cushions of that splendid, comfortable carriage, in the company of three divine women, who all cared for me and whom I mixed together in a mysterious, mystic adoration, blinded by passionate love for one of them, at the very moment when I was about to say farewell to her for ever . . . my thoughts were concentrated on a child who was still carried in people's arms! When I looked into the grey eyes of Laura, whom I adored, it was your green eyes I saw in my heart! My senses were altogether intoxicated with that luxurious, civilized perfume that was about me, but it was our wild, rustic valley that I felt in my heart. . . .

Oh, I am a monster, truly a moral aberration, or I don't know what I am.

Can all men be like that?

Perhaps they are and do not say so.

Joana, my Joana, my dearest Joaninha, my adorable angel, have pity on me, do not curse me. I do not want you to forgive me, neither you nor anyone else, because I do not deserve it. But I want you to be sorry for me and have pity on me.

Ah, that I do deserve. Oh, I do!

I must stop here. I have not the courage to continue looking at myself in this awful moral mirror in which I swore to examine myself as a form of self-punishment and from which I am copying the dreadful portrait of my soul that I am setting down on this paper.

I knew I was a monster, but I had not examined in detail all the hideousness I now find in my features.

I am shocked and horrified by myself.

XLVII

—————— ·:· ——————

Carlos's letter to Joaninha: continuation (4).

W E arrived at the inn, a gloomy, solitary house in the heart of the countryside, at the roadside. The mail coach arrived almost simultaneously.

I handed Laura out of the carriage and into the coach and we had time for only a nervous handshake and to say Goodbye! Goodbye! with the affected coolness demanded by the laws of British convention.

The mail left at a brisk pace. . . . And shall I tell you the truth, or would you rather I lie to you? No, I shall tell you the truth. Well, I felt a desperate relief, a cruel comfort at seeing her go. I felt what I imagine a patient must feel after a painful operation to amputate a part of his body which he could not keep, which he had to lose or lose his life.

Death must be like that too: an apathetic, empty quietude after indescribable suffering.

It was like being dead, so I did not suffer.

And I no longer thought of you, I no longer saw you inside my heart: I did not exist, I was just there.

We returned to the park. I helped my two gentle companions down silently and wént alone on foot, with a firm, resolute step, to my living quarters. Neither of them attempted to stop me, or said anything, or tried to comfort me. What for?

Lord William R. was due next morning from one of his habitual outings to London. He came to see me the moment he arrived and brought me letters from Portugal, which I had been expecting for some time. He told me he was leaving next day for Swansea, the town in Wales where Laura had gone, and that he wished me to keep his daughters company, since they would be alone.

Me! . . .

I did not see them for three days: all I did those three days was write to Laura.

On the fourth day I went to the park. Julia gave a cry of delight when she saw me: a rare example of an exception to the rules laid down to tyrannize English life, prescribing even the facial expression one should die with and measuring the tone in which one should breathe one's last sigh.

But nature occasionally manages to triumph even over British etiquette.

Julia thought that I did not wish to go back to the house: she had resigned herself to not seeing mc again and was unable to restrain the pleasure my unexpected appearance gave her.

We spent the whole day alone together, most of it strolling in the park or sitting in the shadow of its dense coppices, or looking at our reflections in the glassy waters of an enormous dam, inhabited by water-fowl and surrounded by those enormous carpets of green velvet with which the English countryside is perpetually adorned and which disappear only when the winter comes and lays its sheets of snow over them.

She asked to see what I was writing to her sister. I gave her the letter, she read it, mused over it and gave it back to me without a word.

The hours we spent in that silence, that eloquent speechlessness which occurs when the heart feels too strongly and we would say too much if we said anything at all!

That night, when we took leave of one another, she gave me a net pouch which Laura had been making for me and had left for her to give me. I felt something inside the pouch, but decided not to look inside. When I arrived home I discovered that it was the *lucky belt* with black beads I had much admired at a certain ball to which we had gone together, and which Laura had never failed to put on whenever she wore white and dressed for an occasion.

I still have it, that precious belt, Joana; I still have it among my most secret treasures, that gem, that relic. And I love you, and you alone, as I truly never loved anyone nor shall ever love again. But that belt is a charm, a talisman, an amulet which contains my destiny....

I have loved ... that is to say, I have loved.... All right, then, I have loved, since there is no other word in these stupid languages that men speak, I have loved other women, and on occasions when I felt more passionate about them, I never failed to kiss that belt with devotion, to press it to my heart, to commend myself to it – like a Neapolitan footpad commending himself to the image of the Madonna he wears on his breast, with hands stained with blood or carrying the objects he has just stolen.

Ah, Joana, didn't I tell you that I am doomed, irremediably, and that there is and can be no salvation for me, ever?

I lived like that for two months. Laura did not write to me: she received my letters and wrote to Julia in answer; that way we corresponded. Julia was a part of us; she was a part of our love, we lived our life through her. And I soon mingled the two of them in my heart to such an extent that I caught myself not knowing which of them I loved more. Julia seemed happy with this situation; I certainly was. Without noticing, I grew accustomed to it and stopped longing for the past. And when the date of Laura's wedding approached, when she had to return from Wales and I, faithful to my promise, was to allege very urgent business in London which would oblige me to be away until her departure for India, I was so sorry and found it so difficult to keep to my promise, that I felt ashamed.

I left, however, and stayed there a month. Julia wrote to me every day and I to her. On the eve of the fatal day when Laura was to belong to another man, Julia wrote me these words, nothing more: 'Our romance is over; a serious story is beginning. Laura sends you her last farewell.'

And Laura's name was never again mentioned between us, either in letters or by word of mouth.

The galleon that carried the ruins of all my hopes to the East had sailed away already; October came and the English winter with its harsh and that year precocious rigours. I felt as if I should die of sadness and loneliness in the heart of the busy life and crowds of London. Julia sensed it and wrote inviting me to return to ——shire. I went back.

XLVIII

———— ·:· ————

Carlos's letter to Joaninha: conclusion (5).

IMAGINE what I felt, when, despite their being deformed by the three layers of snow that covered them, I began to recognize the places in the vicinity of the park and to place the trees, the meadows and the farms in the neighbourhood!

The physiognomy of the countryside was different, but its beloved features were the same and I distinguished them one by one.

Eventually my stage-coach stopped at the entrance to the park and I set off on foot up the long avenue. It was nine o'clock on a cold, misty morning, but the weather was mild, not *raw*, to use the vivid local expression.

Surrounded by the fog that concealed the old mansion and cloaked the trees on either side with a melancholy, grey shroud, I walked on, almost feeling my way, about half the length of the avenue.

I stopped to reflect on my situation and what place I would occupy in that house which was about to open its hospitable door to me once more, when, through the whitening mist, just where it was less dense, I made out a shape coming towards me from between the trees.

It was the figure of a woman and looked like a shade, a fantastic apparition in the midst of that sad, lonely, mysterious scene.

At a distance, it seemed too tall: it was not Julia, it couldn't be – Julia, the most diminutive, daintiest of all the pretty, charming fairies that have ever carried a wand. Laura . . . ah, Laura was so far away! . . . Who could it be? It could only be. . . . Who?

That elegance, that loose, curling hair, that graceful bearing could only be hers. . . .

But who is 'she'?

I have scarcely mentioned, as yet, the last of the three beautiful

239

sisters who enchanted me. I haven't described her to you; I haven't mentioned her to you by name. It irks me to do so. But it has to be. I find it difficult, but there is no way out. It was Georgina.

Georgina, whom you know, who. . . . It was Georgina who came towards me on that – fatal or fortunate? – morning; Georgina who, of the three, was the one who talked least to me, the one I really knew least.

This heart of mine, as a result of being wounded and inadequately cured, senses and divines changes in the weather from a chronic pain I feel. I divined something indefinable when I saw Georgina approach.

'How good of you to come! I am very happy to see you. And Julia, poor Julia, will be so pleased? She will be completely cured.'

'Why? Is Julia ill?'

'You didn't know?! . . . Ah, of course not, she did not want to tell you. Julia is sick, but it is not serious. But I still wanted to warn you, before you see her, which is why I gauged the time of the coach and came to wait for you here.'

Her words were simple, there was nothing in them to make any untoward impression on me, and yet I felt excited in a way I had never been before. I looked at Georgina as if I were seeing her for the first time, and was amazed to see how beautiful she was.

This is an emotional condition I do not think poets and novelists have yet described; perhaps they ignore it, or maybe they do not recognize it. It is received knowledge that immediate impressions caused by a first meeting are the most interesting and the most poetical.

I do not deny the dramatic effect of these sudden first feelings, but I maintain that there is more interest in that strange, unexpected impression made on us by a previously known object, which we had looked on with indifference until the moment when it suddenly reveals itself to us quite different from what we had always supposed. . . .

But this woman is really beautiful! And I never noticed! But what divine eyes! Where have mine been all this time? But this bearing, these good looks, where has she been hiding them? Etc. etc.

Gradually, little by little, one finds more perfections, more charms, and the resultant feeling is a thousand times more profound, especially more solid, than those much sung and celebrated first impressions.

What more can I tell you after this? We went into the house, I saw Julia, we talked a great deal of Laura. But I no longer talked with the passion, with the exclusive admiration of before. . . .

Julia soon recovered her health and with it her emotional balance. All the pleasure, all the charm of our close conversations and our long walks was resumed. Laura was remembered with nostalgia, but it was a nostalgia that gradually became milder and less acute.

Georgina, who until then seemed to have done her best to be overshadowed by her sister, now that she was no longer there shone with all her brilliance, in attractiveness and intelligence, as a result of her simple, honest nature, an exquisite gentleness of manner, of voice, of facial expression, of everything.

Julia was extremely fond of her and I came to adore her. Eternal shame on me! But it is true: I was more in love with her than with Laura, or so it seemed to me . . . which is the same.

How do I know? . . . No, I was not as much in love, but I loved her.

I loved, I did, and I was loved!

My happiness lasted three months. It is the longest period of happiness I can count in my life. False happiness, but it was happiness.

The tyrannical law of honour obliged us to separate and me to leave for the Azores. I went. No one sacrificed more, no one gave as much as I did for that expedition. History will chronicle many services, many acts of dedication. Who will ever know of mine?

History is a fool.

I cannot open a history book without laughing. Particularly at the historians' cogitations and surmises, which I find irresistibly comic. What do they know of the causes, the motives, the value and importance of almost all the facts they recount?

I still do not know how I left, how I arrived, how I lived those first weeks of my stay on that rock in the middle of the sea called Terceira Island, where the unhappy remains of the constitutional army had taken refuge.

I eventually grew accustomed to it. To what does man not grow accustomed?

One afternoon I was taken to the grille of a nuns' convent there. My sad, absent, indifferent manner aroused the compassion of the good nuns. One of them, who was young, ardent and passionate, decided to undertake the mission of comforting me. She did not succeed, poor girl! My heart was in ——shire, in England; it was in India; it was in the vale of Santarém, 'In pieces scattered round the world',[1] it was everywhere except there, where none of it was or could be.

The little nun's name was Soledade and she stayed as solitary as her name. The gossips, who are never missing, said all they wanted, but they lied, as they nearly always do, and they were wrong, as they always are. I did not love Soledade.

Nevertheless I remember her with compassion and friendliness . . . I am made that way, my God, and I shall die the same!

We came to Portugal. The remainder of my story you already know.

I finally came to our valley. I became oblivious of all the past the moment I saw you. I fell in love with you. . . . No, that is not true. I realized, the moment I saw you among those trees, in the starlight, I realized that it was you I had always loved, that I was born to love you and that I should be yours alone if I still had a heart to give you, if my soul was capable and worthy of being united with the angelic soul that dwells in you.

It is not, Joana, as you see and I see; you feel it and so do I.

I was really born to enjoy the comforts of domestic peace and happiness; I was brought up, I am sure, for the tranquil glory and modest delights of a good family man.

But my star did not wish it to be so. My imagination became intoxicated with poetry and lost its way; I cannot go back. The woman who loves me will inevitably be unhappy; she who puts her fate in my hands is bound to see it ruined. I do not want, cannot and must not love anyone again.

Shame and sorrow have found their way into the heart of our family. I renounce for ever the domestic hearth, everything I desired and everything I can desire. May God punish me if He dare commit an injustice, because I did not make myself what I am; I did not shape my destiny and the fate that pursues me is not of my making.

Goodbye, Joana; goodbye, cousin; goodbye, beloved sister! Stay and look after our grandmother and comfort that poor wretch who is the author of his and our misfortunes. Do it, because you can; and forget me.

And I – who can no longer die, because I see this war end unfortunately at the very moment when I could bless it, when it could give me the happiness of a bullet through the heart –, what shall I do? I think I shall become a politician: talk a lot about my country, which does not matter to me; denounce the ministers, whoever they may be; prate about the services I have rendered, which were never given willingly; and – who knows? – perhaps I shall end up a capitalist, which is the only sort of life left with any excitement for someone who can no longer have any other.

Goodbye, my Joana, my adored Joana; for the last time, goodbye!

XLIX

———— ∴ ————

How Carlos became a baron. – The end of Joaninha's story.
– Georgina an abbess. – Friar Dinis's opinion on the
question of monks and barons. – Cannot go back to the
way it was, but still less can it stay the way it is. – What is to
be, God knows and will ordain. – The author goes on to
Cartaxo to spend the night. – A dream he has there. – He
returns to Lisbon. – Railways and paper. – End of his
travels and of this book.

I finished reading Carlos's letter and handed it back to Friar
Dinis in silence. By way of reply, he said: 'You read it?'

'Yes.'

'What more do you want to know? I feel I can tell you
everything. I do not know you, but...'

'But you must recognize in me a man with a keen interest
in...'

'In what? Elections, financial speculation, national assets?'

'No, sir. I was one of Carlos's comrades. I have not seen him
for several years and...'

'You would not even know him if you saw him now! He has
grown fat, rich and become a baron!'

'A baron?'

'He is a baron and any day now he will be a member of
parliament.'

'What a transformation! How on earth did that happen?! And
Joaninha and Georgina?'

'Joaninha went mad and died. Georgina is the abbess of a
convent in England.'

'Abbess?'

'Yes. She was converted to Catholicism. She was wealthy, so
she founded a convent in ——shire and she is there in the service
of God.'

'And this poor lady, Joaninha's grandmother?'

'She is here just as you see her, she is dead to the world. She neither sees nor hears, she does not speak and recognizes no one. Joaninha came to die here in this fatal house in the valley. I was away, she died in her grandmother's and Georgina's arms. From that moment on, the old lady sank into this condition. She is dead and all I am waiting here for is her physical dissolution so that I can bury her, providing I do not go first, which God forbid! Who would look after her, who would show kindness to the poor, demented old lady? But afterwards ... oh, afterwards, I hope in the Lord, that He will be moved, at last, by all my suffering and take me unto Him.'

'What about Carlos?'

'Carlos is a baron. Did I not tell you already?'

'And because he is a baron? . . .'

'Do you not know what it means to be a baron?'

'Oh, I know! Are there so few of them?'

'Well, the baron is the successor of the . . .'

'The monk. . . . An awful substitute!'

'I saw one of those liberal broadsheets which said that, but it is the only one of those things I have read, years ago. Yet I was given it to read.'

'And what did you think of it?'

'Well written and partly true. We were to blame, certainly, but the liberals were no less.'

'We have both made mistakes.'

'Yes, and they are irreparable. Society is no longer what it was, it cannot go back to the way it was, but still less can it stay the way it is. What is going to happen, I do not know. God will ordain.'

With these words the monk crossed himself, picked up his breviary and began to read. The old woman carried on and on with her winding. I got up and watched the two of them for a few seconds. Neither of them paid any attention to me, nor did they seem conscious of my being there.

I felt as if I were in the presence of death and it scared me.

I made the effort to move, went resolutely to my horse, mounted, spurred him impatiently and did not stop until Cartaxo.

I found my companions there. It was late and we went to stay outside the town, at the hospitable house of Senhor L.S.

We laughed and made merry until late that night and slept the remainder of it like logs.

But I dreamed about the monk, the old woman and an enormous constellation of barons, shining in a paper sky, from which, like snowflakes in a polar night, rained down blue, green, white, yellow notes, notes of all possible shades and colours. There were millions and millions...

I never saw so many millions and never heard of such wealth, except in the *Arabian Nights*.

I woke up next day and did not see a thing.... Only some poor people begging at the door. I put my hand in my pocket and all I found was notes ... pieces of paper!

I left for Lisbon, my mind full of ominous feelings, forebodings and gloomy premonitions. The steamer was almost empty, but did not travel any faster for that. It was past five in the afternoon when we disembarked at the Terreiro do Paço.

So ended our journey to Santarém and so ends this book.

I have seen some parts of the world and recorded something of what I saw. Of all my travels, however, those which have interested me most were still my travels in my homeland.

If you think the same, benevolent reader, who knows, maybe I shall once more take up my pilgrim's staff and go wandering around this Portugal of ours, in search of stories to tell you.

On the barons' railways I swear I shall not travel. My oath is unnecessary, though. If the railways were of paper, they would make them, I do not deny. But of metal?!

Let the government be sensible and make them of stone, which it can, and we shall travel, with great pleasure and to our great advantage and benefit, in our good land.

NOTES

*The author's notes included in the sequence below
are indicated by the appended initials A.G.*

INTRODUCTION

1   Garrett's father was António Bernardo da Silva, his mother Ana Augusta de Almeida Leitão, whence his own surname da Silva Leitão, following normal Portuguese practice. There was nothing, however, to prevent him including Almeida (though he chose to reverse the order) and adding Garrett, the name of his paternal grandmother. He appears to have done this while a student in Coimbra, for by 1822 his name is given in the complete form in the government gazette. The writer was born in Oporto, in 1799, of a well-to-do family who lost most of their possessions in Portugal when they were forced to flee to the Azores at the time of the French invasion.

2   Since Pedro was Emperor of Brazil, he almost immediately abdicated in favour of his seven-year-old daughter, who became queen as Maria II, marrying her uncle, Dom Miguel.

3   The *Foreign Quarterly Review*, no. XX (October 1932), published an outline, with English translations, of Garrett's poem.

4   For information on this complex period in Portuguese history the reader may consult: A. H. de Oliveira Marques, *History of Portugal*, New York and London: Columbia University Press, 2 vols, 1972.

5   The term 'baron' does not, I think, necessarily imply elevation to the peerage. Garrett clearly refers to the *arriviste* opportunists who gain most from revolutionary situations without having shared the ideals in whose name they grow rich, or, at least, having rapidly exchanged them for material advancement. The word is also chosen because it occurs in the first line of *The Lusiads* in its other meaning of 'man of courage': there are enough references to Portugal's national epic in *Travels* to draw attention to the irony.

6   'As Viagens na Minha Terra e a Menina des Rouxinóis', Lisbon, Colóquio/Letras, no. 51, 15–24.

7   In *Almeida Garrett: L'Intime contrainte*, Paris: Didier, 1966.

For useful general information in English on Garrett, Herculano and some of their contemporaries, the reader may consult Anthony Thorlby (ed.), *The Penguin Companion to Literature*, vol. 2, European.

CHAPTER I

1   Terreiro do Paço: when downtown Lisbon was rebuilt after the 1755 earthquake, the square fronting the Tagus was renamed Praça do

Comércio, but the original name has prevailed in general use. Because of the equestrian statue of King José, it used to be known to English people as Black Horse Square.

2 *Dedução Cronológica*: literally 'Chronological Deduction', an attack on the Jesuits attributed to José Seabra e Silva, one of the Marquis of Pombal's ministers, and published in 1768.

3 Bordas-d'Água (literally, Water's Edge or Riverside): a popular name for part of the Ribatejo province, more specifically the meadowlands of the alluvial plains in the vicinity of the River Tagus. By extension the expression is (or was) interchangeable with Ribatejo.

4 An obvious allusion to Xavier de Maistre's popular and inimitable opuscule *Voyage autour de ma chambre*, which was certainly begun in Turin and is supposed by many to have been completed in St Petersburg. – A.G. (The epigraph preceding the present chapter is the opening paragraph of de Maistre's work.)

5 The friend was the politician Passos Manuel (Manuel da Silva Passos, 1801–62) and the invitation was contained in a letter dated 6 July 1843.

6 This is historical fact: it is also true that it was largely responsible for the brutal persecution suffered by the author a few months later. – A.G.

7 'Regata' [*sic*] was the name given, and perhaps still used, in Venice for boat-racing competitions with bets laid. The word and the practice were introduced into England, where it is fashionable and highly popular. – A.G.

8 A metal foundry whose most famous piece of work was probably the casting of the equestrian statue mentioned in n. 1 above. Garrett clearly preferred the pre-Pombaline, more popular eastern area of the city with the view of Alfama from the river.

9 A third-rate heroic poem by Father José Agostinho de Macedo (1761–1831), based on the same subject as Camoens's famous epic *The Lusiads*, which it was meant to supersede.

10 After the 'Vilafrancada' of 1823 (see p. 8), the town's name was changed for a time to Vila Franca da Restauração.

11 *campino*: the word used for the bull-herders of the Ribatejo, especially those from the Vilafranca area, who also take part in the bullfights.

12 cf. Horace, *Odes*, bk I, ode 1: 'pulverem olympicum/collegisse'.

13 Bullfighting expressions used in the *pega*, a part of the entertainment in which one of a group of *forcados*, as they are called, checks the bull's charge, head on, by hurling himself between the animal's horns, at which moment the bull is held fast by the other members of the group, to allow their comrade to extricate himself.

14 *saloio*: name by which the peasants from the outskirts of Lisbon were known.

CHAPTER II

1 Garrett is presumably having a little innocent fun at Hegel's expense.

2 Manuel Álvaro Pegas, a seventeenth-century Portuguese jurist and

author of a book of commentaries on statute laws.

3 *Palito Métrico* (literally, 'Metrical Toothpick'): a book of macaronic verses about student life at Coimbra University, dating back to the middle of the eighteenth century. The mule referred to is the one on which the freshman student rode to Coimbra in order to matriculate.

CHAPTER III

1 A novel by the French author Eugène Sue, published in 1842 and translated soon afterwards into Portuguese (1843–6).

2 These lines are a sort of parody on the famous fragments of Alcaeus, the only record of which is preserved in the commentaries of Eustatius. The lovely fragment in question is translated in my *Flores sem fruto*. – A.G. (Bk I, poem xiv, 'A espada do poeta', i.e. 'The Poet's Sword'.)

3 The reports of the commissions of inquiry, in the last eight to ten years, on the conditions of the working and poor classes in England are absolute proof of the fine estimates made by political economy, a science which I trust to God will soon be discredited. – A.G.

4 In a note Garrett gives a Portuguese version of the lines, which he identifies as being from *Hamlet*.

5 Famous Lisbon café of the period, the haunt of intellectuals and *littérateurs*.

6 'Chourineur', 'Fleur de Marie' – well-known characters from the very popular novel by Eugène Sue, *Les Mystères de Paris*. – A.G.

7 As happens with various other places in the text, Garrett evidently intended to include an explanatory note in a subsequent edition. Unfortunately he went no further than indicating such references in his own copy of the first edition. The present one is obscure.

8 Presumably because the Portuguese form of the anchorite's name, Pacómio, reminded Garrett of the word *pacóvio*, which means a simpleton and thus corresponds to the initial reaction.

9 The reference seems to be to the end of the first act of Molière's play, where M. de Pourceaugnac is subjected to treatment with detergents.

CHAPTER IV

1 Addison, the poet, was one of Queen Anne's ministers and a member of the famous cabinet known as 'All isits' [*sic*]. – A.G.

2 Abbreviation of *dialectus poetica vetera* used in dictionary definitions.

CHAPTER V

1 This forest, planted on the orders of King Dinis (late thirteenth century), stretches from Azambuja to Cartaxo and was famous for the robber bands who infested it as late as the early nineteenth century.

2   Character in Portuguese folk tales, an exaggerated form of Simple Simon.

3   Melodrama by Benjamin Autier *et al.* (1823), whose characters include outlaws.

4   The 1838 Constitution, which lasted for four years, was a compromise between the progressive 1822 Constitution and so-called Charter of 1826, essentially a king's charter, which re-established royal power and the position of the traditionally privileged classes.

5   The horse of the Spanish warrior-knight, El Cid.

CHAPTER VI

1   See ch. I n. 9 above.

2   i.e. in episcopal robes.

3   Title of an important anthology of seventeenth-century Portuguese poetry in the baroque or mannerist style.

4   Important figure in masonic hierarchy.

5   Literally, 'if it is permissible to compare small things with large' (Virgil, *Georgics*, bk IV, l. 176).

6   Canidia is described in *The Oxford Companion to English Literature* as 'a Neapolitan courtesan whom Horace once loved, and whom, after her desertion of him, he holds up to contempt as a sorceress'.

7   Popular form of the common Portuguese given name Manuel. Alfama is the old part of Lisbon, now inhabited mainly by the poorer classes.

8   Name by which the eighteenth-century poet Bocage was known in the literary academy context of the period (see n. 13 below).

9   Name of a sixteenth-century Italian literary academy.

10   References to Aeneas's visit to the underworld in bk VI of the *Aeneid*.

11   Cândido José Xavier Dias da Silva (1769–1833), a liberal general and politician belonging to the opposite faction from Garrett.

12   For the benefit of provincial readers: one of Lisbon's cemeteries, called 'Prazeres' [i.e. pleasures, delights] because of a shrine to Our Lady which existed there before the site was given over to its present use. The coincidence of the name is remarkable. – A.G.

13   António Dinis da Cruz e Silva (1731–99), a founder member of the Arcádia Lusitana, one of the leading eighteenth-century literary academies in Portugal.

14   In the text 'Ricardo Smith'. Did Garrett really mean Richard Smith, who was a military engineer and still alive at the time? Or is there a confusion, possibly intentional, between Adam Smith and David Ricardo?

CHAPTER VII

1   Both references are to theatres: Porte Saint-Martin (in the Boulevard St Martin) was the stronghold of French romantic theatre in the 1830s; Lisbon's Rua dos Condes was the site of a theatre whose repertoire

consisted mainly of translations of French plays.

2   *Alfacinhas*, the nickname given to inhabitants of Lisbon.

3   The political newspaper *Revolução de Setembro*.

4   The local blacksmith was called J(oaquim) P(edro).

5   It is easy to see that the speaker knew of the curious character in the Constable's story not from the chronicles but from the drama which bears his name. – A.G. (Garrett is alluding to his own play, *O Alfageme de Santarém ou a Espada do Condestável* [The Armourer from Santarém or the Constable's Sword], published in 1842 [see Introduction, p. 11]. The Constable was Nun'Álvares Pereira [late fourteenth century to early fifteenth century].)

6   Garrett is presumably punning on various similar words with the initial element 'mirme-', from the Greek *myrmex* (=ant).

7   Members of the constitutionalist party in post-1815 France, whose object was to reconcile authority with liberty, and royalty with national representation.

CHAPTER VIII

1   Writers in the bucolic style: Rodrigues Lobo (1580–1622), Portuguese; Salomon Gessner (1730–88), Swiss.

CHAPTER IX

1   Figueiredo (1726–1801), a member of the Arcádia Lusitana (see ch. VII n. 13 above), hoped to reform the national theatre with his plays. In so far as this reform was achieved, it is owed entirely to Garrett.

2   The expression means something like 'to travel the highways and byways'.

3   This was the derisory name given in Portugal to the French general Loison, who had only one arm. – A.G.

4   The convent of this name in Paris is an establishment for the education of aristocratic young ladies and also for the reclusion of older ladies. – A.G.

CHAPTER X

1   The untitled sixteenth-century sentimental novel by Bernardim Ribeiro, sometimes known as the *Livro de Saudades* (Book of Sad Memories), but better known, from its opening words, as *Menina e Moça* (When I Was a Young Girl). The allusion to the nightingale, later in the chapter, is taken from chapter II of Ribeiro's novel (see also Introduction, p. 11).

2   i.e. *tout fait*, which Garrett translates literally into Portuguese.

CHAPTER XI

1 The passage occurs in the section entitled 'Montriul' (p. 47 in the Camden Classics edition). Garrett stops short of the closing line, 'But in saying this, – sure I am commending the passion, – not myself.', which he might have included to advantage! The words or phrases in square brackets are not in the English original but appear in the Portuguese version, which is presumably Garrett's.

2 A reference to the recent death of his second wife, Adelaide, who left him with a baby daughter.

3 António Ferreira, who lived at the end of the last century and beginning of this one, modelled in clay with the same charm and Flemish naturalness as are found in the painting of the Morgado de Setubal: his little figures are as much admired by connoisseurs as the finest Sèvres or old Saxon *biscuits*★. – A.G.

CHAPTER XII

1 The fable concerning that immortal bird originated in Europe's dark ages when Greek was unknown. What the ancients said about the *phenix*, Greek for 'palm tree', our barbarous ancestors took to be about a bird the former had never dreamt of. – A.G.

CHAPTER XIII

1 *Le juif errant* (1844–5).

CHAPTER XXI

1 i.e. absolutist (supporter of Dom Miguel).

CHAPTER XXVI

1 'I was strolling along the Via Sacra, as is my wont,/Thinking some nonsense or other.'

2 The chronicle of King Fernando (reigned 1367–83) was the work of Fernão Lopes (fifteenth century). Duarte Nunes de Leão was a sixteenth-century historian and grammarian who published his *Crónicas dos Reis de Portugal* (Chronicles of the Kings of Portugal) in 1600.

3 A collection of ancient Germanic rhapsodies, containing the fantasy and poetry of their origins, being for the Teutonic nations the same as the *Iliad* for the Hellenic peoples. What is not known is the name of the German Homer who wrote them down and compiled them as they are today. – A.G.

4   Name of a shallow part of Tagus bordering the beach at Santos, where the carcasses of old, worn-out ships are left to rot. – A.G.

5   In a note Garrett explains the meaning of the word 'fender'.

6   There has been much argument about the alcoholic drink mentioned so frequently with this name by Shakespeare. The most widely held opinion is that it was good old French brandy. – A.G.

7   The war-cry used by all Spanish Christian nations was 'St James!'. When Portugal became allied to England at the time of the accession of the house of Avis, we began to invoke the name of St George. – A.G.

8   i.e. the Paris cemetery where the tomb of Héloise and Abelard is located.

9   Garrett starts reading at stanza 84, where Camoens begins the narration of Vasco da Gama's embarkation. For an accessible English version (in prose), see *The Lusiads*, translated by W. C. Atkinson (Penguin, 1952; 1980); the part in question begins on p. 117.

10   First King of Portugal as Afonso I (reigned 1139–85).

11   A simple, original phrase used by the pious archbishop in an invitation to a friend. The phrase has duly become proverbial. – A.G. (It is not, however, listed in dictionaries. Fr Bartolomeu [1514–90] was Dominican Archbishop of Braga, in northern Portugal.)

CHAPTER XXVII

1   Fr Gil (*c.* 1190–1265) graduated in medicine at the University of Paris, where he also took his doctorate in theology. He entered the Dominican order after a life of licentiousness.

2   i.e. related to the period of Spanish domination of Portugal (1580–1640) by the Philips.

3   Literally, 'Tower of the Marrows', because the church bells are encased in marrow-shaped clay cups meant to increase their sound.

CHAPTER XXVIII

1   Passeio Público, or public promenade, a very fashionable area of Lisbon in Garrett's time, was situated in roughly the same place as the modern Praça dos Restauradores, at the lower end of the Avenida da Liberdade.

2   See ch. I n. 5 above.

3   i.e. common land.

4   English translation by Philip Wayne (Penguin, 1949).

CHAPTER XXIX

1   A native of Santarém, who published (1740) a history of the town.

2   Frei (Friar) Luís de Sousa (*c.* 1555–1632; in civil life Manuel de Sousa Coutinho), Knight of Malta, subsequently entered a Dominican convent; he was much admired by Garrett both for his patriotism and his prose style,

the former of which is exalted in the play *Frei Luís de Sousa* (see Introduction, p. 11). Pedro Álvares Cabral was the discoverer of Brazil. Gil and João D'Ocem were knights of some importance in the early years of the Avis dynasty (fourteenth century).

3 I have not attempted to reproduce the rhyme-scheme of the original, which has a tonic, open /a/, except in the last four couplets, which may, as Garrett suggests (in ch. XXX), be a later addition.

CHAPTER XXX

1 Now Tomar, as Garrett informs us in a note.

2 Scalabis or Scalabicastrum was the original name of Santarém.

3 *endechas*: essentially a formal description, an *endecha* being a four-line stanza with rhyming second and fourth lines; the lines have five or six syllables. As Garrett explains, he believes the six-syllable type should be considered as twelve-syllable couplets.

4 Depping (1784–1853) was a French scholar of German origin who published various works on Iberian balladry.

CHAPTER XXXI

1 'How doth the city sit solitary' (The Lamentations of Jeremiah 1:1.).

2 Garrett 'lusitanized' the English word in the impossible form, *fashionável* (impossible because the group 'sh' is unknown in Portuguese; he would have had to use 'ch', which has roughly the same sound but a different visual appearance).

3 Literally, 'Gateway of the Sun', a vantage-point with a view over the surrounding countryside.

CHAPTER XXXII

1 There were two battles at Pernes, on 11 November 1833 and 20 January 1834, and one at Almoster, on 18 February 1834, in all of which the liberals (i.e. constitutionalists) were victorious.

CHAPTER XXXIII

1 i.e. 'Here comes Crispinus again' – the opening words of Juvenal's first satire.

CHAPTER XXXVI

1 Literally, 'Divine, or Holy, Miracle'. The church known by this name,

more properly St Stephen's (Igreja de Santo Estêvão), is reputed to be one of the finest in Santarém. The 'miracle' occurred in 1266, when a woman desiring to win back her husband's love was advised by a neighbour, who dabbled in magic, to steal a consecrated wafer during communion. When she returned home with it and hid it in a chest, strange manifestations occurred, leading to the declaration of a miracle. The consecrated wafer was preserved in a monstrance which the narrator reports seeing, in the next chapter. The woman, one notes, is said to be Jewish in Garrett's version.

2   Baron of Pombalinho, a liberal peer.

3   One of the town's seven gates. Like the chapel or shrine to Our Lady of the Victory, referred to later in the text, it no longer exists, having indeed been demolished by an 'enlightened' town council.

CHAPTER XXXVII

1   A parody of the opening stanza of *The Lusiads*, presumably by Garrett himself. There appears to be a double irony here, since the Baron of Almeirim would belong to the same faction as Garrett.

2   i.e. the Peninsular War (1808–14).

3   i.e. leaders; Numa Pompilius was second King of the Romans.

CHAPTER XXXVIII

1   i.e. Douro, home of many of Portugal's famous wines, including *vinho verde*.

2   See ch. VII n. 5 above: the chronicle is the *Crónica de D. João I*, by Fernão Lopes.

3   In his work *Les Arts en* [*sic*] *Portugal*, Paris, 1845. – A.G.

4   Since the word *galocha* means a clog and there does not appear to have been a newspaper of that name, I assume Garrett is playing with words. He may, even so, intend an allusion to some contemporary newspaper or magazine.

5   Portugal's national opera-house.

6   In a note Garrett draws attention to the theatrical terms he is using.

7   The etymology is unfounded, according to the Larousse *Dictionnaire Étymologique*.

CHAPTER XXXIX

1   Horace, *Epodes*, ode II, l. 4.

2   'Many brave men lived before Agamemnon.'

3   Frei (Friar) Gil is a character in Garrett's poem of this title.

4   i.e. History of St Dominic, by Frei Luís de Sousa (see ch. XXIX n. 2 above).

CHAPTER XL

1 Psalm 79 in the Authorized Version, which is the source for the English text quoted here.

CHAPTER XLII

1 Camoens, *The Lusiads*, canto V, l. 56.
2 Adaptation of *The Lusiads*, canto III, l. 138.
3 The remains of Camoens were interred in the Jerónimos Monastery, Lisbon, in 1880; Duarte Pacheco Pereira, a sixteenth-century soldier and cosmographer, died in poverty and obscurity.

CHAPTER XLIII

1 Horace, *Ars Poetica*, l. 53: '*Graeco fonte cadent (parce detorta)*'.

CHAPTER XLIV

1 Garrett transposes the English directly into Portuguese, modifying only the spelling of the vowel to a sound closer to that of the English (*flartar*), then proceeds to conjugate the verb according to Portuguese rules.

CHAPTER XLVIII

1 Line from a poem by Camoens, slightly modified (my translation).